BETWEEN THE DEVIL
AND THE DEEP . . .

To Mary –
I hope you can
sink your teeth in this!
Blessings,
Amos K. Sweet Agee

BETWEEN THE DEVIL AND THE DEEP . . .

Memoir of a Maverick Priest

Ames K. Swartsfager, BA, M. DIV

To order additional copies of this book, contact:
Xlibris Corporation
1-888-795-4274
www.Xlibris.com
Orders@Xlibris.com
65597

FOREWORD

All famous people seem to write autobiographies. I keep waiting to be famous, but as yet I have not reached that exalted state in life. Since I am growing older, I decided I would reverse the norm and write my biography before being famous.

This book is as true as my memory and perception will allow. Some of the names used are of living, breathing human beings. To these persons I express my thanks for being a positive influence on my life. Other names have been changed to protect them, or keep me from lawsuits and a lot of work defending myself.

My thanks go to my wife, Judy, for sticking with me through everything and for helping to edit this work. Also my thanks to the Captain and crew of "Nona Rosa," who encouraged me to keep on when I wanted to stop.

Aboard the ketch "Butterfly"
April 15, 1993

I would thank also those people who read and made comments over the years to help me improve the work.

In Granby, Connecticut
June 3, 2009

A NOTE:

"Devil, the caulkers name for the seam in the upper deck planking next to a ship's waterways. It was a particularly difficult place to work and thus the origin of the saying 'Between the devil and the deep blue sea.'" The Oxford Companion to Ships and Sea, Peter Kemp, 1976.

"Maverick: 1. *(Southwestern US)* an unbranded calf, cow, or steer, esp. a motherless calf. 2. A person who takes an independent stand apart from his associates." The Random House College Dictionary, Revised Edition.

CHAPTER ONE

The boat lifts to the ten-foot wave, hesitates at the top with a flap of the mainsail, then dips as it slides down its back side into the trough. A shudder . . . water washing down the lee side from the foredeck, and then she lifts again. The movement is hypnotizing. I lie back and watch the stars swirl through the clouds in the night sky. Fifteen knots of wind from the southwest is on our starboard quarter. Things are going great. The Gulf Stream is just ahead and it looks as if we will have a gentle trip across this fickle river of water that lies off the East coast.

Just a few hours ago we were in the safety of the bay at Beaufort, North Carolina. Close to a hundred boats lay at anchor with us, all cruisers preparing for their voyages to the Virgins, Bermuda, Antigua, and all points south to escape the cold of winter. We had joined them in late October after traveling down the Chesapeake and the Inter Coastal Waterway. The major topic of discussion among the captains on the docks was the weather.

"What do you think?" asks one.

"Dunno. The wind's to the north," suggests another. "Might change soon," hopes a third.

Our problems centered around crossing the Gulf Stream. It can kick up a mighty fuss if the wind blows hard from the north. None of us wanted to face a "fuss" so early in our cruise.

"I think Sunday will be a good day," one skipper forecasts.

"Dunno, Monday might be better. Give the stream time to die down."

"I've made this trip 18 times," said another. "It's always bad and you're always on a port tack."

"Maybe Monday," I mentioned tentatively to Judy to see what her reaction would be. "Any time you think is good."

That was not very helpful, because I did not know what would be a good time. What I really wanted was to have someone, a "Wizard," tell me to go on such a date at such a time and to guarantee me a calm and safe voyage.

There were some who paid for such a wizard. They contracted a private weather service. We would gather around to look over their shoulders and ask them what the situation was. Waving their fax, they would say that today is definitely not a good day. We would all heave a sigh of relief

"What does it say about Monday?" I asked.

"Monday looks OK, but they recommend Sunday." I felt disheartened because we could not leave on Sunday. We had yet to provision, so Monday would have to be the day.

The motion of the boat makes me drowsy and my head keeps dropping to my chest. The auto pilot is doing all the work. My mind drifts in rhythm with the motion of the boat.

I first got interested in boats, especially sailboats, as a method of escape from the situation in which I lived. My father was an Episcopal priest and we had recently moved to a parish in the Mission District of San Francisco. Now the Mission District, to put it in theological terms, was a "white-washed tomb full of dead men's bones." It looked nice in comparison to other slums, but it was just as bad. Up to this time I had lived a very sheltered life in relatively good neighborhoods in Texas. I had fist-fights and arguments with other kids but this did not prepare me for what I faced the first day I went to school at Everett Junior High in the Mission.

I was 12 years old and in the seventh grade. The first day I walked to school and when I got there I was sure it must be the wrong place. It looked like a prison. My last school was a two-story building with a large grass athletic field. Maybe there were 300 students, but I doubt it. What I saw at Everett were 16 foot-high fences enclosing a cement recreation yard. The entrance to the yard had a barred gate. I thought then about running away. I sure did not want to go to a school like this. If I had known the Hell I was about to enter, I do not think I could have walked through that gate.

The noise in the hallways, the hall monitors, and the strangeness of the "black" kids overshadowed everything. In Texas there had been strict segregation, although I was not really aware of it. I never even thought of it. Sure I played with some black kids who lived near us, but I never stopped to think where they went to school. I was very curious to see not only the black kids but also Navahos, Filipinos, Mexicans, Japanese, and kids from other strange places who looked different and spoke assorted languages.

There were two negative experiences that first day. First, my lunch was stolen. The second experience was more than anything else . . . embarrassing. I was trying to find my way to the gymnasium. I had to ask one of the hall monitors where the gym was and he gave me directions. By this time, I was late and ran down the hall muttering, "Left turn at room 103, right turn at room 110, halfway down the hall, first door on left." I went busting in through the door amid screams, squeals and laughter. The monitor had directed me to the girls' gym.

The most serious event at school came the following week. After lunch a bell rang and we all had to line up to go inside. I got in line as usual and was waiting to go in, when the guy in back of me pulled a knife and told me he did not want any prejudiced whitey going to his school. He was African American and was reacting to my southern accent. (In the South, I had gotten into fights because I had a Yankee accent.)

I was terrified. I had been in fights before but no one used weapons. I was angry. It was too much! I hauled off and smashed him in the face. He fell. I grabbed his arm and twisted it hard. He dropped the knife and a friend of his grabbed it and ran. A teacher came and hauled me into the principal's office. I did not have a chance to explain what had happened. It was obvious to the principal that I was at fault because,

"It's clear from your accent you are prejudiced against blacks." My parents were called and my father came to school. He did not believe my story about the knife either. That afternoon,I received a note.

"Because you hurt one of our gang, we are going to beat the shit out of you! Black Beauties."

If I was attacked with a knife on the school grounds, what would they use if they caught me on the way home? After detention, I ran home.

Friday was a strange day at school. No one stole my lunch and I made my first friend, Milo. I received a second threatening note and had to make a mad dash for home again. This time I was chased by about ten members of the Black Beauties but I was too fast for them and made it safe behind the gate to our house.

Saturday Milo came over. He wore his hair in a "DA" style and was dressed in black pegged pants, striped shirt and an imitation leather jacket. His face had a ruddy complexion and his mouth sported a friendly grin. We went out and bought a pack of Phillip Morris cigarettes. I lit up, successfully suppressed a cough, and related my problem. Milo lit his cigarette by flipping open the match book cover and lighting the match and his cigarette with one hand. I was very impressed. He took a deep drag, let the cigarette hang from his lips, and shoved his hands deeper into his pockets as he listened. He frowned as I finished.

"Hell, you have three choices. One, you can continue to run every day. Two, you can face them and probably get killed, or three, you can join a gang who will protect you."

"I've heard about those gangs. You have to be initiated don't you?"

"Yeah, and it's generally hard and painful." Milo took a drag on his cigarette, inhaled, and blew the smoke out his nostrils.

"You belong to a gang?" I asked, attempting to inhale like Milo, but ending up in a fit of coughing. Milo ignored my coughing and I was thankful.

"No, not yet. But if I do I'll join the White Shoe Gang that uses 22nd Street as their turf."

"I don't want to join a gang. There has to be another way. Maybe I could talk to them."

"Ha! That's a sure way to get killed. They have sent you a warning. They can't back down now. They'll lose face. Bad for their rep, ya know."

We smoked in silence.

"I got an idea," Milo said, flicking his cigarette toward the gutter. "Let's explore and map out an escape route. If you can get away from them long enough, maybe they'll forget."

We spent the rest of the day exploring service entrances and alleys between my house on Julian Avenue and the school. I used this escape route with great success most of the time. Once or twice guys who were pursuing would catch at our gate, but I could hold my own against them one at a time.

As we were exploring, Milo asked me if I knew how to French-kiss. I did not have any idea what he was talking about.

"What's a French-kiss?" I felt my face flush with embarrassment.

"It's a very special kind of kiss." Milo winked and smiled craftily.

"Hell yes. Let's go," I replied with more confidence than I really felt.

We walked up a street and Milo rang the bell and waited for the answering buzz that unlocked the door. Rosie lived on the third floor. As we climbed the stairs to her flat, the smell of stale cabbage and urine assaulted me. I could hardly breathe and was ready to turn and run. However, by then, we were at the open door and Rosie was looking at me.

"Hi guys. Whatcha want?" Rosie stood with her hand on her hip and a wad of gum in her mouth. She was wearing a pleated blue skirt and a very tight beige sweater. She was older than we were, maybe thirteen, stacked. She had dark hair and was somewhat plump, but pretty. Her mother yelled from the back of the house.

"Don't just stand there. Get out and don't come back until five!"

"Mom's got company," she said, straightening her raven dark hair with her hand. "Business as usual."

"What kind of business does she run?"

Rosie and Milo started to laugh.

"What's so funny?"

"My mother's business is f—king. She f—ks for money. What rock did you find this cat under, Milo? Don't he know nothing?"

"Ah, he just moved here. He's a country kid, Rose. He don't even know how to French-kiss. In fact, that's what we came here for. Thought you might teach him."

I turned a bright red and wanted to run. But I knew if I ran I would lose Milo as a friend.

Besides, I really did want to learn to French-kiss, whatever that was, might come in handy later.

"I thought so. Treat me to ice cream and a coke and I'll think about it."

We went to a little cafe on the corner of 20th and Mission and had ice cream and cokes. Rosie said we needed to find a quiet place for the lessons.

"Can't you just explain it to me?"

"Jesus Christ, this kid is a real clod. You can't explain a French-kiss. You have to do it."

"I have to kiss you?"

"I don't think you'll find it all that bad. Come on, let's go."

"Where?" asked Milo.

I took a deep breath. "Come to my house. Got lots of places with privacy there."

At home, we went into the basement of the Parish House of the church and I proceeded to learn how to French-kiss. At first, I did not like it but it grew on me . . . in more ways than one.

Under Milo's tutelage, I became a firecracker dealer at school. We would go down to Chinatown and buy cherry bombs and other good things, selling them at school for twice what we paid.

Later we branched out into the pornography business. We wrote pornographic stories, even though we had no idea about real sex. I would type them on the church's typewriter and run them off on the mimeograph. The stories sold for five dollars each. "The Teacher and the Well Endowed Student" was our best seller.

At the Marina Green, I saw sailboats for the first time. They were so beautiful and full of promised adventures. *They look like they're straining at their docklines ready to leave to seek adventure in the South Pacific,* I thought. I would watch for hours as some of the boats sailed past the park toward the Golden Gate Bridge.

I tried to visit the boats every Sunday. I had a fantasy that the captain of one would see me and call out, "Son, you want to be a sailor?"

"Yes sir," I would reply.

"Well, we're heading for Tahiti and are short a cabin boy. We leave in five minutes. Are ya game, boy?"

I would say "Yes, sir," and jump aboard as the lines were thrown off.

I eventually had to join a gang for self-protection. The White Shoe gang's turf was at Twenty-Second Street and Valencia. The initiation was bad, but it was something I had to endure in order to become a member.

I had to beat a kid they pointed out. At least they did not make me use a knife. I had to crawl through the tunnel of fire. That is where you have to crawl between the gang members' legs while they beat you with their belts. It was almost a week before I could sit down again. Then I had to steal a carton of cigarettes from a store and something off a car, preferably the whole car, and be on the front row of the next gang fight. I did it all. I knew my father would kill me if the police caught me and I went to jail. The guys in the gang took pity on me, knowing that my father was a minister. They let me get away with stealing the hubcaps from a '53 Ford. Nevertheless, in the gang fight I got a bad cut on the leg. I told my parents I had fallen and cut it on the sidewalk. I am not sure the doctor who sewed it up bought that story.

So here I was, at the age of thirteen, a street-wise gang member. I did not like it and was terribly angry with my father for placing me in this situation. The only way out was escape. In addition, the only escape I could see was the sea. Someday I knew I would be needed on a ship leaving for Tahiti.

Someday . . .

CHAPTER TWO

I awoke with a start! The sails were complaining mightily by flogging about. Struggling for wakefulness, I checked the horizon for ships and then jibed the mizzen and main. The wind had gone around from southwest to northwest. It was also beginning to strengthen.

My mind began to go over for the umpteenth time emergency actions. *If the bowstay parts, head downwind and use the jib halyard for the stay. If it is the back stay that goes, then head upwind. Use the topping lift for a back stay. If the mizzen goes, cut the triadic immediately and . . .*

I could hardly contain myself. We were kissing and she actually was letting me put my hand inside her bra.

"Oh yeah. This is great," I moaned.

"Mrnrnmrnmm," was the response. She took my hand firmly out of her bra.

Oh no, I thought, *I knew it wouldn't last.* However, she did not let go of my hand. She was moving it lower. She put it under her skirt and placed it right between her thighs.

"Oh yeah," I mumbled. I'm in heaven.

"Oh, ah, oh," she said. We French kissed.

"Yeah, oh, ah." She shuddered. Then to my surprise, she pushed away.

That is not fair. I wanted more.

She said, "Good night," and turned and went inside her flat.

I stood there looking at the empty space where she had stood. I hadn't dreamed it. In fact I was beginning to wonder how I was going to walk down the stairs and get home. My legs were weak. Although we had walked from the church dance where I left her at her flat on Army Street, I took a bus home.

Joining the White Shoe Gang made life easier for me. Anyone wanting to beat me up would have to face the whole gang. This gave me time to explore the possibilities of the opposite sex. The girls of the Mission District were very advanced sexually. Why not? Many of them lived with mothers who, if not prostitutes, were very free and open with their favors.

Their father, stepfather, uncle, or mother's boyfriend had raped some of the girls I knew. Some of them had been sexually abused by all of them. They saw sex as a method of escape. It was not unusual for a sixteen-year-old girl to get pregnant and married. If you were married, you had to live somewhere else. The worst part was that these girls and their young husbands played out the same roles as their own mothers and fathers. It seemed a never-ending cycle.

This intolerable situation had its effect on me. I was in the Mission District, but not of it. My personality became confused. At home or at church, I was an "angel:" helpful, polite, a little gentle man. With the gang, I spoke the language of the streets. Every other word was a swear word, or some four letter word, appropriate for the occasion.

My dress was that of a Pachucho. I wore pegged (rather full at the waist, but narrowing at the ankles) grey slacks and fighting shoes that were black shoes with inch thick soles. In the toe of the shoes, holes were drilled and sharpened eight-penny nails were inserted when a fight was imminent. A wide, thick leather belt, with a large stainless steel buckle, was also worn. One would keep the edges of the buckle razor sharp. You could cut yourself getting dressed! I do not think my parents knew their son was a walking arsenal. Most of the guys also sported "DA" (Duck's Ass) haircuts. I did not feel I could get away with that, but I did get the shuffle-swagger walk down pretty good.

I had been going to church since I could remember and loved the pomp and ceremony of the mass. I could swing incense with the best, and knew the service so well I could recite it by memory. Yet now confusion set in. Even society and its laws seemed to not only permit but encourage the pain and degradation in the Mission. God did not make it, but He permitted it? If so, I did not want any part of Him.

On Mission Street, there were a few fruit and vegetable stores. They all had bins of fruit on the sidewalk. Many times we filched an apple or an orange. One Saturday afternoon Tim, a friend of mine, and I were on the way to the movies. As Tim passed the stand, he took an apple.

"Hey there, you!" a voice shouted.

Tim looked around and saw two cops running toward him. He was frightened so he ran. Now Tim was overweight so he could not run fast enough. The cops caught him and took him into an alley.

I hid in a doorway and watched, shaking allover.

"We'll teach you not to steal, you little bastard!" said the big officer.

"Joe," he said, "get a carrot." The second cop went off around the corner.

"I won't do it again, See, here's the apple. You can have it." Tim had no idea what was happening. Were they going to take him into the station and put him in jail? He could not escape; the officer had an arm lock on him and a fistful of his hair.

"You greasy son of a bitch. We'll teach you, you little f—ker." The second officer returned with a carrot from the stand.

"Pull his pants down," the big one said.

The second officer unbuckled Tim's pants. Then they forced him over and shoved the carrot up his ass, laughing all the time. Tim was screaming and crying, but they covered his mouth. When they had finished, the big one said, "Next time we catch you stealing an apple, we'll shove that up there!" And they left him lying there with that carrot up his rear.

I was thankful they had not caught me, but my knees were weak just the same.

The police did not give a shit for law and order. Why should we bow to that tin god of society? Tim never did get over that and he ended up committing suicide a few years later.

I went to church to keep up the front with my parents and to meet girls. But my belief in God had gone by the boards. He did not exist! Religion was just a way for society to hook me into its moral path. Nevertheless, as a place for meeting girls, it was tops. We had a dance every Sunday night after evensong. You had to attend the service in order to go to the dance. It was the only meeting ground for the gangs where they could talk without a fight, so it was here that the time and place for the rumbles were set.

I managed to survive Junior High and was happy to be accepted at Lowell High School, a magnet school for the college bound. I got my first car, a 1938 Oldsmobile, at the age of sixteen. Having a car made it even more risky to take a girl, especially those from the Mission District, on a date alone. Those of us who were planning to finish high school had to take strict measures. *Never, never, never be alone in a car with one of these girls.* Always double date. Pick up the other guy first and leave him off last. We did a lot of necking and petting in between, but we were safe.

There is not enough room in this memoir to make a full account of these two years in the Mission District of San Francisco. Perhaps some day

I will explore it in more depth. Suffice it to say they had a great influence on my life physically, emotionally and spiritually.

The physical part was the least of my problems, though I had a real fear for my life. I was beaten in fights (lost five teeth and suffered a few cuts), and my father also beat me to "discipline" me, mainly because he was having difficulty dealing with the Mission District himself. Through this, I did learn self-defense and an awareness of danger.

Estranged from my beliefs about family and society, I was emotionally devastated. I learned that I could not trust the authorities, such as the police, to be law abiding. Social constraints meant nothing, because those who made the rules did not abide them. During this time, I attempted to be two persons: the nice gentle "preacher's kid" and the streetwise gang "pachucho." Depression was the result of this conflict in my emotional make-up, and I tried to compensate with illicit drugs.

Lastly, I lost my spiritual foundation. I had gone to church ever since I could remember, attending Sunday school and performing the ministry of acolyte (altar boy). The basis of my faith was a simplistic "God is love" education, with no depth. My surroundings in the Mission brought questions about God, His love, and his caring for his creation. I felt that adults were using religion as another way to control my life. All I saw around me was poverty, drugs, uncaring parents, and violence. How could a loving God permit this? He would not, and therefore God could not exist.

These years were the dark hole—the belly of the whale—that I had to claw my way out of, or go crazy. For the remainder of my life, I feared sliding back down into the black maw of the whale.

Lowell High School was then strictly college prep—no shops, no trades. To get there you had to have excellent grades, and in junior high, I did. However, Lowell turned out to be another shock to my system.

All the kids there were honor students and most were from very wealthy or at least upper middle-class families. In my class, there were about ten of us from the Mission. I found myself met with disdain by those who were not from the Mission. We Missionites were considered the lowest of the low.

I entered a physiology class and found I was the only sophomore and the only Missionite in the class. There were titters and giggles. My peggers were shabby next to flannel slacks and cashmere sweaters. A very pretty girl sat at my lab table. She was a junior and looked luscious in her tight sweater. She looked at me and called out,

"Anyone want to trade? I don't think I can stand sitting next to this uncouth, smelly baby."

I turned beet red. I had taken a bath that morning and I was not smelly! Uncouth I may be, whatever that meant, but not smelly!

All of us from the Mission District had similar experiences. It's funny, but all of us were also attempting to be musicians. The "Band Shack", a block away from the school, became our hang out. The rich kids there seemed to accept us for our talents, so we stayed there as much as we could. I think our music teacher understood our situation.

I was kept back a semester because I had flunked Spanish and Advanced Algebra, although my parents never realized it. I went to summer school to make it up. I felt so bad about this failure that I went to see a girl I had met a few weeks before. I needed some TLC and she, being half Mexican, had the most beautiful dark eyes and a great figure. I knocked on the door and her father opened it.

"I would like to talk to Maria," I said.

"Oh. Well she's on the roof sunbathing in the nude. I'll get her for you."

What fantasies galloped through my head. I wanted to offer to go up and get her myself! Would she come down through the door nude? I was already becoming excited.

The father returned. "She'll be right down," he said with a smile. "I have to go out for awhile," and he left.

There I was alone in a flat with Maria coming down from sunbathing naked on the roof. Wow! I was a little disappointed when she walked in with a bikini on. She looked great. Her long, glistening black hair framed her dark eyes. I knew I was in love.

"Hi ya." She pushed a strand of hair back from her eyes. "I was hoping you'd drop by sometime."

"Yeah," I croaked.

"What's happening?"

By this time, I got myself under some control.

"I wanted to talk to somebody. I really feel miserable."

"You can talk to me, honey. Anytime. Come and sit here beside me." I sat down next to her and it felt like I was sitting next to a furnace.

"What have you been doing?" The question was stupid as the heat of her body was transferring itself to my loins.

"I was taking a sunbath. The all-over kind, you know. Look. No strap marks." With that, she took off the bikini top. Her breasts were beautiful, full but not droopy. I longed to put my hands on them . . . to kiss them . . . to suck them.

She scooted closer, pressed against me, and gave me a kiss. "Lie down and put your head in my lap. Now, tell me what the trouble is and I'll fix it for you, baby."

She kissed me again and all of a sudden a red flag began to wave and alarm bells went off. I knew what she wanted. I knew what I wanted. I also knew what I did not want. I had no business being alone with her. I cut and ran as fast as I could in the condition I was in.

I dated and felt safe with many real nice girls, but I felt that I was missing out on sex. I thought I might even die before having real sex, and that would make me very depressed.

CHAPTER THREE

I look at my watch and see it is time for Judy to get ready to take over. I hear her stirring already. I do not know how she does it, but she always manages to get up before I get a chance to wake her.

I make my way below as Judy struggles into the safety harness that we always wear at night. We kiss briefly as I start to get out of my harness and head for the warm bunk.

The waves sound loud from my bunk, and I wonder if the wind is increasing even more. It is hot and stuffy. We have to keep the hatch closed because of the spray that is coming aboard. We have dorade ventilators, but we closed them up in case we get into bad weather.

It takes awhile for the adrenaline in my system to dissipate. I am tired, very tired, but I cannot sleep. I close my eyes and try to ignore the waves and the sounds of the boat as we plow through the Gulf Stream.

I looked up from the dock at "my boat." At last, I was to take a voyage, and I was only sixteen years old. Well, it was not exactly "my" boat, but I was going to call it home for six weeks. The boat was the SS President Cleveland, a passenger ship that sailed from San Francisco to the Orient.

It was a miracle that this cruise came to be. My father had accepted the position as chaplain for the Christmas cruise. He was a family man and did not want to leave his four children behind for six weeks. He wrote to all his contacts around the country and enough people donated money so we could all go. When he told us this good news, I was ecstatic.

I would escape at last. I might not be escaping permanently, but six weeks was better than nothing. I dreamt of the adventures I would have in Hawaii, with the hula girls in Japan, with the geisha girls in the Philippines, with cute Filipino girls, and, in Hong Kong, with beautiful Chinese girls wearing tight skirts with slits up the sides.

Our parents arranged with the schools for us all to take our books and homework assignments with us. Two weeks of the trip would be over the holiday vacation anyway, and we would be back in time for finals.

I stood on the bridge deck, right under the bridge, where I could hear the captain and mates giving orders. The tugboats were ready. Someone was walking through the ship ringing chimes and shouting, "All ashore that's going ashore!"

Most people were throwing serpentine paper ribbons to shore. I heard the engine telegraph ring to the captain's order of slow astern. However, the boat did not move. It was as if the colorful paper ribbons were holding the ship like a spider web holds its captives. I was impatient to get away. Ever so slowly, the distance between the dock and the ship began to widen and I knew I was not daydreaming this adventure, but really was going for my first sea voyage!

We went under the Golden Gate Bridge headed for Los Angeles and the ship began to roll in the beam seas. There were not very many people at dinner that night.

I soon found a girl my age and was determined to have a shipboard romance. It did not happen.

Then Hawaii was a disappointment to me. Waikiki Beach was a mass of hotels and I did not see any of the native women as pictured in National Geographic. It was explained to me that Hawaii was civilized now and that all the women wore dresses with tops.

We were in Hawaii only for eight hours before we sailed for Yokohama, Japan. Many of the passengers, including the girl I had met, had disembarked at Hawaii. I soon became bored and found myself touring the ship during the night just to see what happened when all the passengers were in bed. It was during one of my nocturnal prowls that I chanced to meet the Third Mate of the Cleveland. He took pity and invited me to the bridge to share his watch from 0000 to 0400.

Just to be on the bridge of such a great ship was a dream come true, and the mate and crew there treated me as a crewmember. The mate showed me the chartroom, gyrocompass, RDF, autopilot, depth sounder, radar, and DECCA navigator. They even let me steer using the small auto pilot wheel. Everyone was sworn to secrecy about my being on the bridge, and especially about my steering.

The area where the crew lived and worked was a whole other ship. It was here that I met Steve, Huey, and John. These three were from the stewards section and were glorified bellhops. They decided they needed to take over my education and we became good friends. The next four weeks I spent more time with the crew than I did with my family or other passengers. I watched movies and munched fried baloney sandwiches while sitting on the reefer hatch. I played cards and observed the varied activities of the crew. This was much more fun than watching the old, rich passengers. I had to show up for some events, but I generally did my own thing.

Steve and his friends were always looking to run some sort of scam. One of the things the passengers looked forward to was the posting of the noon-to-noon mileage. The attraction here was more than just to see how many miles the ship had traveled. For a two-dollar bet you could win twenty if you got the last digit of the mileage right. The crew was not allowed to place bets on the mileage. However, my new friends convinced me to go halves and split the winnings. I had tremendous luck and won most of the pools.

Then the anchor pool was circulated. For ten dollars, you could win 100. All you had to do was guess the minute the anchor was dropped. I won this in Yokohama, Manila, and Hong Kong. I had the strong feeling I would not have been so lucky if the crew had not been in it with me.

Contrary to the Love Boat of TV fame, the crew cannot talk to or fraternize with the passengers. They said it was up to me to get all four of us dates for Manila. We happened to have a famous ice-skating troupe aboard, but the youngest girl was twenty-one. I felt there was no way I could approach these very beautiful women and ask them for a date. Huey, the steward who had a reputation as being the most successful with women, volunteered to give me detailed training on how to approach these skaters and what to say.

"Now Ames, this is how you do it. You be the girl."

"Hi there," Heuey said with a smile.

"Hi," I replied with embarrassment.

"Where you heading?"

"Hell, Huey, we know they're getting off at Manila!"

"Yah, stupid. Do you want to get a date with them or not?"

I thought of the beautiful legs I had seen around the swimming pool. I thought also that these older girls must be experienced. Perhaps . . .

"Oh, all right." I said.

"How long are you going to be on the ship?"

"We are going to Manila for a two-week engagement."

"Now," said Huey, "This next part is important. Ask her about her hometown and where she came from. Stuff like that."

"Why is that important?"

"Oh, for God's sake kid. You don't know anything." Huey was beginning to twist his watchband, a habit of his when he became impatient.

"That makes her see that you are interested in her and it will also make her homesick, and maybe a bit lonely. That's where we come in. We're experts in making lonely people un-lonely," he said with a wink.

Using all these lessons, I managed to get four of the women to go out with us. We would pick them up on the dock the next evening and go out for dinner and dancing.

The ship docked in the late morning and, as usual, Steve, Huey and John were the first crew to leave. I was right behind them. We grabbed a cab and went to an impressive looking hotel. Steve told John and me to wait in the lobby because he and Huey had some business to transact.

"What kind of business they got here?" I asked John after the other two had left.

"Don't talk so loud," John whispered. "What they're doing is changing the crew's dollars for pesos at the black market rate. Instead of getting two for one, they may get two and a half for one."

"What do you mean the crew's money?"

"Shit, man, they got three or four thousand bucks of the crew's pay with them. When we get back, we'll give the crew their exchange and keep ten percent of the difference."

It made me a little nervous knowing we were walking around with all that money. Soon Steve and Huey came down the stairs with big grins on their faces and a full paper sack.

"Let's go." Steve headed for the door.

We left the hotel and got into a cab.

"Metropolitan Life Gardens," he told the driver. "I need a drink to celebrate, and we need to continue Ames' education, don't we boys?"

"There's no place like the Metro Life to learn things," chuckled John as the cab turned down a dingy back street.

I imagined that brown paper bag with the money falling and breaking open. The money would be gone in a minute and my friends would be in deep trouble on the ship.

The Metropolitan Life Gardens was a large dimly lighted bar with only one customer slouching in a corner booth drinking beer. I could not understand what John and Steve were giggling about as we went up the bar.

"Scotch rocks for the three of us," Steve said pointing to the older guys, "and ginger beer for our friend here."

I was sorely disappointed. I wanted Scotch rocks like everyone else. Ginger beer was a non-alcoholic drink and I did not want to be treated like a baby.

Then Huey yelled at the top of his lungs, "Hey girls! We got a cherry boy here! Come get him!"

Ten girls came running down the stairs in the back of the bar. They were yelling and screeching in a language I did not understand.

Most of them came over and pressed up against me. They pressed their breasts, their legs, their thighs and everything against me. They laughed and giggled. My friends were doubled-up with laughter at the expression on my face. "It's on us," said Huey, grinning.

"No, no," said one of the girls. "Cherry boy for free. Uh girls? Cherry boy for all of us for free." Moreover, she planted a big kiss on my lips.

"I can't," I muttered.

I turned flame red and was afraid to put my hand anywhere because there was such an abundance of girl flesh all around me. The girls were not so inhibited. They were putting their hands everywhere on me!

"No," I said. "Not now . . . I can't now!" And the truth was I was so afraid that I really couldn't. I wanted to run away. I just wanted to get out of there as fast as I could.

"We're just joking," Heuey said, and he shooed the girls

"We'll be back tonight," he said, "and you can have him then!" They finished their drinks and left, still chuckling.

That evening we picked up our dates. I do not remember their names, but the one who was stuck with me was definitely not happy. We took them to the Jai Alai games, gambled some, and had many drinks . . . except for me.

After a couple of hours watching Jai Alai and many, many drinks, the girls started complaining.

"If we don't eat soon, we're leaving you guys!" My date reached back to pull her coat on.

We went to the same fancy hotel where we had done our "business" that morning. It was a very expensive restaurant and the girls were happy with the expectation of eating a delicious meal. Steve, Huey and John were unhappy because they wanted the girls and drink, and did not want to pay for an extravagant meal.

Steve noticed a passenger from the ship, a very rich passenger, and his wife sitting at a nearby table.

The passenger saw us and motioned for us to come over. We excused ourselves from the girls and went to say hello. After all, we were not on the ship and we could fraternize if we wanted to.

"Go to the bathroom, or something," the man said to his wife when we got there. She looked angry, but got up and excused herself. We could see the man was drunk.

"Siddown," he slurred. We sat expectantly. "Ya got som' nice girls there."

"Yeah," said Steve, "they're nice." We were still wondering what this was about. Perhaps he was going to turn Steve and the gang in for fraternizing.

"How much do you want for them?"

"What?" Huey was as lost as the rest of us.

"I said how much do you want for them? I'd like to buy them from you."

I could see Steve's brain going around and calculating. I knew he was really considering selling our dates to the rich, drunk man, who had sent his wife to the bathroom so he could buy them. Surely, Steve would not . . .

"Thirty-five each," said Steve.

"Yeah," said Huey.

Without saying a word, the man reached into his pocket, pulled out one hundred and fifty dollars and handed it to Steve.

"We'll call it even at one hundred and fifty," the man said.

"A done deal," said Steve. "Let's go."

We left.

The girls were still sitting there, waiting for us to return and order their expensive meal. We never did go back to the Metropolitan Life Gardens.

CHAPTER FOUR

I struggled to unclose my eyes. I really did not want to wake up. The boat's motion was more erratic now. The wind must be up. As I wondered what time it was, the ship's clock bell struck one bell. It was 0430. There was still time to sleep before going on watch. I turned over and shut out the noise of the wind and waves.

I was disappointed when the ship left for Hong Kong. I was off to Hong Kong without having a chance to go back to the Metropolitan Life Gardens. By now, I had become mentally psyched up for the experience of a lifetime.

The trip to Hong Kong was a short one. Early the next morning we anchored in the outer roads to wait for clearance and a pilot. I was still depressed and could not face visiting the crew area, where I was sure I had become a laughingstock. As I leaned on the rail looking through the misty morning at the strange Island of Victoria, a hand was laid on my shoulder. I turned and Steve was standing there.

"Be ready to go at 4:00 p.m. tonight," he said.

"You really want me to go with you tonight? I mean, after Manila I thought you guys wouldn't want me around."

"Well, we weren't very nice," he sounded repentant. "But tonight we'll have a ball. Oh, I almost forgot. You won the anchor pool again."

At four, I met Steve, Huey, and John at the crew's gangway and we headed for the Kowloon Hotel for drinks. We had a few beers (I was allowed real beer!), and ate some snacks. Most of the people there were crew from our ship.

There were a lot of girls there also. Some were pretty Eurasian girls with beautiful eyes, some Chinese women, and a few who looked Filipino. They wore tight fitting dresses with slits up the sides to the waist. Our table conversation revolved around these girls and their various attributes.

"We gotta get Ames here laid," says Huey.

"Tonight's the night," he said to me.

"You pick the girl, old buddy," Steve said. "You get first choice."

"Look at the one with the large tits, you want that one?" says John. "If you don't, I do. I like them big like that."

"Pick one with full lips," says Huey. "They're more passionate."

"Let him alone. Let him pick one for himself," said Steve.

I looked around the room and fought being afraid. The beers had helped, but I had never been told before to pick out a girl and screw her.

"How do I know that the girl I pick would want anything to do with me?" I looked around nervously.

Steve laughed. "They're all whores. They'll do anything for money."

"Oh," I said as I attempted to sort the situation out. I had dreamt of having sex for the first time with someone I loved. This seemed to verge on being dirty.

"Stop stallin', man," said Huey. "I got the feeling I'm gonna have to choose one for myself soon."

"Yeah, kid, get on the stick!" said John with a laugh.

I looked around. *Big breasts? Nice legs? Full lips? What should I pick?*

Hurry, Ames," said Steve. "They aren't going to bite you."

There was great hilarity at the table. About that time, one of the room stewards came by the table. He had a young girl with him who had the biggest, deepest eyes I had ever seen. We all talked for a while, mostly about how we hated the Chief Steward (that was traditional opinion among the crew). After we all agreed he was a low-down bastard, I turned to Huey and whispered:

"I want that one," and nodded toward the girl.

"That's Jack's girl. I don't know if he will give her up."

"Find out, will you . . . . Please." I had begun to feel that I could really enjoy being "successful" with this girl. Huey asked Jack to step away from the table for a minute to talk with him. The discussion took about five minutes. Then they came back.

"Ames, this here is Juanita, my girlfriend. We get together every time I come to port. She isn't a prostitute, I wantcha ta know. But because it is your first time . . . and you want her . . . I'll lend her to you for the night, but that's all."

I was overjoyed, and embarrassed. "Thanks, thanks a lot. How can I ever repay you?"

"Just have a good time and don't hurt her."

"I won't . . . uh I will . . . I will have a good time and I won't hurt her."

He called Juanita over to us. "Juanita, my love, I am going to lend you to my friend Ames for tonight. He has never had a woman and he likes you. Is it OK with you?"

"Sure, honey. Anything you say." Juanita turned to me. "How you say name?"

Soon we were in deep conversation and I began to feel more at ease. Suddenly the door to the bar slammed open and two Chinese men walked in. They headed in our direction but turned at the last minute to the table next to us, and pulled guns.

Blam!

Blam! Blam! Three shots rang out.

Screams.

A man who was sitting behind me slumped, his head hitting the table.

He was one of us, a crewman from our ship. The gunmen turned and started walking out as calm as you like.

"Let's get the f—kers!" John yelled, jumping up. All of us jumped up and ran after them. The bar was on the second floor so we chased them down the stairs. They had a black car waiting at the entrance. John was a madman at the front of the mob chasing the gunmen, who jumped into the car and slammed the doors. Before the car could get away, John slammed his fist through the back seat window. The car burnt rubber amidst the crashing of glass and sped off.

"God dammed bastards," John said as he wrapped a handkerchief around his knuckles to stop the bleeding. "F—king bastards!"

"Let's get out of here before the police come," said Steve as he hailed a rickshaw. It took four rickshaws to transport the girls and us to Steve's friend's house.

The shock of the events, especially running after men with guns in their hands, finally settled in and I began to shake. Juanita put her arms around me as we rode and told me how brave I had been to chase those bad men. She began to kiss me, and soon I began to kiss back. When we arrived at our destination, Juanita paid the rickshaw coolie, and we followed Steve into the house.

"There's plenty of room," Steve said as we entered, "but Ames gets the big bedroom." We sat around having drinks and discussing the shooting.

It was explained to me that there was a lot of gambling on the ship and a seaman could pile up a lot of debt. Loans were made to cover the debt, but the interest was so high that soon the only way to payoff the debt was to agree to smuggle heroin or gold into the U.S.

"If you don't want to do it," said John, "or if you try to deal in smuggling on your own, you can get beat up badly."

"Or killed," Steve added. "That was an execution. They did it in front of everyone to set an example. Never, never gamble on a ship. That's my advice. Just don't do it."

Soon pairs began to drift into other areas of the house. Juanita kept tugging at my arm.

"Come on," she said happily, "we get the big room." She pulled me up and led me into the bedroom. We sat on the bed, because I did not know what to do next.

"How much do I pay you?" I asked.

"For whole night?"

"I donno, I guess so."

"Ten Hong Kong dollars," she said. This was about fifteen dollars US. I thought perhaps that I should bargain.

"That's a lot of money."

"I'm lot of girl. For whole night too," she said with a grin.

"I guess that's all right. Do I pay you now or later?"

"Pay me now because I honest girl. Don't do it with any other girl. They run and not stay whole night."

I was very embarrassed when I opened my wallet. It had a juvenile cowboy motif on the front. Here I was about to become a MAN, and she saw my kid's wallet! I wanted to hide. I pulled out the ten Hong Kong and gave it to her.

"Stay here honey," she said, "I be right back."

As she left the room, I thought, *well, that's it. My money's gone and so is the girl*. However, a few minutes later she came back.

"How come you not undressed? We can't do it with your clothes on."

I turned my back and took off my clothes.

"Aren't we supposed to kiss or something?" I asked.

"We kiss, sure, if you want."

An hour later, someone started pounding on the bedroom door.

"Come on you guys, don't take all night. We're going to the Princess Club."

We got up and got dressed.

Juanita kissed me. "You not act like you never have girl before. You sure I am first?"

"Yes." I was flattered, but not feeling too happy. I did not want to go the Princess Club. After all, I had paid for the "whole night."

The Princess Club was a dinner-dance club in Kowloon. I danced almost every dance with Juanita and, when the club closed down at 2:00 a.m., we headed back to the house. I had drunk too much beer and had trouble negotiating the stairs. Juanita took me in and put me to bed.

For the second time I fell into her arms.

I awoke with a start and panicked. I was disorientated and not sure where I was. Who was this girl and how did she get in my bed? Soon I remembered the events of the night before and I also remembered my family expected me to take a tour with them at eight in the morning. I looked at my watch it was already three in the morning. I had to get back to the ship in a hurry.

I climbed over Juanita and got dressed as quickly as I could. With shoes in hand I walked over and around the tangled sleeping bodies and out the door. My head hurt and I was sick at my stomach. I vomited, and then, head reeling, got my shoes on somehow.

A light fog drifted down the street. I had no earthly idea where I was, but started walking. I walked for about half an hour and did not see a soul. There were not many streetlights, and it was very dark and shadowy. I was frightened, my head felt like it was going to explode, and my stomach . . . I knelt down and retched into the gutter. Under a streetlight, I looked at my watch. It was almost four and I was lost in Kowloon. I went on walking until I finally found a rickshaw with its driver sleeping under it. I woke him up and tried to explain where I wanted to go.

"The ship!" I yelled. There was no response from the coolie. "The ship!" I figured the louder I yelled the easier it would be for him to understand. Eventually he set up the rickshaw and motioned for me to get in.

"The ship," I said again.

"Ah so," he nodded as he took off at a trot. I prayed we were really going to the ship and not to some dark alley where I could be murdered—painfully. To my great relief, we came to a part of town I recognized. There at the dock was the USS President Cleveland. What relief! I gave the coolie five U.S. Dollars (way too much) and ran for the ship.

The telephone by the bed rang and rang. I picked it up.

"Where are you?" It was my father and he was using his rough voice. I was in trouble. "Do you know what time it is? Why weren't you at breakfast? Get down to the gangplank now. It's already eight-ten and Fr. Jones is waiting to take us on the tour."

I shook my head trying to clear the fuzziness That was a great mistake. Going into the bathroom, I drank some water and got dressed. It was going to be a bad day.

CHAPTER FIVE

"Come on honey, get up," a voice said.

"Ugh."

"Get up, it's your watch."

As I swam out of my dreams I began to realize that Judy was trying to get me up for my watch.

"What time is it?"

"Ten to six."

I noticed a different movement to the boat as I pulled on my clothes and asked Judy what was happening outside.

"The wind has moved to the southeast. It's beginning to build also . . . to twenty knots." She looked very tired.

"Go on to bed. I've got it."

After I finished getting my clothes and foul weather gear on, I went to the galley where I kept my safety harness. *Six o'clock and still pitch black outside*, I grumbled to myself. Then I saw Judy had made hot water for my coffee. *She is a wonderful mate*, I thought. My heart felt full of love.

The rain began.

I had foul weather gear and my coffee, and I was too lazy to move. Let it rain! The wind was coming directly from the direction we wanted to go.

At least we were making six knots. We had run all night with the working jib and the mizzen. *If the wind increases I will reef the mizzen*, I told myself. I stood up again and looked around the horizon for shipping. A gust of wind laced with rain hit my face. I took a sip of coffee. It was getting cold.

We left Hong Kong in pouring rain. I did not personally experience this, as I was in bed exhausted. The day spent with the family was difficult because of my hangover and not having much sleep the night before. Off the coast of Japan the next morning, I went on deck to get some air.

"Thank God you're alright!" a voice said behind me. "You sure as hell gave us a scare!" It was Steve. "What happened? When we woke up you had disappeared. When we got back to the ship, you were not there either. And we couldn't raise you in your cabin when we sailed yesterday. God, you gave us a fright."

I told him of my adventures finding a rickshaw and how I was not sure I would arrive back at the ship.

""You're lucky you didn't get your throat slit. Do you realize that even armed service personnel are not allowed in Kowloon after dark because it's so dangerous?"

"I knew that it was dangerous, but I had to get back to the ship in time to go with my family," I replied.

"Still, that was crazy. Oh, by-the-way, take these for a week." Steve handed me some little white pills. "Take two a day."

"What are they?"

"Penicillin. That's so you don't get VD and have your tool drop off."

I had not thought of that. *What if I got syphilis or gonorrhea? Then what?* I took the pills and put them into my pocket. I vowed I would take two a day until they were gone.

"Hey, you must have made a good impression on Juanita. She was sorry she didn't get a chance to say goodbye. She also said to tell you to look her up when you come back."

After we parted, I went straight to the stateroom and did a careful examination. I did not see anything, but I took my first pill. Then I scrubbed in the shower for about forty-five minutes.

Later that day the ship docked in Japan at Kobe and I toured the emperor's palace with my family. That evening my parents and older sister Dianne decided to take the fast train overland and spend the night in Tokyo. I was placed in charge of my two younger sisters. When our ship arrived the next day at Yokohama, I hailed a taxi and we all climbed in for the ride rejoin our parents. I told the driver we wanted to go to Tokyo and gave him the name of the hotel.

He said, "Oh yes, I know."

"Do you speak English?"

"Oh yes, I know."

"You have a beautiful country here," I said, attempting to be friendly.

"Oh yes, I know." He smiled. I was beginning to have doubts about his English. It was a beautiful chilly, cloudless day.

"Looks like it's going to rain soon," I tested.

"Oh yes, I know."

We were driving through an industrial area when the driver took a sharp turn off the main road.

"Where are you going?" I asked, becoming worried.

"Oh yes, I know," was the response.

The taxi made many turns down smaller and smaller streets. I was now greatly concerned and could see my sisters starting to panic.

"What are you doing? Where are you going?" I tried to keep my own panic in check.

"Oh yes, I know." He turned and smiled at me. "Oh yes, I know."

"You can get in a lot of trouble if you hurt us!" I was becoming desperate now. I could see my sisters being kidnapped and sold to houses of prostitution. I, of course, would get my throat slit.

"Stop the car now!" I yelled, trying to open the door, but it would not budge.

He looked back with his toothy smile.

"Oh yes, I know." He pulled the car into a dark garage. I locked the doors. My sisters were beginning to cry. The driver left the car and went through a door.

Perhaps we should run. But to where? Surely they would catch us.

The man came out of the door with a five-gallon can. He brought it to the window and showed it to me. He smiled and said, "Oh yes, I know," and proceeded to pour the gas into the car. I nearly fainted with relief. He had run low on gas and had to go to a black market source in order to get more. I felt like a fool.

The ship left the next day for Hawaii. I was still involved in crewing, and, at the same time, did all the normal things passengers do. I would have rather just stood my watches but my parents were unhappy with my being gone so much and my sisters were jealous of the independence I had. I was also aware that the cruise was ending. There was one thing I did every day and that was a self-examination looking for the dreaded VD.

By the time we reached Hawaii, I was exhausted. I became ill and missed two days of sailing. The day before we arrived in San Francisco, I became deeply depressed thinking about going back to the Mission to live and to Lowell to study. I went below to the crew area and talked with Steve.

"How can I get a job like yours?" We were munching on hot baloney and egg sandwiches.

"You have to join the union and you gotta get training at the Maritime Academy at Vallejo. But most of all you have to be at least eighteen," he said with some sympathy. You can talk to that bastard of a Chief Steward, but he'll tell you the same. Why don't you finish high school and then sign on?"

I turned away because tears were filling my eyes. I did not want him to 'see me acting like a kid.

"I guess I got to go and pack." I left, throwing a "See yah" over my shoulder.

I finally packed up and was ready to leave. I went to the gangplank with my family as we prepared to disembark.

"Somehow," I vowed to myself, "I'll come back to sea. I don't know how and I don't know when, but I'll be back."

CHAPTER SIX

All day long the wind had been increasing and blowing from the southeast. Every two minutes or so a wave would come on deck and roll down the starboard side, ending in a swirl in the foot well.

Night was approaching and Judy was resting up for her watch. You could not tell when the sun set. It just became pitch black. No stars. No moon. The only company was the wind whistling in the rigging, the waves roaring up to the boat and smashing themselves on the hull, and the luminescence of the clouds above.

My anxieties always increase when sailing at night. So many things can go wrong and they would be harder to fix in the darkness. The darker the night the more fearful I am. What if we ran into a log or a container off a ship and holed the hull? What would I do?

The ship's clock rang five bells. I went to awaken Judy, but as usual she was already stirring. I charted my latest DR and GPS fix, turned on the gas under the teakettle to make water for Judy's tea, and started removing enough clothes so I could sleep. The boat lurched and the teakettle went flying out of its holder to the back of the stove.

"Well, I guess I'll have to hold the darned thing," I mumbled.

"What did you say?" asked Judy.

"Nothing. You have to be careful with the pots on the stove. Tea will be ready soon."

"Go on to bed," she said. "I'll finish the tea. I'll call you if anything happens."

"I love you," I said, lurching toward the bunk.

Ever since coming back from my ocean voyage on the President Cleveland, my interests had changed from girls and sex to music and sex. I had been playing clarinet since seventh grade, but in high school branched out to saxophone. I had a mind for organizing so as a junior in high school I set out to start a dance band. I was able to borrow music from the high school, as they no longer had an official dance band. The music the band teacher loaned me was wonderful stuff: arrangements for the great forties songs like Sing, Sing, Sing; Stardust; Celery Stalks at Midnight; and almost a hundred more. The difficulty was they were arranged for eighteen piece bands and all I could gather were seven musicians.

The musicians were mostly from the Mission District contingent of Lowell, as the "good musicians" would have nothing to do with us. However, the "Blue Notes" band was born. We had Nancy, Clark and me on sax, Manny on trumpet, Irene on bass, Dick on drums, and Kenny on piano. (These last two were not from the Mission.)

Then we asked the De Molay if they would like to have their own band for dances. They were ecstatic. We said we would play if they financed some equipment and music. They agreed and we did play two dances before we absconded with the equipment for two years. We figured we had rented it.

We played good music for dancing and tried to keep our prices within reason. Soon we had the Lowell contract for school dances, three contracts with Jewish Temples for their dances, and two contracts at the University of California in Berkeley. We were playing four to five nights a week and making fair money.

The band became a family unit. We went to school together, we worked together and we had fun together. After we finished a gig we would go to a pizza parlor on the corner of Divisidero and Hayes. We held jam sessions there and as a reward the owner gave us pizza.

I graduated from Lowell in the spring. My friends in the Mission District were all planning to go into the Armed Forces. They felt they would be drafted anyway and besides it was a way out.

My friends at Lowell were planning to go to Stanford or the University of California, Berkeley, and they figured they could get deferments. I could not afford, nor did I have the grades, to go to either of these two universities. I chose joining the Air Force instead of going to college.

I figured it would be the cleanest of the services. I wanted to learn Meteorology. The recruiter said he was sure I could get training in it and arranged for my physical the following day.

"Strip down to your under shorts and get in line," said the man in a white smock. There were about fifty of us waiting for a physical. We stripped down and put our clothes in a basket that we carried with us. Then we proceeded from one room to the other doing vision and hearing tests, "bend over and spread 'em," tests, and "turn your head to the right and cough" exams. And it continued with blood, breathing, and, finally, written tests.

They called me into a room to be interviewed by a doctor, who wanted a history of medical problems. Although I had experienced foot problems and frequent nosebleeds, I did not tell him about those. I mentioned the fact the doctors thought I had an ulcer when I was ten years old. I returned to the waiting room. While I waited, I visualized myself in uniform with glistening medals. I fantasized my goodbye with my girl friend:

"Honey, I have sad news," I would say.

"What's the matter, darling," she inquires as she draws me close.

"I'm going . . . I leave tomorrow morning."

"What? Where are you going?" There is panic in her voice.

"I'm going to serve my country. I don't want any Godless communists coming over here. I'm going to fight for liberty, freedom and the pursuit of happiness. I joined the Air Force."

"Oh baby, I don't what you to go. Is there anything I can do before you go?" Tears begin to brim over her eyes and spill down her cheeks. "Anything at all?"

"Swartsbaker," someone shouted, pulling me from my daydream. As it was close enough to my name, I came forward.

"This way." I followed the uniformed man into an office. "Well now, let's see," he says as we sit. "Umm . . . ummm. Well, you made the highest score on the written test. Very good. Umm," he read my file more. "Not bad physical shape either. Ummm . . . uh,oh . . . well now, that's too bad."

"What's too bad?" I asked.

"Well now . . . we can't accept you. You said you had an ulcer, so we can't accept you."

"What!" I exclaimed. I was shocked. My fantasies died." What do you mean?"

"Well now, don't get excited. I know you're disappointed, but you are '4F'."

"Didn't you just say I was physically fit?"

"Well yes, but that was before we found out about your ulcer."

"But it was just suspected and that was eight years ago. I haven't had any trouble with my stomach in years."

"Ah, but you might and it would be our responsibility, wouldn't it?"

"Isn't there anything I can do?" I pleaded. *I was being rejected. I was not wanted. What could I tell my friends?*

"Well now, you could get three doctors to certify you don't have an ulcer, and we would take another look at you then."

"F—k you," I said, getting up to leave.

"Wait a minute," the man said, "don't forget your free meal ticket."

I went out of the office and slammed the door. I felt like crying. As I walked down the street, I saw a wino sitting on the curb. I gave him my free lunch ticket and went home.

I went looking for work. The only jobs I could find were for fifty cents an hour and looked like hard work. I entered San Francisco City College the following fall semester.

It was the grand opening of the Old Spaghetti Cafe and Excelsior Coffee House (OSC/ECH) and there was a lot of noise. We had worked like dogs to get the place ready for the opening. There were seven of us sitting around the large circular oak table: Tina, Joseph and his friend Tom, John, Pat, Jack and myself.

"Man, what a crowd," said Tina. I had been running around with Tina since meeting her at work. She was a plump woman in her thirties. A Beatnik, she lived and made sandals in a loft near the Embarcadero, and had been my introduction to the very different life of North Beach.

"Yea, it's a gas," Joseph, a burly, tough looking man, said. "I gotta get back in the kitchen and make sure they don't put too much food on the plates."

Joseph was Tina's husband. She had left him when his boyfriend Tom moved in with them. It was not that Tina did not like Tom, but she had been insulted when Joseph asked her to use the spare bedroom so Tom could sleep with him. Joseph and Tom were co-owners of the OSC/ECH.

"Tell them they're putting too much oregano in the sauce," Tom said. He was the worrier of the group.

"Best spaghetti I've ever tasted," said John, the only African-American at the table. All you could order at the OSC/ECH was spaghetti, salad, sandwiches, wine, and beer. John was an actor working as a clerk in an accounting office. He had been in several plays produced by the Actors' Workshop.

"These people came tonight out of curiosity," said Pat, wiping some spaghetti sauce off her sweater. "What's gonna keep them coming back?" She was a very pretty woman in her twenties, and was one of many airline flight attendants who had become involved in the North Beach scene.

Jack, who was trying to write a book, came out of his silent stupor. "Screw them," he mumbled, his mouth full of spaghetti.

The restaurant was located in an old spaghetti factory building, hence the name. "Yea, man," I said in my newly acquired "Beatnikeese." "We need some entertainment."

"Cost too much." Tom shook his head and reached for the bread

"Oh Tom, quit your bitchin'," said Tina, scooting her chair back from the table as a signal she was finished, then changing her mind and reaching for more crusty sourdough bread.

"Hell," said John, "it wouldn't cost much if anything. There are always actors wanting to perform. We could get guys from the Workshop to do improvisations."

"String quartets," said Pat. "I know some guys would love to come and play some quartets. They're good and they like performing."

"Don't forget jazz, man," I added. "All you have to do is go down to The Cellar a half a block away and find guys who would love to come and jam." I had been there but was not good enough to join in with my tenor sax.

Our discussion on what to do for entertainment solidified into a plan. Friday evenings there would be jazz, Saturday afternoon improvisations, and Sunday afternoon, string quartets. The spaghetti factory soon became the meeting place for the late Beatnik era in North Beach.

Running around with Tina introduced me to all kinds of beatniks. We went to wine and marijuana parties. It was great fun, but I took the scene very seriously.

Thirty or more people would gather in a loft sitting on the floor and drinking cheap wine or puffing a roach. Almost every male sported a Jungian beard and a turtleneck sweater. The women wore loose fitting dresses. After all, they were nonconformists. I did not grow a beard, as I was not willing to conform to their non-conformity. During all this babble there would generally be someone strumming a guitar in a corner. It was mellow!

"Have you read Plato's 'Republic'?" asks one. "You need to! All men need to be governed according to Plato. Those other philosophers just don't cut it."

"Hey man," says another, "Plato was a fag. You don't want that kind of government."

"Don't forget Descartes," someone interjected, but was ignored.

"Didn't you read William James on the 'Nature of Man'?" asks another.

"What we have is a democratic dictatorship, ya dig?" says another.

"Yah, I dig." This goes on for a long time, while I wonder who Plato is and who Descartes is, and who is this guy James? I am impressed. After all, I was accepted by these great philosophical thinkers. About this time a man jumps to his feet and recites,

> "All or nothing,
> Nothing or all,
> It makes no difference
> Who cares?"

He sits down and everyone claps. While I attempt to make sense of this, another guy stands and says,

> "The big
> The little
> Both"

Again, everyone claps. I am impressed again. I am not sure what I am impressed about, but I am.

I met Jack, who was also a copy boy, and we became friends. Jack was an aspiring artist and we shared the same attraction to the Beatnik movement. During the summer, he and I rented a loft, and he painted while I composed my great symphony. We went the rounds of the parties and gab sessions as much as we were able. I was relieved to find that Jack had no idea what these people were talking about either.

Jack and I finally admitted to each other we felt stupid, so we went to the library and checked out the books that everyone discussed. As we read them, we discovered that these "intellectuals" could not possibly have read the books they quoted. They were just repeating what other people had said about them.

Tina and I broke up. The reasons our platonic relationship went down the tubes were two-fold. First, she took me to Miss Smith's Tea Room.

As we were walking down Grant Avenue in North Beach, Tina asked if we could stop in for a cup of coffee. We were outside a little restaurant I had never really noticed before named Miss Smith's Tea Room.

"Sure," I said. We went inside and sat at a table. At first, I thought I was in a motorcycle bar. There were a lot of guys dressed in leather at the bar. Then I began to notice that there was a strange sound to their voices.

"Excuse me," Tina said, her mouth seemed to be suppressing grin. "I left something at the spaghetti factory. I'll be right back." We were only a half a block away so I knew it would not take her long.

Soon I noticed that the people at the bar were looking at me. If they had been animals, they would have been growling. Then it came to me that these people were Lesbians, butches.

"What the hell are you doing here?" said the biggest, meanest looking woman I had ever seen.

"I'm waiting for someone," I stammered.

One of the women in a dress came over and put her arm around my shoulder.

"He's sweet, Billy," she said, "and cute."

She was obviously teasing her "friend," who I could see was becoming very angry.

I squirmed in my seat.

"No, I'm just waiting for my girl friend."

"Can't I be your girl friend?" asked the teaser.

Billy the butch grabbed me by the shirt collar and shouted, "Get out of here you father f—king son of a bitch. Don't mess with my girl." She pulled me out of the chair and threw me toward the door. The other butches were glaring and moving toward me. I ran out the door and down the street.

Tina was standing on the corner doubled over with laughter. I had been set up. She had bet that I would not last more than five minutes in there alone. She won ten bucks.

The second reason we split was that her husband, John, wanted her to come back. He still had his boyfriend living with him, but they promised to do the cooking if she did the cleaning.

"What the hell, it's cheap rent," she said. I was happy to be out of the relationship.

By the middle of my first semester in college, I dropped out of the beatnik scene. I was disgusted with the pseudo intellectualism and the growing commercialism surrounding these "non-conformists." I found college was great fun. High school had been boring, having to attend the same classes day after day, but in college, you went to class three times a week and were left on your own to learn. My grades went to honor roll status.

CHAPTER SEVEN

There was a loud crash and then I was flying through the air. The lee cloth had given way and I dropped with a bang. I had landed on my elbow and the pain was excruciating. Had I broken something? No, all my body parts seemed intact, but I was lying on the cabin sole.

Judy came below at the noise and was frightened to see me on the floor.

"What was that?" I asked, shaking my head to clear it.

"Just a large wave." Her foul weather gear was dripping and she looked very tired. "The wind is getting up. Are you all right?"

"No broken bones. I hurt my arm, but it'll be all right." I looked at the lee cloth dangling from where it was tied to the overhead. All the screws had torn out of it.

"How's it going with you?"

"I'm fine," she said and then added in her mothering tone of voice, "You still have another hour before your watch. Go back to bed."

"I'll be damned if I'll climb back in bed! I'll just sleep here." I grumbled.

"Get up, Ames, it's happened," someone was shaking me awake. I struggled up from a deep sleep.

"What happened?" I mumbled. My mother was standing by the bed, still shaking. There were tears in her eyes. As I became more awake, I understood what had happened. My father had died. He had been dying for a year or more from intestinal cancer. I had watched him deteriorate slowly.

"Dad's gone?"

46

"Yes, early this morning . . . the doctor just called. I need your help."

"I'll be right there," I said as I got up to get dressed. A sense of relief came over me. My father was gone . . . dead. At least he was out of his pain. The rest of the day and week were busy with funeral plans, the funeral and the aftermath of emotional exhaustion.

My mainstay during this time was my girl friend Judy.

She did not say much, but she was a good listener. She had stood by me during this year of waiting and pain. It had been a tough year.

Theologically, I had gone through some interesting changes and experiences. Although still attending church, I had rejected God, church and society for many years. During this past year, however, I had felt the need to explore religion. I had discussed religion with John, a journalism classmate, and he was very cynical about it all. He said he believed if one did attend church it should be fun.

"Come with me to my church," he urged. "I think you'll like it."

"I really don't want to go to any church. I only go to ours so I won't disappoint my parents."

"Come just once. I guarantee you'll enjoy yourself."

"OK, I'll come just once. What time on Sunday?"

"Oh it doesn't meet on Sunday. We meet at eight o'clock Friday evenings. I'll pick you up at seven."

We arrived at the church just before the service was to start. The building did not look like a church, but it had a sign in front, "THE CHURCH OF THE BLUE FLAME."

"What religion is this?" I asked.

"This is a special religion. You'll find it interesting."

We went in and the church looked like a theater with rows of seats. On the stage there was what looked like a fire pit, with some benches around the sides of the stage. We took our seats in the third row.

"You'll really love this," John whispered.

Strange music played over the PA system.

A man came out in a dark blue robe, bowed to us and said, "Oh wise ones. May the light of the blue flame enkindle love in your hearts. May it warm your loins. May the seed be ready to flow. Amen."

He left the stage and the lights dimmed. Ushers came down the aisles taking up a collection.

"Put ten bucks in," whispered John.

I did, and the usher handed me a paper with something wrapped up inside.

"What's this?" I whispered to John.

"Marijuana." he replied, "Light up."

I am not an aficionado of the weed, but it seemed like it was a sacrament of some kind. So I took a deep toke, held it and then exhaled. Meanwhile the music picked up its beat and a blue glow came from the fire pit.

Three girls came out, each dressed only in a flowing scarf.

They danced around the blue flame for a few minutes and, dropping their scarves, leaped and cart-wheeled over the fire pit. As they went over the top, they seemed to turn blue. It was interesting, and between this dance and the marijuana, I felt my lust growing.

The man in the blue robe came out and said,

"Oh wise men of good will, you have experienced the holy Dance of the Blue Flame. Now let your seed flow. The priestesses are waiting. Don't forget to make your offering as you enter the chamber of love."

"Let's go." I started out of my seat. The show was repulsive to me.

"Go . . . the back rooms?" John looked at me quizzically.

"Hell no, let's get out of here."

"Why?"

"This is not religion. It's just a whorehouse," I started walking toward the church door.

"I'm staying," John said with a laugh. "I'm going to celebrate the flesh. See you later."

I left the church and got a bus for home. There must be something, some strength outside ourselves. I could just not believe in a God who would let the world get so bad. I felt like a hypocrite.

"A God of love." they say. *"If that is true then why all the pain?"* This was my continuing question.

I noticed a sign on a college bulletin board announcing a meeting of the Vedanta Society. I asked around and found that this is a sect of Hinduism. They emphasize the philosophical aspects of Hinduism. I decided to attend and see what they had to say.

The meeting was held in the back room of a restaurant in North Beach. We discussed the Vedic scriptures and the Bhagavad-Gita. I was drawn to their image of God. It was so outside of man's reality that there was no possible definition. In fact the word "god" so limited the unlimited that all one could do when speaking of "god" was to breathe: "Ahhhh".

Man's role was to fulfill his destiny according to the karma set out for him. I went to Vedanta meetings for six months or more before I began to feel something was missing.

Then I found out about Taoism and, as I was beginning to explore that, found a Christian Taoism church on California Street. Taoism helped me understand the need for evil in the world as a balance for the good. However, this mixture of Taoism and Christianity did not fulfill my spiritual needs.

Being very mixed up, I decided to talk to a dear friend of the family, an Episcopal priest by the name of The Rev. Leon P. Harris. I went to visit him at his church on Waller Street in the Haight Ashbury District. He was about sixty years old, trim and slightly bald. I explained my dilemma.

I had written an article against Christianity and sent it to him. When we met I attempted to be honest, but I also was openly hostile.

"Ames," he said softly, "I understand you are angry. I also understand you want to walk your path of karma. I would like to help you."

I was shocked. *He wanted to help me with my karma? An Episcopal priest? He is surely snowing me*, I thought.

"How are you going to help me with my karma?"

"Well, a lot of the Gentiles in Jesus' time believed in karma and they felt Jesus spoke to them in relationship to it. Have you ever read the Gospel of Mark?"

"No," I admitted. I was raised a Christian, but I had never really read the Bible. I had read the Bhagavad-Gita, Vedic sutras, Confucius, and Buddhist scriptures, but never the Bible.

"I think you will find in Mark, the oldest gospel, that the apostles also had a hard time with their karma. Why don't you read it this week and let's get together to discuss it next week, and it would help immensely if you would footnote your paper to the bible."

I spent the week reading and re-reading Mark. I found the apostles were as stupid as I, and they found it as difficult as I did to follow their own special karma. They were there with Jesus, and they still betrayed him.

Fr. Harris and I spent several months discussing the gospels and what they meant concerning my karma. My paper was all wrong. It was based on "Sunday School" knowledge of the bible. I realized that what I was lacking in my spiritual life was forgiveness. Hinduism, Taoism, Buddhism, etc, all relied on man becoming God-like. Christianity recognized that man is made in the image of God, but is fallible and has a nature that inhibits him from being sinless. Man cannot follow his own karma and ever expect to have union with God, but Jesus did it for him and offered forgiveness and mercy for falling off the path set out for us.

Still rebelling against my father and "the church," I decided to look for a better Christian church. I went to many Protestant denominations, to Roman Catholic and Orthodox churches, but I could find none to suit my spiritual needs.

A new understanding was unraveling in my mind. "The Church" (whatever denomination) is fallible. God ordained the need for a social structure with the gathering of the apostles and disciples by Jesus. However, after the death of Jesus the church was man-maintained. Since men are fallible, the church became fallible and filled with error. God did not promote evil and suffering in the world. Indeed, mostly man and his greed and sin created this. God wants us to choose love, but we generally settle for the opposite. He tried to make it easy for us through Jesus the Christ, but we crucified even him.

I struggled with these concepts for a year wondering if this was just a rationalization. I was fighting for discernment, faith and peace.

It was over a very crooked road that I traveled back to the Episcopal Church, which fulfilled my needs for worship and yet had a broad enough theology I could feel comfortable with.

When my father was diagnosed with cancer and was going to die within the year, my mother discussed it with my sisters and me.

"The doctor says that when he operated they found cancer. It had metastasized throughout your father's intestines, pancreas, and spleen. He has less than a year to live," she said, with tears in her eyes. Then she broke down and wept.

We were shocked.

Fathers were supposed to live forever. I could not believe this news.

"But," mother said, "and this is very important, we're not going to tell him. Not one word. The doctor has not told him and he does not know. No one's to know, except the bishop."

Thus began the "year of the lie." We did as mother wished, but I knew that he knew. Mother knew that he knew. However, none of us (my sisters or I, my mother or father) admitted we knew what was happening. I cannot think of a worse way to live. We all kept up a brave front, but we all knew.

As the year went by more responsibilities fell into my hands. Mom and dad would leave for a vacation and I would stay home to take care of my younger sisters. My older sister was married and not in town. I was working one full time job and two part time jobs. On top of this, I was taking a full load at college.

Church responsibilities began to fall on me also. As my father got worse, I began to take on some of his duties at the church.

The bishop called me into his office and told me the facts of life.

"When your father dies," he said, after offering his sympathy to me and our family, "I want you to know you can stay in the rectory for awhile. At least until the new rector is selected."

I was shocked. I had never thought about this. We would not have a place to live and the only income we would probably have would be mine.

"Meanwhile," he continued in a solemn voice, "I am going to make you a lay reader and put you in charge of the parish. I am making an exception for your age because I think you can handle the situation. You will need to arrange for priests to come for the communion services at eight o'clock on Sunday mornings and eleven o'clock the first Sunday of the month. You will be in charge of the other services and the visitation of the sick. I will make sure your father's salary is paid until another rector is chosen." I knew he was trying to be generous. After all, he would not throw us out immediately, just wait awhile.

I was angry and depressed. Since one does not yell at a bishop, and since I realized he was doing as much as he thought he could, I got up, thanked him and left.

How were we going to make it? Would I have to leave college? I would have to bear the burden myself. I knew my mother could not, but I did not know how we would manage.

My father's condition worsened and he became more difficult to manage. Mother and I would take turns staying up with him at night. We would read to him from Eugene Sue's great book, "The Wandering Jew." However, the medication soon was unable to control the pain. One night he jumped out of bed three times, and I could hardly manage to get him back. We decided he had to go to the hospital because the doctor would not allow heavy medication at home. We sent for an ambulance and they placed him on the stretcher. He fought them all the way.

"I don't want to go . . . don't take me away!" he yelled. As they carried him down the stairs, he looked at me and screamed, "Don't do this to me, you bastard!"

That was the last time I saw him alive. He lingered in the hospital under heavy medication for a week, but I did not visit him. Then, he died.

CHAPTER EIGHT

The rain was easing off but the wind was blowing a steady twenty-five knots with gusts to thirty. The waves were running about twelve feet, with a sixteen footer every so often. I felt miserable—wet and miserable.

A wave broke aboard the port deck, came swirling down to the cockpit and filled the foot well. I just barely got my feet up in time. I chuckled. My feet were already soaked.

Out of the corner of my eye, I noticed a flickering movement. I looked around, but was not able to spot anything. A few minutes later I again saw something move. It was a tiny land bird, about two inches long, brown in color and with a sharp pointed beak.

He kept landing on a lifeline, losing his balance, and flying away. Finally, he came and landed on the deck of the cockpit and stood there on unsteady legs. He pecked at the seawater and I knew he was tired and thirsty.

"Judy, come and see this," I called. Judy, braced in a corner of a bunk, was trying to read.

"Isn't he cute?" she said, coming to the companionway.

"He's thirsty, and tired."

"I'll get him some water." She disappeared down the companionway. After a few seconds the bird followed her below. I waited. What was happening? Judy's head popped out of the companionway door.

"He finally drank some water. I had to drip some on his head before he would touch it. Then he took a bath in it. I think he's hungry too."

"Why don't you give him that roll with sesame seeds on it? Maybe he'll eat the seeds." A few minutes later, she stuck her head out and reported that the bird was eating the bread. I was sure he would leave after resting a few minutes.

When I got off watch, I went below and lay on the bunk. I was not sleepy, just tired. Soon the bird, who we named Stormalong or Stormy for short, came and sat on my stomach. He looked at me and pecked at my shirt. I held out a finger and, with some hesitation, he climbed up on it.

"Chirp," he said, "Chirp, chirp."

Not knowing for sure what he was talking about, I agreed with him anyway.

During my early morning watch, along about dawn I heard Stormy's "chirp" again. There he was, sitting in the doorway to the companionway. He looked at me and chirped. Then he turned around, looked down into the cabin, and chirped. It was clear that Stormy wanted something.

I went below. He had water from the day before, but he would not touch it.

"Chirp," he said sternly.

I understood. No self-respecting sailing bird would use yesterday's water. Renewing the water made Stormy happy and with a joyous chirp, he dived in.

For several days, Stormy stayed with us and helped us do our many chores.

It was New Years Eve and I did not have a date. The party this year was being held at the home of one of the old Blue Note Band group. After attending the midnight service, I went by myself. It was not one of the most uproarious parties I ever attended. Everyone was sitting around and talking.

I went into the kitchen and found a girl I did not know doing dishes. *This is ridiculous. There is more action here than anywhere else. Maybe I will just go home.*

However, the girl doing dishes was pretty and we talked a while as I helped her by drying the dishes. Her name was Judy, she went to San Francisco State, was a musician, and attended the Episcopal Church. All this, particularly the latter, was as good a recommendation as anyone could get with me. When we finished dishes, we went to the family room and began dancing. Judy was a fair dancer and we had a great time. I was able to sneak in a kiss before the party broke up at dawn.

When I left the place with my friend Manny, I told him I was going to marry that girl.

"*What was her name, anyway?*" I wondered when I arrived home. I had her phone number, but I could not remember her name. It began with a "J" like Jean or Jane. *Yeah, Jane sounded right.*

For the next few weeks, I was busy doing term papers and getting through finals. I felt like I was up to my ears in alligators and sinking fast. The exams were soon over and I made a call to . . . *think her name is Jane.*

"Hello," a woman's voice answered.

"Hello," I replied, "Is Jane there?"

"Yes, this is Jane."

"Hi Jane, this is Ames."

Silence.

"It's Ames. Don't you remember me from the party?"

More silence. *Some impression I must have made.*

"I thought maybe we could go out to a movie tonight," I said.

"I think you must be calling for my sister Judy. Just a minute."

I was sure the phone glowed red in my hands. I was so embarrassed. Jane was Judy's older sister.

Boy, do I know how to *make a good impression on a girl!*

Judy and I dated steadily. She lived In Oakland, a good forty minutes drive from my house over the Bay Bridge. She was fun and very naive, which was refreshing to me, so I did not mind the drive.

While in college, I had been able to get a full time job on The San Francisco Call-Bulletin, a Hearst afternoon paper. It was great, especially for a journalism major. I was a copy boy, which was the lowest of life forms in the newsroom. A reporter who wanted something would shout,

"Boy!"

One of the copy boys had to run, not walk, to his desk. He might want a cup of coffee, to have his wastebasket emptied, or to hand us a piece of copy for the city editor. This last was what we aspiring reporters looked forward to. As we ran from the reporter to the city desk, we would try to find out what he had written. This was news, real news before anyone else knew about it!

Copy boys had other duties: counting the fire bells and reporting the location of the fire to the city desk, cutting out local stories from competitive papers, running copy to the news services, and we all tried to write our own stories, which seldom were published. One of the benefits of working for a paper was the "Annie Oaklies" (free tickets) to plays, operas, movies, and sometimes ball games. This made it easy to date Judy. We went to the symphony, the opera, and plays.

Working on the Call-Bulletin was very exciting, although it did not pay much. Samuel Clemens (Mark Twain) had worked there when the paper was called The Daily Call, and you could go into the back files and read his copy.

I led an exhausting life, especially right after my father's death. On Fridays, I would generally play music until midnight with a small combo we formed at college. I would go home for a couple of hours sleep and be at work by three in the morning. I would get off work at eleven and beat it home for two more hours sleep. In the afternoon, I would clean the church until five-thirty, and then head for a date with Judy.

She never wanted me to go home after the date, so I would not get away until three in the morning. I would put the car on autopilot and head for home to catch three hours sleep since I had to be at church by seven-thirty. There were times I overslept and came to church wearing my pajamas under my cassock. It was one of the benefits of living practically in the church.

Things eased up a little when we moved from the rectory. We discovered a few small insurance policies and gathered enough money to buy a small house south of San Francisco in Colma. This made my drive to Judy's more than an hour. With my income, Social Security and my father's very small pension, we lived fairly well. One sister married and the other graduated high school, and my mother found a job cooking for a retreat house near Russian River during the summers.

I was already tired of being "the man of the house." I did not want the responsibility of my mother and sisters. I wanted to marry Judy, but responsibilities held me back. I had talked to my father about marriage before he died.

"Son," he said, "If you ever go into the priesthood, don't get married. If you do get married, marry a rich girl." He knew I was going to marry Judy, who was far from being a rich girl.

Judy made it very hard for me to keep to my dating rules. She lived so far away it was difficult to double date, and when we did, none of the guys wanted to ride with me for two extra hours just to pick her up and deliver her home. She did not like to double date anyway. I was reduced to exercising self-control, which did not always work too well.

I asked Judy to marry me and we were married in July, just before my summer finals at college. Our honeymoon consisted of one night in a motel in Sacramento. On Monday morning, I took my first final exam and aced it.

After much searching, we found a little apartment on O'Farrell Street in downtown San Francisco. It had a bed that dropped down from the wall and fell down to the floor if our lovemaking became too energetic. Both of us registered for San Francisco State College in August.

I continued to work for the Call-Bulletin full time in the evenings. That summer the managing editor assigned me to the "Night Desk" from two to ten, Sunday through Thursday. I was in charge of the activities for the evening, kind of being night City Editor.

I was in charge of a reporter and a photographer. All I really did was keep an ear on the police radio and watch the teletypes. If anything came in that needed coverage, I would radio the photographer. The reporter usually came into the office and did some re-writing if nothing else was happening.

One evening a huge fire was reported in the city of San Rafael across the bay. The fire got out of control and they started calling units of the San Francisco Fire Department to the scene. Rick, our reporter, had not shown up. He was almost two hours late. I had covered for him many times in the past, but I could not cover for him this night. I sent the photographer to San Rafael and called in another reporter. I had to tell the Managing Editor about the replacement.

I had done the right thing, but they fired the reporter. He was a strange man anyway. When Rick did get to work, he would spend hours in the morgue, where old newspaper stories and photographs were filed.

Rick was very angry about being fired and blamed me. He called one night and threatened me, but I did not take him very seriously. The next day the Managing Editor asked if I had heard from him and I told him about the call. He did not say much, so I thought nothing of it.

Later that night I was busy rewriting press releases when I heard a noise. I was by myself since the reporter and photographer were out on a society story. I looked up and there was Rick.

"I told you I was going to get you!" He had something in his hand, but I could not see it too well since the city room was large and he was at the other end of it.

"You got me fired and now you're going to pay!" He took a few steps toward me. It was then I saw the gun in his hand. I was behind the big city desk and tried to figure out how I could get down before he fired.

"You god dammed son of a bitch." He continued moving forward waving the pistol around, "I'm gonna kill you!"

I thought if I got down behind the desk I might crawl to the pressroom doors. There were more places to hide in there.

Just then, several men from the sports section office, the drama critic's office, and the men's room ran in, jumped on him, and took the gun away and hand-cuffed him in seconds.

I just stood there with wet pants. The Managing Editor came in.

"How ya doin' Ames? Couldn't let you know what was happening. I needed you for bait. It worked."

"Thanks," I mumbled as I walked directly to the men's room and vomited in the sink. When I came out, the Managing Editor was still there, with a couple of glasses of whisky in his hand. I drank one straight down and he poured another one for me.

"You did real well. Rick had called the paper this afternoon and threatened to kill you if he didn't get his job back. That's why I asked you if you had heard from him. The police staked out the place at five. They did a good job."

"What if they hadn't?" I asked.

"Well . . ." There was silence for a minute. "Have another drink."

Charley, a heavyset man in his early thirties with curly blond hair, which would not stay combed, was the next reporter assigned to us. He was a good Catholic and had ten kids. We became great friends. He had a very lively imagination and was a terrific writer. There was no way he could support his family on his salary at the Call-Bulletin, so he used to write a novel a week.

"How can you possible write a novel a week?" I asked him.

He smiled. "I go to garage sales and buy up used paperbacks. You can get them for a penny a piece sometimes. My basement is full of them. I have a stack of westerns, a stack of sci-fi, and a stack of murder mysteries."

"How does that help you?"

"Well, on Friday morning I go down to the basement and turn the lights off. I reach out and grab a book from each stack. Then I go into the dining room, take parts from each book, and make a new one. It's just like rewriting. I have one worry, though."

"What's that?"

"Some day I'm going to come up from the basement with three of my own books and end up reproducing one of the originals!"

Charley was also an opera buff. He tried out every year for the San Francisco Opera Chorus, but was never accepted. He had a great voice, though. I know, because he would break out singing The Anvil Chorus from La Traviata at unexpected times.

One Sunday he came to work looking beat.

"Boy, you look exhausted," I said as he settled his bulk into a seat at the rewrite desk across from me.

"I am. I almost called in sick." Charley never called in sick. He could be dying, but he would be to work on time. "Let me give you some advice," he continued.

"Shoot."

"Ames, never, never, never attempt to make love while listening to the Ride of the Valkyries."

Judy was pregnant, which made for a change in our young marriage. We never had much money. She had been able to make some playing percussion for several symphonies, and even got to play at the first Monterey Jazz Festival, but we were definitely broke most of the time.

Our dinner menu was spaghetti without meat six days a week. On Sundays, we went out to eat in China Town, where we would dine on beef or pork noodles and tea. Our apartment was not very great either. When I came home at midnight, I would gather all the drunks in the lobby and deliver them to their apartments.

We had noticed the ceiling of our apartment had indentations in it, but we thought it was some kind of design. Judy's mom and dad came over for dinner one Saturday. We had splurged and bought some unidentifiable meat for the spaghetti in their honor. We wanted to show them how well we were doing. Then it happened . . .

"You g-d d—n!" shouted a woman's voice from above.

"Ah, shut up you bitch!" There was a crashing sound.

Judy and I pretended we heard nothing. Her parents followed our lead.

"Don't you hit me you sh-t head!"

"I'll do any f—kin' thing I want!" Another crash sounded louder than the last, followed by the sound of a window opening into the air well.

A scream penetrated our apartment.

"I'll get that nice young man from downstairs and he'll whip your ass."

Eventually, Judy's parents left and I pounded the ceiling with the broom, adding to the ceiling's design. We were embarrassed and exhausted. We went to bed and, as usual, it fell down.

I did not know how we were going to support a baby, and I certainly did not want to raise a baby here. I would have to find another job.

CHAPTER NINE

The HAM radio was giving me trouble. Water had dripped on it from a leak under the cabin window. It would operate fine for a while and then cut out, or static would interfere with my reception.

"North Atlantic weather," the man said in slow speed so all could understand. "Synopsis: There are several lows in the North Atlantic causing gale and storm conditions. These lows are moving to the north-east. Positions of lows are as follows . . . (static for about two minutes) . . . coast of North America and out past the 1000 fathom line . . . (static)"

O drat, I think, *here we go again.* I fiddled with the knobs and the radio decided to go on its own and change its frequencies as if on the scan mode. The only way I could stop it was to turn it off. Eventually, I reach the weather again.

" . . . and south of this system for three hundred miles gale and storm winds are forecast, with winds from the east and south-east forty to fifty knots and seas to twenty feet (static)."

We're in for it now! I tried for a few minutes to recapture the weather, but I had the information we needed. Forty to 50 knot winds were forecast! I was not ready for this. We had not been able to afford a storm trysail, so what could I do now to make the boat safer in such heavy winds?

Panic clawed around the edges of my consciousness.

"Chirp," said Stormy, as he fluttered to the chart table. He looked at me with his big eyes as if to say, "You can handle this."

"All right Stormy, but don't be so cheery. You can abandon ship easier than we can," I grumbled.

My encroaching panic subsided. "I'll take the jib down now, and run on engine and mizzen," I mumbled to Stormy. Making these plans eased my anxiety to some extent, but thinking about taking the jib down raised it again.

Our boat has a six-foot bowsprit and the sail is hanked on in the old-fashioned way. I would have to go out on that blasted bowsprit.

Judy came on deck to handle the wheel, and I secured my safety harness to the tack line and went forward. I cringed, seeing the bowsprit burying itself in the huge waves.

"It's got to be done," I said aloud to no one, and gave Judy the hand sign to come upwind. Releasing the halyard, I crawled out to the end of the bowsprit to haul the sail down. Then, lying prone on the grating of the bowsprit, I slowly unhanked the jib while being immersed by a wave one minute and tossed about a foot above the platform the next. After unhanking each fastening, I stuffed the sail under me to keep it in control. After what seemed like hours, I was able to get the sail stuffed down the fore hatch.

I was tired. I started the engine and stumbled down the companionway to rest keeping my wet clothes on and lying on the floor in the forward cabin. Stormy came in to check on me, then with a chirp perched on a bungee cord, tucked his head under his wing, and fell asleep. With this show of confidence, what could I do but follow his example.

Finding another better paying job was not difficult. One day the City Editor called me in to tell me of a job he had heard of in Vallejo. I went for an interview and found the job was for a reporter/photographer in a bureau office in Fairfield, California. I could report, but I had never been a photographer.

"We need a good photographer there," said the burly Managing Editor of the Vallejo Times-Herald and News-Chronicle. "Can you do news photos and handle a Graphflex camera?"

I had been taught by one of my first journalism professors to never admit you do not know something. I hardly knew how to take a picture with a Brownie camera, but I replied, "Sure."

"Have you any experience with a teletype? You'll have to file your stories on a teletype."

Well, I did have experience with a teletype. I had torn stories off them and changed the paper and ribbons in them plenty of times as a copy boy. How much harder would it be to file stories on one?

"I've had about three years experience on them."

"You'll have to work out of the Fairfield bureau. That's the county seat of Solano County. You would be in charge, along with Bernie the other reporter, in making sure all the county news gets reported. The important thing is for us not to let the Solano Republican scoop us on anything. Above all I don't want you to fraternize with those other reporters. Stay clear away from them."

"Sounds great to me."

"Can you start in two weeks?"

"Sure." I said. My mind was racing. How was I going to learn to operate a camera in two weeks?

Back at the Call-Bulletin, I told the Managing Editor about my job and gave two weeks' notice. Then I went into the photography department and asked for help. All twelve of the photographers, some Pulitzer Prize winners, volunteered to teach me.

"Sure," said Johnny, one of the Call-Bulletin photographers, "you can learn enough to get by in two weeks. The rest is just practice and experience. All you have to know is how to load negative holders, take a picture, develop the negative, and make a print."

"You've got only one chance for a picture with a Graphflex. These young modern photographers with their Roliflex cameras aren't real news photographers," said Bill, the Call's oldest cameraman. "They just take a lot of pictures and hope one of them is good. With the Graphflex, you have one chance and it better be a good picture."

"Now Ames," said Johnny one afternoon, "you can sometimes fix up a poor photo when you print it by fading the light on the background." As he said this, he took a negative and placed it in the enlarger. As he pressed down on the foot switch, he waved his hands over it. When the picture was printed, the main focus was definitely on the mayor and all the background was less distinct.

I'll never learn all this, I thought.

I was taught twelve ways of taking a news photo, seven ways of developing the negatives, and five ways of loading the holders in daylight. In a few more days I was going to have to do all this by myself.

We had arranged for the baby to be born at a San Francisco hospital, so Judy stayed in Oakland with her parents for the remaining month before her due date. I went to Fairfield and moved into the cheapest motel in town, the El Rancho Deluxe. *Some deluxe,* I thought. There were separate cabins equipped with a bed, a washbasin and cockroaches. The bathrooms and telephones were about half a block away.

On checking in, the desk person informed me, "No women are allowed in the room over night, don't wash condoms down the sink, and don't pee out the window." I knew I was in for some interesting nights.

The bureau office was on the upper floor of a two-story building, the second tallest building in town.

"I don't take pictures and I don't work weekends," Bernie, my new coworker, said with a frown. He was a large man in his 40's, and he had a habit of trying to comb his hair, of which he had very little. He did not talk much and didn't seem very happy. The office was an eight by ten foot room with a small window, a desk, a table piled three foot high with newspapers, and a teletype.

Pointing to the pile of newspapers, he said, "This here's the morgue. Better read back a few weeks so you'll know what's happening. The camera is over there. I'm going to lunch."

After Bernie left, I looked over the camera I was to use. It was a regular, but old, Graphflex. I was very disappointed to see it used flash bulbs. Flash bulbs slow down the rate of picture-taking. In the camera bag there were two negative holders (four negatives) and four flash bulbs.

I started reading back files, but Bernie stormed through the door before I had read very much.

"Grab the camera and come with me. Hurry!" We ran down the stairs and across the street to the county court house. "They're going to move him any minute," he said.

"Move who?" I asked.

"The kidnapper. The sheriff's going to parade him down the hall so we can get a good picture. I hope you can take a good one."

At this point, the Sheriff opened a door and escorted a hand-cuffed man down the hallway. A handful of big city photographers took six pictures to my one. I was not sure I had even gotten one. Then it was over. The other photographers ran out the door.

"Let's get those on the bus," said Bernie. "I'll teletype the caption."

"Get what on the bus?" I asked.

"The photographs you took."

"Make that singular," I said.

"Those other guys took three or four. I hope yours turns out good, or I'll have to wait again while they replace you."

I wondered how much I could take of Bernie. Was he the reason for the opening I was filling?

The news that I would not have to develop or print the pictures was a two edged-sword. How would I find out how good the pictures were? How could I wave my hands over the enlarger to correct any mistakes? On the other hand, over-developing the negative would no longer be a nightmare.

My first Friday at work, I was assigned to cover the arrival of the first B-52G SAC bomber to Travis Air Force Base near Fairfield. The huge droopy winged bomber landed right on time. We stood around and waited for the disembarkation of the Base Commander who had brought the plane in, Colonel William Powell. The crew and important base personnel gathered under the mighty wing for a picture. All of us photographers got ready to take pictures. A hand tapped me on the shoulder,

"You can't use a flash bulb here," said an officer in a polite but firm manner. "Too much jet fuel . . . might blow us up." He smiled.

I was flustered. Everyone else was madly taking pictures and I had to reset my camera. I got my picture and was shuffled off to the cocktail reception and press conference. The booze was flowing. I stood around with my bourbon on the rocks waiting for some action. I was feeling pretty satisfied with myself. I had written most of the lead story and several sidebars from handouts and interviews with high-ranking officers during the week, so all I had to do was write the lead and caption.

Then my stomach sank. I had forgotten to get the names of all those people in the photograph. There had been about twelve. Since I would not be developing the photos myself, I would not be able to figure it out by looking at the picture. I would be fired. The Solano Republican would scoop us!

I felt like a clod.

How could I get the caption? I looked around the room and my eyes fell on the short stooped thin figure of the Solano Republican photographer, Frank. I went over to him.

"Nice night."

"Yea," he said, looking disparagingly at the plate of finger sandwiches in his hand. "Wish they had more to eat."

"Tell you what, after this is over let's go have a good dinner and get to know one another." His eyes lit up. He was used to being snubbed by the Times-Herald reporters.

"Sure, that sounds great! But I got to develop these pictures first. It'll be awful late."

"That's OK. I'll come and give you a hand."

We left after the press conference. I stopped by the bus station and dropped the film off with a note that the story and caption would be on the way later.

I met Frank at the door of the Solano Republican. "While you're developing the pix, I'll write the caption for you," I said.

"Hey, that's great. Here are the names." I put two pieces of paper with carbon in the typewriter and quickly wrote the caption. In half an hour we were done.

"I have to stop by my office for a minute to file my story." I was feeling pretty satisfied with myself. All I had to do was write the lead and caption.

"I'll meet you at the Grange Restaurant in fifteen minutes," I said. After filing my story and the caption, I joined Frank and treated myself to a steak.

A week later I was covering a very boring school board meeting. The editor of the Solano Republican was there and after the meeting we introduced ourselves.

"I've been looking forward to meeting you," he said, showing a boyish grin. "I'm Bill Shepherd." He was about my age and I liked his style right away.

"You sure put one over on Frank last week."

"I did?"

"Yah, stealing that caption from him."

"How did you know about that?"

"Oh it was easy. You goofed. You took the original with you and he filed the carbon. He doesn't have much smarts. I'll have to watch you carefully."

"Well, let's start by having a drink."

"Come on over to my place." He started putting on his coat. "I'd like you to meet Mary, my wife."

"I don't know. I'm not supposed to fraternize with the enemy," I laughed.

"I won't tell if you don't."

Thus began a long friendship with Bill continually trying to scoop me and I him. I ended up living at his house for about two weeks until one morning Bill woke me up saying Judy was on the way to the hospital.

"Oh God," I cried, and rushed to get dressed. I hopped into my '52 Hudson and headed for San Francisco. The trip from Fairfield to San Francisco usually took an hour and a half, but it took less than an hour that day.

I ran up to the receptionist and asked for my wife. She said there was no Judy Swartsfager in the hospital. I began to panic. I did not remember seeing any accidents on the way, but maybe something went wrong with the car. I could see her having the baby on the floor of a greasy, grimy mechanic's garage floor.

"Perhaps," the receptionist was saying, "you might check the emergency room. They may know something."

I ran down the corridor and into the emergency room.

"Do you have Judy?" I shouted.

"Judy who?" the nurse asked patiently. I explained the situation and she checked the labor room. They said she had been taken in just fifteen minutes before and I was directed to the obstetrics department. As I exited the elevator I saw her being wheeled down the corridor with a baby in her arms.

"Stop!" I shouted. The nurses looked anxious. "That's my wife."

"So," said a big African-American frowning nurse, "the father's finally gotten here. Well, you'll just have to wait a few minutes until we get her settled. She's doing fine." And they were gone.

I did not even know if it was a girl or a boy. The ten minutes it took for them to get her settled seemed like a year. I had my chance to pace the floor with the other waiting fathers.

"Mr. Swartsfager?" asked a nurse.

"Come this way." She took me to Judy's room and there they were.

"I'm OK," Judy said with a tired smile. "Look at her; she's so small and beautiful."

I looked and saw a red, wrinkled, squirming little creature. She definitely was not cute, but Judy and I had made her and this made her beautiful. We named her Debra Ann.

A few weeks after Debra was born, we moved to Fairfield and into a tiny house. For the first time I felt like a real husband and father.

After nine months, I had a yearning to get a better job and return to college. I applied to various papers, and finally the Call-Bulletin said they would hire me as a reporter, starting in a month. I needed a vacation so I gave two weeks notice and we moved in with my mother while we looked for an apartment. The day before I was to report to work I received a telegram:

"THIS IS TO ADVISE YOU THAT THE SAN FRANCISCO CALL-BULLETIN AND THE SAN FRANCISCO NEWS HAVE JUST MERGED. THE CLASSIFIED DEPARTMENT, CIRCULATION DEPARTMENT, BUSINESS OFFICE OF THE CALL-BULLETIN WILL BE RETAINED ALONG WITH THE EDITORIAL AND PRINTING STAFF OF THE NEWS. THEREFORE, WE ARE SORRY TO INFORM YOU THAT YOUR SERVICES WILL NO LONGER BE NEEDED."

Nothing like being fired before I even start!

CHAPTER TEN

"Ames, dinner is ready," Judy called from the galley. "Hurry Ames. Dinner's ready." I heard her say again.

We had been beating to windward for five days now with winds consistently from the south-east. We had not seen the sun, stars, moon, or even the horizon since we left Beaufort. Although we never did get that huge storm, we were tired and exhausted.

Again Judy called to me. As I unwound myself from the corner of the cockpit that protected me somewhat from the wind and spray, I thought it strange for her to make dinner at two in the morning.

I danced across the bucking cockpit and leaped over the wash of water left from a wave that had crashed aboard. Making my way down the ladder, I saw that the galley was dark and Judy was snuggled in her bunk sound asleep.

I shook my head, clambered back into my watch position and attempted to get comfortable again. *Must have dreamt it.* I scanned the horizon for ships and settled down to complete my watch.

The next day I told Judy about the experience, half—hoping she would indeed cook a big dinner. I was to be disappointed, as it was well-nigh impossible to make much of anything except peanut butter sandwiches as the waves that tossed the boat also tossed our pans from the stove.

Judy said she had also heard voices, except it was our daughters calling to her.

The following night we both heard whole choirs singing in the rigging and started looking forward to the company of these ghoulish, disembodied voices that kept us company during our watches.

All the noise of the boat crashing through the waves and the banging of pots and pans that no towel would quiet was wearing us out. I looked at the chart and found we were one hundred-fifty miles from Bermuda.

The following morning I asked Judy, "Do you want to go to Bermuda? The weather report is not encouraging for the next few days. We are able to make our easting, but if we try to go south we'll end up in the Bahamas."

"I'm tired," she said, "but you do what you think is best." This is typical Judy. She never lets me off the hook.

So, I thought. *What is best?* I was also very tired, but did not want to admit it. If only the sun would come out. What I needed was a sign.

At this point Stormy fluttered down from his perch on the bookcase and tapped his beak on the island of Bermuda. Then he looked at me.

"Looks like Stormy's voted," said Judy with a laugh. "Chirp," said Stormy, pecking the chart again. Who was I not to accept such a sign? Besides, I felt if I did not go to Bermuda, I might face a mutiny, at least from Stormy.

"Let's go." I threw up my hands in fake surrender although I was ready to get out of this mess also.

The next morning, I watched for Stormy to make his usual early morning demands for water and fresh bread. However, he did not show up. I went down and looked for him in his usual haunts below decks, but he was not there either.

When Judy got up a few hours later, she searched the boat for him. He had gone. He must have slipped by me at first light and headed for Bermuda.

I was overcome with grief.

I missed him. The only positive thing that helped both Judy and me was knowing he had probably made it to shore and was lying on the beach with his fellow birds, getting a tan and telling tall sea tales.

They say that job hunting is the hardest work you can do and I am a real believer. Where is a young green reporter going to find a job when fifty journeymen reporters and photographers from the Call-Bulletin were flooding the market? Every day at eight, I would set out and not get home until evening.

I applied for all kinds of jobs: newspapers, public relations, industry magazines. I had a wife and child to support and very little savings.

I even went to Southern Pacific, which had advertised for a clerk.

"How fast do you type?" asked the employment officer.

"I don't know. Pretty fast I think."

"We'll give you a typing test." She took me to a typing table with a manual typewriter and gave me a printed letter. Now I am not a touch typist, but I finished fast and turned in my results. She counted and said "Ahum" several times.

"Well, how did I do?"

"Not bad. You type about forty words a minute, but you completely rewrote the letter."

I was not hired.

Later in the week, I heard about a temporary job with a publicity campaign for the next mayor of San Francisco. I went and applied.

I had heard about smoke-filled rooms. Men with cigars stuffed in their faces, with bands around their sleeves to keep the cuffs up, green visors on their heads, making political moves as if they were playing chess. I never believed, until I opened the door to their office, that these back rooms existed. It was in such a room that I had my interview with a famous political consultant. He was conducting a campaign against the incumbent mayor.

"The job should take two days and the pay is fifty dollars a day. Take it or leave it," he said in a cloud of cigar smoke. He was fat, his tie was loose, and he made that cigar produce more smoke than a three-alarm fire.

We needed the money. I had not worked for almost a month.

"What's the job?"

"I'll explain it after you make your decision," he said, as he hooked his thumbs under his suspenders. If he had not had a cigar between his lips, I would have sworn he was smiling. I felt that something was not right, but . . .

"I'll take the job."

I was to go to the National Gay Liberation Convention then meeting in San Francisco.

"Try to get them to introduce and pass a resolution in support of the incumbent Mayor." The words seemed to explode from a cloud of cigar smoke.

Listen to your gut stupid! You have been trapped. I have never felt so insecure in my life. I went and talked to "men," "women," I was not sure.

Several times, I was propositioned, but was able to evade the invitations and circumvent any hard feeling by saying I was in mourning for my lover who had died recently. They were sensitive to my feelings and did not bother me. In two days, I was successful in getting the resolution passed.

The next morning the resolution was printed in the local newspapers in a full page advertisement with the caption:

"WOULD YOU VOTE FOR A MAYOR LIKE THIS?"

Apparently they would, as they re-elected the old mayor. I was one hundred dollars richer, and had learned that I did not like dirty political campaigning.

Eventually I found a job with Standard Oil of California, Inc. The job was originally for a mailroom clerk, but almost immediately, I was promoted to a Junior Clerk in the Retail Pricing Section.

Boring! I spent eight hours a day figuring price rebates to Chevron gas stations. But the pay was not bad and we were able to afford to move to a house in the Sunset District. Part of our rent was paid by baby-sitting the owner's son when he came home from school each day. In the meantime, I re-entered college in evening classes.

I was ambitious. I wanted to get ahead in the world. If I was going to work in business, I wanted to get to the top and right now!

A chance to be a substitute in a Senior Clerk's position was offered me. The work was easy, but still boring. My co-workers were a lot of fun and, although other sections we located in large open rooms, our department was privileged in having its own private room. Some days we were rowdy, which was a way of breaking up our boredom.

My ambition still drove me. They sent a young Canadian they had hired to fill the vacant position of Senior Clerk and I was told to train him. He was getting the position because he had a degree in accounting. I was angry because I had been doing the work and felt they should have given me the job. So when I found out that he did not know the difference between a debit and a credit in our accounting system, I taught him to record them backwards. A month later, they moved him to another department since he was continually screwing up in ours, thanks to me.

When he left, they gave the job to me. It was my second promotion in three months! However, I was still not satisfied. I called a friend in the department to which the new man had been reassigned and suggested they continue giving him false information. They did, and eventually he was fired.

When I heard he had been fired I felt as I did when I was about eight years old and had my first BB gun. Seeing a sparrow in a tree, I took aim and fired. For a second nothing happened. Then a drop of blood fell to the ground, followed by the bird. I was shocked and saddened by what I had done and never shot at another living thing.

This was a similar experience, and it left me feeling evil and dirty. My ambition and inclination toward evil scared me. Both had gotten out of control. Had I not erased the Mission District in me after all? Was I sliding back? Ever since leaving the Mission District I had felt like a man hanging from a cliff by his fingertips. *Had I finally regressed and fallen back into that gaping maw of the whale?*

Over the next few months, what I had done weighed heavily on me.

CHAPTER ELEVEN

"Gibbs Hill light five miles to starboard," I wrote in the log. "Wind SE twenty to twenty-five knots." At last, we were able to bear off and sailing was easier.

Looking to starboard, I could see the lights of Bermuda. They seemed so bright and friendly, especially after so many days at sea. Nevertheless, I knew that between us and the lights were coral reefs, which could grab our keel and kill us. I longed for a calm harbor and a good meal.

Soon the Great Head Light's red zone came into view. We could not turn in toward the island until it became green. Dawn came at last and we saw the sun for the first time in a week. We soon entered the green zone of Great Head, and changed course for the harbor entrance.

The customs dock was on the far side on Ordinance Island and I did not notice there was a boat at the dock until I came around the point. On the shore, a black man was waving to us wildly and pointing to a likely docking spot along the quay. We docked there and a man, who introduced himself as Bama, helped to tie our lines. It was eight in the morning and I was extremely tired.

"Wel'come Bermuda," Bama said with a huge smile. "You been here afore?"

"No, this is our first time." Judy answered, feeling strange talking to someone other than me.

I had gone down to shut off the engine. The compression shut-off cable had broken and I had to climb over the hot running engine to shut it off with a large screwdriver. I accidentally dropped the screwdriver in the bilge after getting the engine turned off. *What's the difference?* I thought. *We are tied up anyway.*

"We can stay here?" I asked Bama when I got back on deck.

"Sure mon," he said, showing his broad grin marred only by a few missing teeth. "This is a good place. We check your lines at night. The last man so happy he give me a whole bottle of rum, Mon."

Judy looked at me. We were wondering if this was a hint. I did not have any rum and certainly was not going to part with anything else in the way of booze. I finally gave Bama a dollar.

Then a man on a motor scooter drove up and welcomed us. In the nicest way possible, he told us we could not dock where we were but had to go to the customs dock across the way to clear in. I was confused.

"Bama said we could stay here," I said, looking around for him.

"Oh Bama," said the man, "he drinks a lot. Don't get too friendly with him or you'll never be rid of him. I'll help you with your lines. It looks like the other boat is leaving."

After clearing in we pulled in our lines and motored across the bay to anchor. We had a sandwich and then hit the bunk for some serious sleeping, feeling safe and secure, with the wind still whistling through the rigging.

That I could be so evil weighed heavily upon me. I knew that I could be evil; I had proved it to myself in the Mission District. I attempted to analyze why I had done this, but never could find the answer.

We had been attending All Saints Episcopal church, where my good friend and spiritual advisor Fr. Harris was rector. I helped as lay reader and acolyte while Judy sang in the choir. Week after week, I would go and pray that something would happen to change me. I was indeed frightened of myself and my actions. I remembered the things I had done in the Mission and knew I had a great tendency toward evil. I felt that if I just let up my guard a little, I might do something terrible.

From time to time, I had felt pulled to the ministry. Every time I felt this, I was able to banish the thought by remembering how my father had been treated, the parish and diocesan politics, the low pay, the difficulty in taking care of a family, and finally nothing, at the end, for the family. No, I was not interested in the ministry. I talked it over with Judy, but all she would say was that it was my decision.

I could not decide. I would wait to be called, but I did not really believe I would be called.

It was traditional to have an all night vigil during Holy Week on Holy Thursday. I signed up for a couple of hours in the early morning between two and four. The church was very quiet. There was a candle burning on a small table before the altar and the tabernacle where the sacrament was kept was open. I prayed and read scripture. Then I fought my sleepy eyelids for a while. The question of ministry floated back into my mind.

"0 Lord, I know you can't use me," I prayed. "You know how bad and evil I really am. Give me peace in my spirit. Forgive me for my sins." Then I went back to reading scriptures.

My favorite Gospel is Mark and I read about the events of Holy Thursday evening: the Last Supper, Jesus praying in the garden while his closest and best friends were sleeping, His arrest and capture, and Peter's denial of Jesus in the courtyard of the High Priest.

A voice, intuitive thought, a feeling, I do not know exactly what I heard or experienced. I did get the feeling that God was telling me that he wanted me just because of my unworthiness and sinfulness. I attempted to argue the point; God being God won the argument. An assurance came that God wanted me as I was and entering the ministry was not only the right thing to do, but that it was imperative. I was not worthy, but then neither were the apostles and they knew Jesus personally!

Finally, I felt that everything would come out all right. The pain would not be so much that I could not bear it. In addition, my family would survive. I would see to that.

With the decision made, I went to see The Rt. Rev. James A. Pike, our Diocesan Bishop, and demanded that I be considered for the priesthood. He smiled and said, "I've been waiting for you to say that. You will first have to complete college and be sure to take a year of Latin," he continued.

"But if I do all that and try to support my family, I'll not graduate from college for four more years. I'm only able to take six credits a semester at night school."

"Son, if you are meant to go to seminary and become a priest, God will make a way for you. Now don't worry."

I left the cathedral grounds in a deep depression. I did not think I would be able to make it through four or more years of evening classes. Some of my courses, Latin for example, were not even given at night. I could not quit work; we needed the money to survive. I was angry with the bishop.

For the next month or so I deliberated. One day I was getting gas at a Standard Station service station when a strange thought came to me. The next day I requested a meeting with my department head at Standard Oil.

"Mr. James," I said, "It's very nice of you to give me this time."

"That's all right, Ames. What can I do for you?"

"Well sir, it's hard to explain, but I've decided to go into the ministry . . . the priesthood in the Episcopal Church, to be exact. To do that I must finish college and go to seminary. I'm already taking a full load at college in the evenings, but I feel the need to speed things up. Is there any way I can be transferred to Standard Stations, Inc? That way I can attend college during the day and work in the evenings."

"Have you thought this out? I mean really thought this out?" Mr. James asked. "We have very high regard for you and your work here. No one has ever been promoted as fast in this division. I was thinking of putting you in the Junior Executive Training program. You have a great future here. Won't you reconsider?"

I thanked him for his kind support and assured him I felt I really had to make this move.

"Well, let's see what we can do. Come by my office tomorrow morning at ten."

The next day I returned.

"Here's what we're going to do," he said. "There are three stations that need a night Assistant Manager. You pick the one you want. We'll transfer you at an Assistant Manager's salary and commission, which will most likely equal your pay here. Next, we'll put you into our College Scholarship Program. As long as your grade average is "B" or better we will pay seventy-five percent of books and tuition."

"I don't know how to thank you," I said, humbled.

"When do you want to begin?"

"As soon as possible so that I can get my training done and be ready for the summer semester."

"Fine. I'll set you up for a special training course in two weeks. Tell me tomorrow which of these stations you want to work at and I'll call and tell them you are to set your own hours. Keep in touch."

"Thanks, thanks a lot."

"Oh and Ames, if you ever want to come back here, you're welcome."

The bishop had said God would provide and he sure had come through on this one. I took a full load on both summer sessions and then started with a twenty-four and a half unit fall semester, with three philosophy courses and Latin. I worked from midnight to eight in the morning, started classes at nine, and finished at four. Then home for study and a couple hours of sleep and back to work. I had taken Tuesdays and Wednesdays off, so on those two days it was not so bad. I had little time to study or sleep, and frequently napped in class. We had moved to Oakland and lived with my in-laws. Judy went to work and I stopped working.

Most of the time, my mother-in-law took care of our daughter. There were times when she could not, and then I had a choice of not going to classes or taking her with me. At college I could usually find someone to baby-sit for an hour or so when I would be in a class, but sometimes I had to take her to class. She was good and quiet, so most of the professors did not mind. However, my Latin Professor did not like it at all.

I must admit I let Debra do what she wanted in this class. There were only two students, so she did not disturb us by writing on the black boards, but it drove our professor crazy.

"Must you bring that child to class?" he would ask.

"Well, sir, it was either bringing her or not coming."

"In Harvard they would never permit such a thing."

"Yes," I replied, "but this isn't Harvard, or Yale, or Princeton. It's just a little state college and I am just a struggling poor student. If you want to expel me from your class, it's all right with me." I knew he could not expel me because he would find himself without a job. The administration had granted our petition to keep the class as long as there were two of us who required Latin for graduate school.

I finished college and graduated in June of 1961. I had again gotten straight "A's", except for Latin, where I had made a "C". Well, in any case, I had fulfilled my requirements.

I applied and was accepted at the Church Divinity School of the Pacific in Berkeley, California. However, the problem of money still reared its ugly head. The rules of the seminary did not allow students to work while in school. Judy's work was bringing in just enough to live on and we had moved to a little house in East Oakland, but we did not have enough money for tuition and books for two semesters. I had to find a job for the summer.

I heard of a cannery job and applied for it. They assigned me to the end of the gallon can assembly line. Dole leased the cannery and we were canning fruit cocktail in gallon cans. As I stumbled out into the early morning light after working the first night, I found I could not open my hands. They were locked into the position of holding the tool that I used to pick up the cans. A young college student who was working as a sweeper on my shift came over to help me unlock my car, but there was no way I could drive. He was very kind and took me home.

I came into the house and got into a hot bath. After soaking for an hour, I was able to move my hands. And so it went until I had saved up enough to pay tuition for both semesters, and then I quit. Since that time I have not been able to eat fruit cocktail.

CHAPTER TWELVE

At last, a peaceful night's sleep without interruption! The simplest things are the best things. A full night in bed asleep is a true luxury. Going up on deck with a cup of coffee, I looked at the beautiful morning and surveyed the harbor. The smell of bacon and eggs came up out of the galley. *This is what it is all about!*

Maybe it was worth the effort to get here. As one sailing friend asked philosophically, "Why does one have to go through Hell to get to Paradise?"

This did indeed look like paradise. The wind was light and the bay, which is surrounded by land, had just a ripple on it. The sun was warm on my back. A quaint looking village lay on the opposite shore and more than sixty boats were anchored around us, some getting ready to put out to sea. It looked as if the weather had broken.

Maybe we should have kept on, I wondered. However, I quickly pushed that thought aside. We were here and I was happy. Cruising is the only way we could visit such wonderful places. We have never had enough money to take vacations in distant places, except by sailing there.

"Butterfly, Butterfly, Sea Level," squawked our VHF radio.

"Go ahead Sea Level," I answered. Sea Level was one of the boats that left Beaufort the same day we had.

"Hey Butterfly, we are having a get-together on Queen of Hearts tonight to compare our trips. Can you make it?"

"Love to. What time?"

"Cocktails and snacks at six."

After breakfast, we moved the boat alongside the wall over by the village of St. George. This is one thing nice about Bermuda. They do not charge you for tying up to the wall. Everything else is very expensive.

After tying up, the man who had told us to move our boat the day before stopped by. He introduced himself as Bernie and told us he was the dock master for the port. He was dressed in Bermuda shorts, sports shirt, and motorcycle helmet.

76

"I was just going to call you and tell you to come over here by the wall," he said. "This is a good place to tie up unless a south-west or south-east wind begins to blow. The best place then is behind Ordinance Island. You know, where the customs dock is."

"Please come aboard and have some ginger bread and coffee," Judy invited.

"I will be glad to, but I've got to do something now. I'll be back in ten minutes."

Judy and I wondered about this man Bernie. Should we tip him? Was he another one like Bama? We really were not sure what to do. Why had he come by?

Bernie came back with a paper bag in his hand. "You like fish stew?" he asked, pulling a jar out of the bag. "My wife made fish stew last night. It takes her forever, but it's sure good."

"Sure we like it," I said already beginning to drool.

"Brought you a jar of it. Save the jar for me, will you? They're hard to come by."

Bernie came on board and we sat, drinking coffee and eating ginger bread. I love ginger bread. Bernie told us that in the Bermuda prison they get gingerbread every morning for breakfast. In fact, one time they stopped serving gingerbread and it provoked a riot.

After Bernie had gone, Judy and I laughed about our paranoia. Bernie was just being nice.

That evening the cruisers gathered on Queen of Hearts for drinks. There were crews from five boats. As we sat on the deck and watched the sunset, we began to discuss our various experiences. We were happy to find that all of the other crews had also heard voices.

"I was tired and very discouraged," said one.

"I spent most of one watch petting our dog. It relaxed me and I felt much better." He continued with a laugh, "Until I remembered we had no dog!"

Another captain told us of how his compass kept reassuring him that everything was going to be O.K. Still others shared stories of voices and music they had heard while on watch or resting. Although all of us experienced these auditory illusions, none of us seemed frightened by them.

As often happens in these sundown parties, we decided to go ashore for dinner. As we walked into the restaurant, Judy decided to call our youngest daughter, Laura. She had been feeling sick when we left so we were concerned about her health. The call went through and we received the crushing news that she had multiple sclerosis.

Here we were, thousands of miles from her. We went out for a walk, as we were in no condition to have dinner with our friends. After walking for a while, we decided Judy would go back to the States to be with Laura while I stayed on the boat. With that decision made, we went back to the boat and ate that wonderful fish stew Bernie's wife had made.

The next day we moved the boat behind Ordinance Island and Judy flew to the **U.S.**

Somehow, we managed to get through seminary. I was able to do public relations for the seminary in return for my tuition. Judy went to work for Nabisco and I studied, studied and studied. Debra stayed with her grandmother during the day. Money was always a problem.

The seminary had a rule against working during the school year, but towards the end of the second semester our funds were running low. I took a part-time job at the University of California in their entomology laboratory. When the summer finally arrived, they put me on full-time status and promoted me to Lab Assistant. My main job was raising cockroaches and mosquitoes. The lab was working on identifying a replacement for DDT and at one point I spent weeks beheading mosquitoes so we could find out whether a new chemical pesticide worked on their systemic system or nervous system.

I did find out something interesting. Only female mosquitoes bite. Therefore, if one is in the woods, all one has to do is stay away from female mosquitoes. You can tell the females because of the white spots on their breasts.

The job at UC was great and paid well, but when the fall semester started I was not able to keep up with work and seminary and had to quit work. The next summer I worked for Standard Stations, Inc. in Oakland.

I also interned at two churches while in seminary. The first was St. Paul's, Oakland. The rector was a kindly and loving man, but overworked and not getting much support from the congregation. They had one assistant priest, but needed at least one other. As there was no funding, the rector used up to seven seminarians in his programs. We worked for the experience: in other words, for free. My assignment, besides calling on possible new members, was the Young People's Fellowship group. The

YPF had about fifty active high school teenagers, and I enjoyed working with them.

During the Cuban Missile incident the kids were scared to death. So was I.

"Every time I go to sleep," one told me, "I am never sure I'll wake up. If they bomb us, you know."

We spent many hours discussing this fear, and the second highest concern on their list: sex. They were at an age when they were pressured to have sex. In the early sixties parents were not too good about explaining the facts of sex and outside the locker room there was no information given in the schools.

I had the brilliant idea of setting up a seminar on sex. After clearing it with the rector, I arranged five lectures: First, the physical aspects of sex. For this lecture, I obtained two doctors, a male for the boys and a female for the girls. I planned to split the boys and girls into two separate rooms. These doctors were to describe accurately the sexual physiology of humans. The second lecture was to be a psychologist who discussed the psychological ramifications of teenage sex. The third lecture, by a lawyer, discussed the legal responsibilities of sex (rape, paternity suits, child support, etc); and the fourth lecture would be a social worker who talked about the problems of unwed mothers. I would give the final lecture, dealing with the moral responsibilities of sex.

The whole seminar almost fell apart at the beginning because of a slight error on my part. The first lecture had gone very well. The girls met in the Women's Guild Room and I stayed with the boys and listened while the doctor talked to us and filled the blackboard with all kinds of very graphic drawings of sex organs. After the lecture was over, I carefully erased the board.

The next morning I was called out of my seminary classes by the Dean and told to report immediately to the church. The rector was very angry with me, but I did not understand why. I had cleared the seminar with him. Had the parents complained?

"I don't know what to do," he said to me. He opened a drawer, took out two pills and swallowed them without water. "How could you do this to me, Ames?"

"What did I do, sir?"

"Oh God," he said as his eyes rolled heavenward, "What did he do? I'll tell you what you did. You forgot to erase the blackboard in the Women's Guild Room! They met for coffee and prayer this morning and were greeted with pornographic pictures allover their blackboard!"

"I'm sorry, sir," I said mournfully, realizing my mistake. I could picture the little old ladies coming into the guild room and being confronted with drawings of penises, vaginas, and both together.

"Do you think they learned anything?" I asked.

For a minute, I thought he would explode, then a smile broke, and soon we were both laughing heartily.

"Don't do that to me again," he said with finality.

I did pretty well in seminary, except for one class, where I got an incomplete. The class was Devotional Life and taught by a wonderful old Chinese missionary, who was not quite up with the modern seminarian. The average age of my class was 35 and 80% of us were married. The days of the young naive seminarian were no longer as more and more people were beginning to be called to the ministry late in life.

Good Dr. Benson was discussing prayers to use in married life.

"We should pray at every occasion," he said. "Even when we have intimate relations with our wives. We should pray before, during and after sexual relations. For example, before intercourse one might pray, 'Dear Lord help us make this act of intercourse be to your honor and glory. Amen.'

"Now, he continued, "do any of you have any special prayer you would like to share?"

There was a great silence. I do not think any of us had ever prayed before, during, or after intercourse. Then an idea entered my mind. I held up my hand.

"Yes, Ames."

"Well, sir," I said hesitantly, "when I reach a climax I yell 'Oh God! Oh God!'" The whole class roared and could not stop laughing. Dr. Benson gave me an incomplete. I appealed it to the Dean, who had it changed and told the old professor that if he did not ask questions like that he would not get responses like that.

At the end of my middler (second) year of seminary our second daughter was born, Alaina Beth. At least she waited until after the finals.

In my senior year, I worked for Trinity Church in San Francisco for pay. We needed every cent we could get, as our funds were at rock bottom. By this time we had moved into a housing project and, due to the baby, Judy could not work. I had a great time working at Trinity and was able to do a specialized ministry with the thousands of young adults who lived around the church. These young people were lonely and had many stresses on their lives. Most of them lived in rooming houses or residences and responded well when the church made contact with them. Although I had a great time in this ministry, there was no guarantee it would continue after gradation.

I was drawn to work in the ghetto, but I refused to place my family in the same environment in which I had lived. My best friend at seminary, Don Ball, told me I should go into prison ministry, but I did not think much of the idea. It was too easy to see myself sitting in a cell, where many of my friends from the Mission district had ended up.

I have always been a romantic person and had read a lot about missionaries. I visualized myself traipsing through the jungle with pith helmet and collar, ready to save the natives, or sailing to some far off South Pacific island with my collar and sarong. Therefore when I saw a notice about Foreign Missions I quickly applied.

It took months and months of physical examinations for the whole family. Acceptance was based on our ability to pass the physical as well as the need for missionaries. May came, there were less than four weeks until graduation, and I still had not heard whether we were accepted. When Trinity Church asked me to stay on as an assistant, I was in a quandary. If I was not accepted as a missionary, I would like to work with this church. I told the rector I would inform him of my decision the following morning.

When I got home that night, there was a letter advising that we had been appointed as missionaries. We would be going to Costa Rica for language training in August.

CHAPTER THIRTEEN

Making the decision to continue one's journey is sometimes very difficult. We were ready to go as far as boat preparation. Judy had returned from visiting our daughter, who was going into remission. The boat was stocked with food and ready to go, but we stayed in port.

Should we continue with our daughter being so ill? If we were to live close to her, we could provide some moral support. However, we could do nothing about her illness. It would be with her for the rest of her life, or until some drug could be found to control it. Perhaps living close by would be a hindrance to Laura and make her feel more handicapped than she really was.

No, we should not stop to go live near her. We could fly back to see her if she became really ill or depressed or if Judy could not stand not being by her side. To complicate our decision, the Bureau of Prisons wanted me to come back on contract for six months at a prison in Florida. We were short on money, thanks to the federal government taking my lump-sum retirement payment two months before I was eligible to retire. We were stretched very thin, trying to cruise and payoff the boat while on retirement pay.

But I didn't want to go back to work.

We did not want to leave Bermuda because we were afraid. After the beating we took getting here, what would the trip to St. Thomas be like? It was a nine hundred mile sail.

We had some great times visiting the churches and getting to know the people and the island. My biggest thrill was preaching in the oldest Anglican Church with a continuing congregation in the Western Hemisphere, St. Peter. It was exciting to mount the three-tier pulpit and look out over the congregation.

December came and several boats got their courage together and left, while we looked more closely at the weather. The hardships of our voyage here had begun to fade and the time was nearing for us to leave. We felt it in our bones and grew restless and at times even bored. Therefore, every morning we would go to the customs office and pick up the current five-day forecast.

At last, we knew we would leave the following morning. It really did not make any difference what the weather was. We knew we had to leave and discover what lay in front of our bow.

We got off the plane, stiff from sitting the six hours from Houston, Texas to San Jose, Costa Rica with two squirmy daughters. We were tired and disorientated. As we went through customs, I saw a friendly face through the glass door. The Rev. Jose Carlo, an old friend of mine who had graduated from Church Divinity School of the Pacific the year I started, had come to meet us. It was great seeing a familiar face in a crowd of Spanish-speaking people.

Jose graciously drove us to what would be our new home for the nine months we attended language school. He dropped us off and told us that a woman, Maria, would come over the next day and be our maid. Then, seeing our exhaustion, he left us to our own devises.

The thought of having a maid shattered my self-image of a struggling missionary. You cannot tell your friends about it because they would not think you were suffering.

However, there is a very good reason for having a maid.

Everything is more complicated in a Latin country. Each vegetable you eat has to be peeled or rinsed in an iodine solution. Water must be boiled for twenty minutes and then put through a filter before it can be drunk. Besides this, we needed a baby sitter, as both of us were to attend the language school.

I was awakened by the doorbell ringing. Glancing at my watch as I got into some clothes, I saw that it was only 6:00 a.m. I went to the door and opened it.

"Buenos días," a woman in her middle thirties said, "me llama Maria, su empliada." She pushed past me into the house. I did not understand a word she said.

When they had told me I was going to Central America, I replied that I had trouble with Spanish and had flunked it in high school.

"Don't worry," they said. "You'll learn it quickly in Costa Rica."

I spoke, using the only phrase I knew.

"Como . . . está . . . usted?"

"Muy bien, gracias," she said, pushing on into the kitchen.

She put on an apron and started boiling water on the stove, all the time talking in Spanish. I left her and went upstairs.

Judy was sitting up in bed. "Who was that?" she asked.

"I'm not sure," I replied. "There is a woman in the kitchen speaking Spanish a mile a minute. Why don't you go down and see who she is?"

"That must be the lady José was talking about. What was her name?"

"I don't remember."

"Maria, I think," said Judy.

"I think I heard her say something that sounded like Maria." Judy got dressed and we went down stairs together, seeking each other's company in this strange situation. When Maria saw Judy, she ran to her, spouting more Spanish and giving her a big hug. Judy looked at me with astonishment and questioning eyes. All I could do was shrug my shoulders.

Soon the girls were up and dressed. When they came down Maria gave each a hug, and then fed us all a huge breakfast. She never stopped speaking Spanish and we had no earthly idea what she was saying. I was becoming frustrated. After all, how much can one communicate with the only phrase I knew: "How are you?"

At one point, my oldest daughter Debra turned to me and asked, "What's wrong with that lady, Daddy? She doesn't speak right."

"There is nothing wrong with her," I replied. "She is speaking another language. We will have to learn it also."

"Oh," Debra replied with a vagueness that indicated I did not know anything. *The woman has something wrong with her,* her eyes said.

After much arm-waving with Maria shouting in Spanish and me shouting in English, I finally figured out she was saying there was a severe lack of food in the house. I understood this only after she grabbed my arm and showed me empty shelves in the kitchen.

We were eager to go to the store, but this was complicated by the fact we had no Costa Rican money. We were supposed to have been met by a Big Brother who would show us how to do these things, but he had not shown up.

Maria gave us money for the bus so we could go downtown to a bank and change our money to Colonies.

It took us forever to find the bus stop and then figure out where a bank was, and by the time we got there, it was closed. We came back home depressed, without food or even Maria's money.

Later that afternoon the Bishop's wife who came to visit brightened our day. She explained that the "Supermarket" near the school took US Dollars. She drove us there and we made some purchases.

Language school was a combination of fun and frustration. Baptist and Assembly of God churches ran it. Many of the teachers were converted Catholics who were down on the Catholic Church.

We were watched carefully to see if we were Catholics in disguise and were prayed for daily for our wantonness in smoking cigarettes and drinking liquor. Even so, the school was very good. All the courses were taught in Spanish. We started school at the early hour of seven and were through by noon. After lunch, we would go to town to shop in the market or to see a movie in Spanish. While we were gone, Maria would watch over the children and make dinner.

As the weeks went by, our communication skills began to improve slightly, but I still had problems. About a month into the course, I was coming home from town by myself on a bus. Riding a bus was a unique experience. The buses were old and rattled and banged more than they moved ahead on the road. None of them had batteries, and all the buses were started with one battery. If the bus stalled, all the men got off and pushed to get it going again. One could see that faith in God was necessary, because every bus had a Crucifix and a Madonna lit up with Christmas tree lights. There were sure to be several St. Christopher medals and rosaries hung around the windshield. I noticed many people crossing themselves as they entered the door.

The drivers were gentlemen. They would wait five minutes, if necessary, for a woman to walk a block to catch the bus. No woman would run, of course. On the other hand, men, to prove their manliness, generally had to run and jump on the bus as it was moving.

The pull cord that rings the bell to tell the driver to stop was broken on all the buses. When a woman wanted to get off, she would quietly tell a man next to her "esquina" (corner). The man would whistle a shrill whistle and the bus would stop. A man would never call esquina if he wanted off. He would just whistle.

I cannot whistle, never have been able to.

When I rode a bus, I would pray that someone else would be getting off at my stop. Generally this would work. On this particular day, my stop was coming up and no one whistled. I tried, but was unable to produce any noise that even resembled a whistle. We passed my stop. As we passed the next stop, I decided I would have to swallow my pride and callout the word.

What was that word? I asked myself.

"Escoba (broom)!" I yelled. Everyone looked at me. The bus rolled on.

"Must not be the right word," I mumbled to myself.

"Esposa (wife)!" I called. There was some giggling, but the bus kept rolling. I heard one person say in a low voice, "Gringo."

Finally, a woman in front of me said the magic word, esquina, a man whistled, and we both got off.

I walked back a mile and a half to get home that evening, but at least I had learned a word that I would not forget.

On December 22, I was ordained to the priesthood by the Right Rev. David Richards, Bishop of Central America. It was a great service in English and Spanish. Judy's parents and my mother had flown down to be there. The next Sunday I was to preach at the Spanish service in San Jose.

It was a fine sermon and most of the people understood what I was attempting to say in Spanish, I think. There was one bad moment in the sermon. I had strayed away from my written text and gotten lost in my faltering Spanish. I could not remember a certain word. I was embarrassed and said to the congregation:

"Siento mucho, soy embarrizado."

This should have meant, "I'm sorry, I'm embarrassed." There was tittering throughout the congregation. Some of the younger folks had to put handkerchiefs in their mouths to keep from laughing aloud. A few doubled over in their pews in silent convulsions of hilarity.

I did not know the cause for all this until after the service, when my friend Jose said that what I had really said was, "I'm sorry, I am pregnant."

Part of my ministry after ordination was in the jungle on the east coast of Costa Rica. On Friday, I would leave at noon on the train, head to the coast and fly back to San Jose on Monday morning.

Sometimes I flew with very strange passengers. One time a man and his sick wife got on board with many people helping her. I felt sorry for the wife, as she must have had a terrible back problem. She could not sit upright in her seat and was stiff as a board. Her husband lovingly put a washcloth over her face and held her in the seat through the flight. After we landed people came aboard and helped get her off the plane. I thought it was strange she had not moved during the flight and I asked the plane's crew what had happened to her.

"Oh, she's dead," the pilot said. "It's cheaper to bring the body to San Jose for burial as a passenger than as freight."

The time came for my assignment to the mission field. I had the choice of a mission in the Dominican Republic or one in Puerto Cortes, Honduras. I chose the one in Honduras because I liked the bishop and Honduras had only two priests attempting to take care of six missions.

With great excitement, I wrote home to my friends telling them of my assignment. I was very disappointed in the replies I received. No one seemed to know where the Republic of Honduras was. Some thought it was in Africa, others got it confused with British Honduras (now Belize). Actually, it is the largest Central American country and located south of Guatemala and north of Nicaragua. Puerto Cortes is on the northern coast near the Guatemalan border.

As we boarded the plane for Honduras, I wondered if we would ever return to Costa Rica.

CHAPTER FOURTEEN

This was the day. We got up early and I went out on deck with my coffee in hand to see what the weather looked like. *"Hum,"* I thought, *"what are those clouds over there? No, they are in the east. They've passed us."* I stepped off the boat and walked down to the customs office, still sipping my coffee.

"Good morning," I said to the nattily dressed officer in his white starched shirt and Bermuda shorts.

"Morning Captain. What can I do for you?" asked the officer.

"Is the morning weather report in yet?"

"Yes sir, it just now came in. Have a copy. Are you planning on leaving today?"

"If the weather is right. Can I bring my papers by here, or must I bring the boat to the customs dock? We're tied up just down the quay."

"No sir, just bring the papers by when you're ready."

After thanking him, I walked back to the boat, relieved that I would not have to move the 100 yards to the customs dock.

"Judy," I called as I got on the boat, "let's get going. The weather report looks great."

"Wait a minute. I'm not ready yet and we have to eat breakfast before we leave."

After a quick breakfast and another trip to customs for clearance, we gathered in the lines and got the boat that was side-tied to us out of the way. Somehow we got away from the dock without getting tangled in all the dock lines running over our decks and without hitting the bridge ten feet off our bowsprit. We were on our way.

We requested permission to leave the harbor through Town Cut. And, after asking the usual questions about our radio and navigation equipment they said, "Butterfly, you have permission to leave the harbor."

As we cleared the end of Town Cut, the boat seemed to leap for joy. There was no wind and the sea was as calm as glass with a low ground swell gently heaving us every so often. I do not think I have ever seen such a blue sky, with hardly a cloud in it. It was ten-thirty and it had taken us four hours to get ready to go.

All day long we ran under the "Iron Genny."

During the evening watch the precariousness of our situation took hold of my mind and would not let go. I tried to think of other things, but every time I go offshore, I get a strange feeling. I realize that between me and the ocean floor, a thousand fathoms down, is only one and a quarter inch of fiberglass. Pulling the boat down is the 8,000 lbs of lead in the keel plus the engine, fuel tanks, anchor chain and the tons of equipment. All of this stuff wants to go to the bottom, but cannot because of this one and a quarter inch of fiberglass. I feel suspended above the rocky and craggy floor of the ocean and hope that none of the fiberglass gives way.

In addition, I know that the wind is trying to blow me over. It hits the sails, masts, and rigging and actually tries to roll the boat over so the ocean can get in and fill the thin fiberglass hull. If enough water gets in, the boat will refuse to float and we will head for the bottom below. Rationally, I know that the ballast and the hull and the rigging all work together to make the boat sail. I just hope it will keep on doing so.

I get up, look around the horizon, set the alarm for fifteen minutes and decide to take a short nap to free me of these thoughts.

We arrived in Honduras and were met at the airport in Tegucigalpa by the Archdeacon, an Englishman in his late forties. He took us to his house and made us comfortable.

We spent a week filling out forms repeatedly. The night before we were to leave for Puerto Cortes, we sat out on the balcony watching the sunset and the latest revolution. The revolution had started that afternoon and consisted of some university students raising hell with the government.

"Nothing to worry about," the archdeacon said to Judy, who was looking anxious. "This happens all the time."

On the hill opposite us was an armory. We sipped our scotch and sodas and watched an attack on the armory.

"Zing/splat . . ." something landed on the balcony. "Zing/splat/zong . . ."

"My dears," said the archdeacon, "I think it is time for us to retire."

"It's still early," I said.

Yes," he replied, "but it's becoming a little dangerous with these spent bullets hitting the balcony, you know."

We all went to bed.

The next morning, the revolution being over, we went to the airport and caught a plane for San Pedro Sula, the second largest city in Honduras. Members of the English-speaking congregation who lived there met us. That evening we went to a dinner party for us-I think. It may have been a going-away party for someone else. They had parties almost every night for someone coming or going, but I did not know this at the time and thought the party was for us. I would be having services for the English-speaking congregation on Sundays at the little church/house they rented.

We spent the night with one of the families from the States, and the next morning left for Puerto Cortes thirty-five miles away by car. Puerto Cortes is the third largest city in Honduras. Having seen the largest, Tegucigalpa, and the second largest, San Pedro Sula, I did not expect Puerto Cortes to be the small dusty dirty banana port it was.

There were only two paved streets and they both led to the docks. The church, La Iglesia San Juan Bautista, a wooden frame building with a steeple and set on high pilings, was old and the rectory was brand new. The first thing I did when we arrived was to climb the stairs to the church. It was on stilts so the cool breezes could try to reach the congregation above. I opened the door and was met with oven like heat and the heavy smell of rotting, dead flowers. The women of the church had tried to make it pretty for our arrival, but with everything closed up and hot, the altar flowers drooped and the candles had melted.

The rectory was also up on stilts (cement block columns) so air could flow through the house. The windows had wooden louvers, except in the living room, where there were glass louvers. It was a spacious house but sparsely furnished. The chairs were too hard to sit on, the beds sagged, and the lighting consisted of fifteen-watt bulbs dangling from the ceiling. It was furnished like the homes of our congregation, but it was almost too primitive for us. The first thing I did was buy some one hundred-watt light bulbs.

I put my foot on the brake, just a little, and the jeep began to fishtail all over the dirt road. I got her stopped before running head-on to a truck coming from the other direction. He had beaten us to the one lane bridge that narrowed the road in front of us.

"Que esta haciendo!" cried Mario, a member of my Honduran congregation and my guide to the Honduran town of Tela. He was asking what I was doing. We were headed to Tela so I could perform a wedding and had been traveling since six in the morning. It was nine now and we were still several hours from Tela, according to Mario. The wedding was set for eleven.

"What do you mean?" I growled back out of irritation and tiredness. "I had to stop or we would have hit that truck head-on."

"No, Padre," Mario said in English, "you don' know how to drive here. You keep on goin' fast. The first one gets to the bridge gets to cross. The other has to turn on his lights. It like playing 'pollo'." I have never been one to play "pollo," or chicken.

I worked the jeep back up through the gears and we shook and rattled on down the road. Ahead was another one-lane bridge—and another car heading for it.

"Go faster," yelled Mario. I went faster.

"Go faster, man!" shouted Mario again.

I tried to go faster, but I did not think I could make it.

"You can make it!" Mario screamed as he read my mind. "You can make it!"

I could not make it. It was clear to me I just was not going to make it. I braked ever so lightly and we went into a spin in a cloud of dust. As the other car passed I heard part of a shout,

"No cajones!"

I looked at Mario, who looked as depressed as a person could get.

"What did he say?" I asked.

"You could have made it," he replied.

"What did that man say?" I asked again.

"We're never going to get to the wedding on time if you keep stopping like this."

I started up the car and we crossed the bridge.

"What did that man say as he passed us back there?" I repeated.

"He said you didn't have any . . . balls!"

Up ahead was another bridge and another car coming towards us. This time I would make it. I would show him who had balls. I gunned the engine and floored it. As we went faster, I had to fight to keep the car on the road as the dust and gravel made it slippery as ice. I was determined to be the first at the bridge.

"Slow down, Padre!" yelled Mario. "You can't make this one."

"Shut up," I yelled back.

"Alto! Para! Stop!" yelled Mario.

We got closer and closer. I prayed, as I felt I was soon to meet my maker. It is always best to meet him with a prayer on your lips.

The other car's lights went on and he skidded to a stop leaving me inches to pass him. As we did, I yelled out the window, "No cojones!" and looked over at Mario. He had passed out.

We soon entered an area of jungle and had to slow down even more. We came across a river, which looked simple enough to cross. It was about hundred yards across and the road went in one side and out the other. As I started into the river, Mario, who had recovered by this time, said, "Stop."

I did. Then I turned to him and asked why.

"Because you cannot cross this river straight. We go in and turn left, go for about one-half a kilometer and cross, then come back the other side and out over there."

"Are you sure?" I asked.

"Sure I'm sure. That's why you brought me, isn't it?"

I put the jeep into compound low four-wheel drive and floored the gas pedal. We ground into the river, made a left, went for a ways, and sure enough there was a sand bar. We crossed over, up the other side of the river and out where the car tracks left the river opposite of where we went in. Several months later, while traveling this same road, I saw a car top in the middle of the river. They had not taken Mario with them.

At the next river we came to a truck stuck in the middle. After waiting an eternity, the traffic began to move, but as we left the river there was an awful bang and our jeep tilted. I got out and saw that our right rear wheel had fallen off. The holes for the wheel lugs were so out of round we could not put it back on. We got the spare out and put it on. These lug nuts were also in bad shape, with one of them broken off, so we could not secure the spare wheel very well.

We limped off with a clang added to our rattle. At about one in the afternoon we pulled up to the church and as I stopped, the wheel fell off again. We had made it, but where were the people? I did not know what to do.

"Ring the bell," said Mario.

"What?"

"Ring the church bell. People will come."

After the wedding, we got the lug nuts fixed and had a sandwich.

"Let's get going," I said to Mario, when I had finished eating.

"You can't go back," said an elderly man. "It's too late."

"It's only," I looked at my watch, "four o'clock."

"It'll be dark soon. Can't drive that road in the dark. How you gonna cross the rivers in the dark?"

"I'm sure we'll be able to. I have to get back to do Sunday services tomorrow."

"It is too late to start now," said a short, fat man the color of fine fudge. "There's the robbers, you know."

"What robbers?" I asked. I had not heard of robbers.

"Them what waits in the road and robs ya," was the answer. "Sometimes they lay in the road like they is sick or somethin'. You get out and look, and another man come and chop you head with a machete!"

"What if your tire breaks again?" asked a kindly woman with grey hair. "Them tigers might get you . . . or the snakes."

"Oh woman," said the elderly man, "you know there ain't tigers there. There's some ocelots, puma and panthers, but no tigers. He don't have to worry about no tigers!"

"I'm sorry, but I feel we really have to get back to Puerto Cortes tonight. They're expecting me there in the morning for mass."

"OK, but you be very careful," admonished the old woman.

I grabbed Mario, who had been hoping to stay, and started. He was very quiet for a long time. As it got darker, his eyes got whiter.

"Maybe we should go back," he said.

"We've got cajones, don't we? We can make it." I said with more confidence than I felt.

Somehow, we made it through the rivers and back home, but I saw thieves and tigers around every bend. The only thing that saved us was that they knew we had "cojones" and did not want to mess with us.

After my trip to the wedding in Tela, I asked the bishop if we could buy a new car. He said that the car was only two years old.

"But the wheels fell off twice in one trip. The emergency brake does nothing but pull up the muffler, the clutch is slipping, and I'm afraid to drive the thing." A month later, the bishop gave permission to buy a new car. I had my eye on a brand new Landrover, which was quite inexpensive. It was a beautiful red one too!

CHAPTER FIFTEEN

As I swam up from a deep sleep, I heard the monotonous throb of the engine. *Still not any wind!* I thought. I lay in the bunk and visualized the diesel fuel leaving the tanks. When they were dry, we would be becalmed in the middle of the Atlantic. This vision got the adrenaline going in my system and I leaped out of bed to check my calculations on fuel consumption.

"What's the matter, Ames?" called Judy from the cockpit. She had heard me scrambling around below.

"Nothing, honey." I went back to my bunk and stared at the overhead.

"Come on lord, we need a little wind!" I prayed. Soon the constant noise of the engine sang me to sleep.

"Ames, Ames, get up." Judy was shaking me.

"What's wrong?" I said as I quickly sat up.

"Nothing's wrong, but I think we have a little wind."

I stumbled in my sleep out into the cockpit. There were a few small clouds and maybe a little breeze. The waves had a ruffled effect, so maybe the wind was here.

I went on the foredeck and raised the jib. Judy turned off the engine. We were doing 2 knots. The wind was aft and the jib was flapping and banging. The wind dropped again and the boat barely made a knot, so I went up forward and took the jib down while Judy, with sadness, turned the engine back on. I was tired, frustrated and hungry.

Several times that day we stopped the engine, hoping the wind would carry us on. The fear the engine would break or the wind would never come up and we would run out of fuel, pursued me.

I went to my bunk for my watch off. We had used twenty-nine point two gallons, and leaving only seventy point eight in the tanks. I tossed and turned for what seemed like hours before falling asleep.

A red Landrover. Landrovers were the very best. They had an aluminum body that would not rust out like that Willis Jeep had. My new one was sporty looking and I felt great driving it back from San Pedro to Puerto Cortes. Later that week I visited the taxi driver member of my vestry. I was eager to show off my car.

"You going to get it painted?" he asked with a scowl.

"What do you mean?" I said defensively. "It's a brand new car. The paint's great." I walked around the car, checking for bad paint. It looked all right to me.

"Should get it painted," he repeated.

"Why? What's wrong?" I looked closer.

"Because, Father, red is the color of the ruling political party. You ride in a red car and there is a revolution, they shoot you all up. Blue's bad too. You ride in a blue car and the ruling party shoot you up before you start a revolution. Better get the car painted, Father. Yellow's a nice color."

"No wonder the car was inexpensive."

"Nobody buy red or blue cars here, Father."

I never did get that car repainted. I probably should have, but at the time I didn't have the money, and later . . . well, no one had shot at me yet.

Every morning I had a mass at five-thirty. After mass, I would have breakfast and then head for town. I walked through a different section every day, greeting my parishioners and getting to know people in general. My favorite section was the docks. Here the great white fleet of the banana companies came to load boxes upon boxes of bananas. The banana docks were the largest industry in Puerto Cortes. The second largest industry was prostitution.

One day as I was walking down the docks, a very young prostitute came over and grabbed my hand. I could see some others had put her up to propositioning a priest. Since I was wearing my collar, she assumed I was a Roman Catholic priest.

"¿Quiere ir conmigo, Padre? Pienso que te amo." (Would you like to come with me, Father? I think I love you.)

"Well," I said in Spanish, "you are very good looking. But I think I prefer being with my wife."

Her mouth dropped. A Roman Catholic priest does not have a wife, at least not openly. Her face turned red and she ran back to the other girls. I was never bothered again.

It was in this part of the city that the local fishing boats landed with their catches. There was a small shed where they sold conchs and the many varieties of fish they caught. The longing to sail had returned, but this time, not to escape.

One knurled and weathered fisherman named Ron asked me if I wanted to buy his boat.

"It's a good boat, mon, only a few years old."

"What would you want for it?" I asked cautiously.

"Oh, I don't know, mon . . . maybe two thousand Lempira."

My heart started beating very fast. Two thousand Lempira was only about one thousand US dollars. *A thirty-foot boat for that price! I might be able to buy one.*

"I don't know," I replied. "I'll have to think about it."

"She is a good boat. I'll take you for a sail next week. You see she's a good boat."

I agreed to a test sail the following Friday after the fish market closed. While waiting I discussed the venture with several parishioners and friends.

"Well, Father," said one, "she's a good enough boat, but don't you want a new one?"

By the time Friday rolled around, I was beginning to doubt the wisdom of buying this boat. I brought Judy down to the fish market and we waited in the shade of a palm tree for Ron to take us for a sail. Judy was very silent. Too silent.

"What are you thinking about?" I asked.

"Oh, nothing."

"Nothing?"

"Well, I was thinking about buying a boat," she said.

"Do you think it's a bad idea?" I asked, afraid she would tell me she did not want me to have a sailboat.

"No. It's just that we've never sailed before."

"Just you wait," I said. "I know you'll like it."

About this time, Ron came over and took us out to his boat in a cayuca or dugout canoe.

"You have to watch the boom when she tack," Ron said. The boom went rather low across the deck. I was proud I knew what a "tack" was from reading a lot about sailboats and even constructing a few sailing models. I felt good being able to explain these things to Judy and thought it would give her more confidence in my abilities.

We raised the sails and hoisted the anchor. For the first time in my life, I was sailing!

"She foots nicely, don't she mon."

"She does what?" I asked.

"She go well."

"Yes, it's wonderful." We were moving through the ship anchorage.

"How do you steer?" I asked, as I looked for a wheel or tiller.

"By these ropes. You pull this one and we go this way. Hey, watch out the boom!"

We ducked barely in time as the six-inch diameter boom swung within inches of our head.

"She tacks nice, don't she?" Ron said with great pride.

"Watch out!" yelled Judy. "That ship . . . we're going to hit that ship!"

Sure enough, we were headed for the side of one of the great white banana boats.

"Duck!" yelled Ron as he tacked hard over.

The sailboat, now winded by the freighter, turned from its course very slowly, but finally she tacked with the boom just brushing the side of the ship.

"I told you she tacks nice," said Ron with a sheepish grin. After about an hour, we returned to shore. "See," Ron said, "she's a good boat. You gonna buy her?"

I looked at Judy and she gave me that look she has which says, "Do what you want, I won't be responsible for it."

"I don't know," I replied. "Let me think about it for awhile."

In the weeks that followed the word got around that I was interested in buying a boat. Many fishermen came to offer their boats, and many friends suggested I buy a new one. They would never say anything against another person.

At last, I got the message and decided to see how much a new boat would cost. I wrote out a list of specifications that I got out of a "Rudder" magazine and set it off with a request for a quote to boat builders in Belize and the Bay Islands.

Then I waited.

I waited a month. I thought that perhaps the boat was too small to attract any boat builders. About the time I was completely discouraged and contemplating buying Ron's boat, a man arrived at the door.

"Good mornin' sir, my name is Freddy Jarvis, and I'm a boat builder."

"Come on in. I'll get you some coffee." He stood five foot-two inches, dressed in a worn and weathered black suit, a plaid shirt and a red tie. He was very wrinkled and bald, but his eyes were youthful and bright. I was not sure how old he was, but he looked very old.

"You sent a letter about building a boat. I came on over straight away to talk to you."

"Where are you from?"

"Me and my boys live in Coxen Hole . . . that's on Roatan, you know."

"You have a ship yard there?"

"Ah, yes sir. We build lots of boats. The 'Suyappa,' the 'Anna Maria,' and many more." He pulled out some grimy and well-creased photographs that showed some coastal powerboats of the type that plied between Puerto Cortes, the Bay Islands and Belize.

"Have you ever built a sailboat?"

"Sure I've build plenty sail boats, you know."

"Tell me about your yard."

"It's a good yard. We have lots of good dry lumber, well-seasoned."

"How many employees?"

"Ah, just me and my two sons."

"If I were to give you the job, when could you start on it?"

"We could start now. We just finish a boat this week. That's why I couldn't come see you before now."

For the next several hours we discussed the kind of boat I wanted and I showed him pictures of a thirty-foot ketch I had seen in Rudder Magazine. Some things bothered him. For example, I thought it would be good to have an auxiliary engine in the boat.

"What for you want an engine? This gonna be a sailboat."

"Yes," I said, "but I've noticed the wind drops every evening and the sailboats have to row in or wait until morning to get into port. I will have to get in when I want to get in."

"Oh." He scratched his baldhead. "What you want is a motor boat. We build you a fine motor boat."

"No, I want a sailboat with a small motor."

"I never build a sail boat with a motor. I build sail boats and I build motor boats, but I never built a sailboat with a motor."

"Well, I want a sail boat with a small motor in it."

"I guess it can be done." Mr. Jarvis looked at me as if I were crazy. "I'll come back tomorrow and we'll talk again," he said, getting up.

I showed him to the door, thinking I would probably never see him again. I moped around the house that afternoon, getting into Judy's way. She shooed me out of the house in desperation. "Oh Ames, go work on your sermon or something. If you're meant to have a sailboat you'll get one."

I went downstairs to my study to pray.

About nine the next morning, Mr. Jarvis appeared at the door holding a package wrapped in newspapers.

We went into my office. I watched his knurled and calloused hands untie the coarse string that held the paper together. I felt this must be a momentous occasion since Mr. Jarvis had not yet spoken a word. As the string loosened, the paper fell off and there before my eyes was a half-hull model of what was to be my boat.

"I made this last night," he said with pride.

"It's beautiful." I feasted my eyes on the mahogany model.

It was just as we had talked about. It had a hard chine for shallow draft with a centerboard. The centerboard was not on the half-hull, but in my mind's eye I could see it, along with her two masts rising from the deck.

"How much would it cost?" My voice was low and the words came out with great hesitation, fearful that the cost of this beautiful boat would be beyond my reach.

"I could build it for you . . . let's see. I'll put a seven and a half horse power Briggs and Stratton engine. You still want an engine? OK, two masts and sails . . . I'll do the whole thing for . . ."

I could hardly wait. I wanted to scream, *"Tell me how much!"*

"We'll put a big hatch in the middle."

"What do we need a big hatch for?" I replied, thinking he had better tell me how much before I had a heart attack.

"For the cargo. Ya got to have a hatch for the cargo."

I tried to explain the boat was to be used for pleasure only and not to carry cargo. He said he had never heard of a boat that did not carry cargo. I could wait no longer.

"But what could you build it for? How much?"

"Oh, we could do it for 4,500 Lempira."

My mind quickly divided that sum by two and I knew instantly that I could afford the boat. I could not believe it. I could buy a new thirty-foot boat for only two thousand two hundred and twenty five dollars! I was ecstatic. In three months, I would take possession of a brand new sailing ketch!

After a month had gone by, I received a letter from Mr. Jarvis.

Dear Rev. Ames,

    I hope this letter find you and your wife in good health. The weather here has been fine and I in good health. Please to buy some oakum, tar, white lead paint, four-four inch blocks and two, four part six-inch blocks and send them to me soon as possible.

Sincerely yours, Freddy Jarvis

He must really be making progress, I thought, if he needs oakum for caulking already. I spent several days gathering the items. Honduras did not have a great deal of boating gear in its stores.

I hauled the materials down to the "Anna Maria" and shipped them to Mr. Jarvis with a letter saying the costs would be taken out of the final payment.

At the end of the second month:

Dear Rev. Ames,

    I hope this letter finds you well. All is going good here. The keel is laid and ready to close in. We will be done soon. Could you send me a shaft and propeller for your engine? We could use some ballast at least 500 lbs—perhaps more. Please send two gallons red lead paint . . . .

It was obvious that Mr. Jarvis was behind schedule. The boat was supposed to be two-thirds done, and it sounded as if he had only the keel and frames done. I decided to fly out and see what was happening.

Arriving in Roatan, the only taxi, indeed the only vehicle, on the island met me. It took me to the Williams Hotel (grocery store, restaurant, etc). After checking in, I asked for the Jarvis Boat Yard. The man behind the counter smiled a funny smile and said,

"You the man having a boat built here?"

"That's right," I said proudly.

"Well, go out the door to the right and walk two houses down. You'll find Freddy there."

I had not remembered seeing a boat yard when we came down this street, and it was the only street in town. Then, between two houses and under a gigantic almond tree, I saw the keel and frame of my boat. As I stood looking at it, Mr. Jarvis came running from another house.

"Rev. Ames! Rev. Ames!" he called, panting. "Why didn't you write and tell me you was coming? I would have met you at the airport."

"That's OK, Mr. Jarvis. It looks as if you're not going to be finished by next month."

"No sir. We're a little behind. Thank you for sending me that stuff."

"That's all right," I said greatly discouraged. "I'll deduct it from the final payment."

"All I got to do is plank and deck her. She be ready in no time. No time at all. You have the second payment?"

I was trapped. The contract said nothing about the amount of work to be finished after two months. I had to pay the second payment or lose the money from the first payment.

I took a hike across the island to visit with Mr. James, an uncle of a member of my congregation. It was an interesting hike through the jungle and along the shore. After about two miles, I arrived at Mr. James' house.

Mr. James, who gave me a cool drink of coconut milk and rum, greeted me warmly. We discussed Mr. Jarvis.

"Dat man has many problems," he said. "I wish you come here and talked to me before doing business with him."

"What's his problem? Does he drink?"

"Oh no sir . . . he don't drink. He has the womans problem."

"What do you mean?"

"He likes womans too much. Dat ol' man . . ." He chuckled. "He's eighty-three you know. Well, after getting your payment, well he upped and married a thirty-five year old woman. She took his money and split. Now he got no woman, no money and a boat to build."

"He better build it, too." I said with determination. "What about his two sons?"

"They good men. Seventh Day Adventists, you know. They mad at ol' Freddy and won't work for him no more."

"What am I going to do?"

"Oh, he build it. If you want I look after him to make sure he do."

"That's a good idea. I would appreciate it if you would."

"No problem, mon."

CHAPTER SIXTEEN

I love the morning (2:00-8:00) watch because I get to see the sunrise, which in December was not until six forty-five. I frequently like to hand steer, so this morning I shut down our hard working auto pilot and became one with the boat and sea.

As the dawn crept over the horizon, I kept my eye on the glassy waves. Would the wind come today? I hoped so, as we were now down to fifty-six gallons of diesel. By eight o'clock, I began to notice some ripples on the glassy waves. Soon the ripples became wavelets and fifteen minutes later I was raising the jib and mizzen and shutting down the engine. By the time Judy got up, we were doing five knots and, expecting the wind to strengthen further, we took down the mainsail.

We could have really moved out if I had kept the main up but the remembrance of the high winds going to Bermuda kept me from adding more sail. Heck, five knots under sail is better than having to expend diesel we might need later on. Soon we saw the puffy little cumulus clouds floating seemingly at masthead height, which indicated we were indeed in the trade winds.

For the next several days, we watched these clouds marching in rows toward the west. Our watch system during the day depended on how we were feeling. Both of us like to steer under sail, so we generally took two hours on and two hours off, although we did not keep a hard and fast schedule. It was a wonderful "time to." Time to read. Time to talk. Time to sex. Time to relearn how to navigate. I loved "time to" days.

Take reading, for example. We love to read and it is very hard for us to keep enough books in stock. One I ran across was about the old days of sailing ships and the hardships of the crew. There were mates with their "sticks," bo's'ns with their "starters," and, of course, the ultimate punishment, the cat-of-nine-tails.

"Judy, you have it easy."

She looked up from her book. It was a book dealing with the psychological aspects of something or other. She likes that kind book.

"What?"

"I said that you have it easy."

"I don't know what you mean."

"I was reading how the poor old sailors were treated in the olden days. You know . . . they would hit them with rope ends at every whim of the bo's'n. If they disobeyed an order, the captain would order them whipped with the cat-o-nine-tails, or keel haul them."

"Oh yeah? Do you want to keep me as crew?"

"Sure."

"You hit me with a rope end and I'll knock your head off and jump ship by the jib down haul." She had evidently been reading some sailing books herself. We have this great relationship. I am the captain and can give her any order she wants me to give. If I give what she considers an incorrect order, she simply looks at me and says no.

"Yeah," I said exuding bravado, "perhaps I should punish you now just to get you used to it."

"You just try," she said with a sparkle in her eye.

I caught her, disrobed her (she did not have much on so it was not much of a job), and tied her to the pin rail.

"Ho, ho!" said I in my best pirate voice. "How shall I carry out the punishment?"

It was situations like these that made me enjoy the "time to" days.

Dear Rev. Ames,

I hope this letter finds you well and that your family is in good health. Well, things are going well on the boat and we will be ready to launch in two weeks. Please send me some chain plates . . . .

After nine months, Freddy Jarvis was finally finishing the boat. I gathered all the equipment together we would use on the trip back by boat, my own boat! Food, a small stove, bucket, anchor, and other assorted necessities added up to three huge cartons full. I took them down to the dock and put them aboard the "Anna Maria" bound for Coxen Hole.

I had been preparing for this trip for nine months now. My brother-in-law sent me a very old copy of Chapman's "Piloting, Seamanship, and Small Boat Handling," but the best information I got from the mates of the banana freighters. I would ride out with my friend the customs officer when a ship cleared in and go aboard to ask for help in navigation.

Although I did not think I was an expert navigator, I felt I would be able to find my way home from Roatan. Besides, as part of the contract, Freddy Jarvis was to accompany us the one hundred eighteen miles back to Puerto Cortes. If he came, I figured the boat was seaworthy.

Judy and I flew to Coxen Hole on a Monday, expecting to sail the boat back home by Friday at the latest.

When we arrived under the almond tree, we saw our boat. It had not been painted, the spars weren't ready, and,

"That shaft you send us," said Mr. Jarvis, "weren't the right size. Much too big. Did you bring us another?"

I felt like screaming. "You didn't tell me that . . . you didn't ask me for another."

"Guess I forgot. But we can't launch till we got a shaft."

"Where can we get a shaft?"

"Don't know. Perhaps there's one up French Harbor way."

I left Judy painting the boat while I hired a motorized cayuca to take me the twenty miles over to French Harbor.

In French Harbor, we went house to house looking for a four foot long, three-fourth inch shaft. It was surprising what people had stowed under their houses. There were portholes from ships, old blocks, complete binnacles from old sailing ships and a lifeboat compass among other things. They must have stripped a lot of wrecks. I bought the lifeboat compass in a box, as I had not been able to find a boat compass in all of Honduras. We finally found two shafts and couplings that were three feet long.

When I got back, Judy was on her hands and knees painting the deck. Mr. Jarvis eyed the shafts and said they would do but asked, "Did you get the stuffing box?"

I had foiled him this time and had indeed bought a stuffing box to match the shaft. So he had to set to work. I talked his sons into helping him and soon the shaft log had been drilled by hand. I covered the cabin top with canvas and painted the bottom while Judy painted the topsides.

As the week wore on the masts were constructed, chain plates installed and the sails, made by Captain Gene, were delivered.

Captain Gene was an interesting character. He was missing all the fingers on his left hand from the second joint on out. I asked him what had happened.

"It were a long time ago," he said, as he spit a chaw of tobacco to leeward. "I used to sail the square riggers when I was a boy. The grain route, we went. To Australia and England and back again. We would go around the Cape of Good Hope on the way down and come back by way of the Horn."

He spit again and hitched up his pants.

"It always was bad around the Horn. Ice and snow and wind . . . oh lord there was a wind. And waves . . . they come near as high as our top mast at times. 'Cause the Captain wants to make time we was always changin' sail."

He looked away into the distance as if he was there again, hanging from the hundred foot steel mainyard in the freezing wind.

"We was putting a second reef in the main tops'l. I had to hang on tight with me left hand while I gathered sail with me right. T'were a mistake."

"How's that?" I asked.

"'Cause me left hand froze to the steel yard. The only way I could get down was to take me knife and cut the fingers off at the joints."

Even without all his fingers, Captain Gene had done a fine job sewing sails out of cotton duck canvas for our boat.

At last, on Thursday morning, the time came for launching and the whole town gathered for the event. I passed rum around. Freddy Jarvis, a few others, and I made speeches. Judy smashed a bottle of Coca Cola on the bow (we did not want to waste rum and could not get champagne) and named the boat "El Marinero" as she touched the water.

"You can't name the boat that," complained Captain Freddy.

"What's wrong with the name? It means 'The Sailor.'"

"It's a man's name. You got to name it after a woman. It's bad luck to name it after a man. You'll see."

That afternoon the masts were stepped and she began to look like a real sailboat. I had a hard time sleeping that night. We were going to sail in the morning. I repeated variation and deviation in my head repeatedly until I fell asleep.

We arose at dawn and I ran to the window to look at our beautiful boat at the dock. I stood, staring.

"What's wrong?" asked Judy. "Is the boat still there?"

"It's there all right." I turned from the window and Judy saw my expression.

"My God, what's wrong, Ames!"

"Come and see for yourself."

"Oh. What do we do now?" Judy asked.

"Let's go swimming down at the beach."

The vision from the window was sickening. EI Marinero was there all right, but she had sunk in five feet of water. We walked down the beach in silence.

"What are we going to do now?" Judy asked.

"I don't know. Let's just swim for awhile."

Several hours later, we arrived back at the dock. The boat, bailed out now, was floating again.

"I expected her to sink," Mr. Jarvis said confidently. "She needed to take up a bit. All new boats do. She's OK now."

"Humph! I could have told you this would happen. Named it after a man. Had to sink," said another well-wisher.

It was obvious we were not going to sail the boat back this weekend, but I was not about to leave without it.

The following week we found the leak. Someone had drilled two holes in the bottom, possibly out of jealousy.

While the holes were being repaired, I busied myself getting the paperwork for the boat completed and finding a crew for the sail home. I hired a lawyer to get the boat's papers straightened out for the Honduran government. He was a fat jolly man about thirty-five years old, who had been a judge under the prior administration and was now stranded on Roatan. In exchange for the paperwork, I agreed he could go with us on EI Marinero.

I hired a younger captain to be in charge of the trip, Captain Jim, who was in his forties. Captains Freddy and Gene were also coming, but they were so old I thought I had better engage a younger man as the official captain. To fill out the crew bill, I found two young men in their twenties,

"We've got lots of sailing experience, mon." they assured me.

We departed Coxen Hole at three on a very starry morning the following Saturday. Since I felt I needed to be in church the next morning we had not had time for a trial voyage. With the hired captain, the lawyer for ballast, two crewmen, Freddy Jarvis, Captain Gene and I, we were seven aboard.

We had not been at sea very long before the lawyer, who had advised me he was prone to seasickness, and the two "experienced" crewmen were actively sea sick. They turned out to be entirely useless the whole trip.

I had not slept all night and was exhausted. At dawn, we had our first landfall, an island that lay right on our course. I quickly went below, made a few calculations and brought up a course change that would bring us to the mainland near our destination. This stimulated a heated discussion between the other three captains, who had never used charts: "Don't trust 'em!"

"Son, I been sailing these waters for fifty years. Never needed a chart then; don't need one now. The course is clear: 160°." Captain Gene pulled the brim down on his baseball cap and dared the others to contradict him.

"That's not right!" Captain Jim, the one I had hired, pointed to the compass. "The course is 187°."

"No." Captain Jarvis shook his hand in anger. "We always take a course of 180° to get there."

Now my calculations said we should go 190° True, but I was a novice and figured one of them was probably right. I went with Captain Jim's course. After all, he was the hired captain.

Time passed and we moved right along, reaching in the trades with seas six to eight feet. Every time the boat was in the trough, I wondered whether it would continue down as it had done when it was launched or whether it would rise on the swell.

Late in the afternoon, we made landfall on the mainland. The captain's course had taken us too far to the east. My course would have brought us where we wanted to be. There were many red faces that afternoon. We arrived at Puerto Cortes at eleven at night and headed right for the dock between two freighters. At the last second, the anchor was dropped from the stern and the boat came to rest with the bowsprit just over the dock. As I stepped ashore, one of the captains called to me.

"Padre Captain! Good Night!" I had made it. The crew had given me this title in recognition of my navigational genius.

We had problems with El Marinero. Because the little gasoline engine was air-cooled and had no exterior exhaust, every time I ran it we could not go below into the cabin. A carpenter extended the exhaust to the stern, bracing the pipe with wooden braces. Then every time we ran the engine, we had to keep bailing water on the wooden support to keep it from catching fire. After the stuffing box fell out and the long three-quarter inch shaft bent, I bought a new engine.

The new engine was a twenty-five horsepower Wisconsin Marine air-cooled gasoline engine. After having it wired by some Americans for an electric starter, we installed it. The engine did not work properly because the fuel was gravity fed and the tank, as installed, was lower than the engine. A simple solution was to place the tank over the engine.

This worked fine until the day the engine wiring, which had been improperly installed, caught fire. I grabbed the fire extinguisher, proud of myself because I had met the safety requirements that Chapman detailed. I aimed the fire extinguisher at the fire and a dribble of water came out. In desperation, I grabbed the wires with my bare hands and yanked them out. This stopped the fire, burned my hands and forehead, and traumatized Judy. It would be seven years before she enjoyed sailing again.

The last straw was when Henry, our boat watchman, who had caused me no end of problems, was arrested for stealing an ice-shaving machine. The police caught him, with the machine in my dingy, rowing away from town. I went to the boat to get his identification papers for him and found many things that had been missing from our house. I went back to the jail, (1) fired Henry, and (2) pressed charges for theft.

By this time, I was discouraged about boating and did not feel too bad when we sold El Marinero the day before we left Honduras.

CHAPTER SEVENTEEN

For the next several days, we sailed south. I had set the course further east than was really needed. This was probably a reaction to the Bermuda trip experience. I did not want to beat upwind at all, especially in the easterly trade winds. Our speed with the jib and mizzen was a steady five knots and I felt no need to go faster.

During the day, we watched those neat little trade wind clouds and during the night the stars filled the sky from horizon to horizon. I am never as fulfilled as when I am sailing. When I am in a boat miles from shore, I know our safety and survival are up to me. If something breaks I cannot call someone to come and fix it, I have to repair it. It is frightening, yet it makes me feel good about myself. I am not dependent on the whims of a boss and I can go where I want to, when I want to.

I could alter the heading of the boat right now and go anywhere I want. I set the goals and I am the one who must meet them. If I decide I do not like a goal, as in the case when I changed course for Bermuda, I can do that too. No guilt. No feelings of failure.

I have to take Judy's thoughts and feelings into consideration also. She is not too sure about this cruising life. Her goal is a year of cruising, and then she will decide if she wants to cruise longer. One of her worries before we left was meeting other people.

"1 don't know, Ames," Judy had said. "Are there going to be people there? People who will become friends? We will be moving all the time."

"I don't know, hon. All I've read says people become friends quickly while cruising. Sometimes they sail together and sometimes they just meet up every so often when they arrive in the same port."

"1 don't think I could take it without friends."

So far, we had become acquaintances with about fifteen boats and made friends with three cruising families. Our closest cruising friends, Judy and Jim and their three sons, were cruising on a boat named Nona Rosa and planned to sail for two years. We first met them when we had to tie up alongside them in Annapolis after our engine gave up the ghost in a cloud of smoke.

Nona Rosa was a very active ship. The two younger boys, Devon and Joseph, scampered around the decks sword fighting with homemade swords. The smell of fresh baked bread wafted through the hatches and across our decks as Judy, the mate of Nona Rosa, cooked a daily ration of fresh bread for her crew.

On deck Jim, the captain, helped us side-tie to his boat so we would not crash into each other when a wake from a passing boat threw us together. He was a veterinarian who had sold his practice to go sailing with his family.

A head popped up through the fore hatch.

"Mom said to ask you if you want any fresh bread." This, we learned, was Jeremy, sixteen, the eldest of the three sons on board. Their mother was teaching him, along with his brothers, from a curriculum she developed herself.

"We sure would," I replied already drooling. We enjoyed it so much that we cruised with Nona Rosa down the Intracoastal Waterway to Beaufort, North Carolina. As we sailed along, we watched Jim make final repairs on his boat in preparation for the voyage to the Virgin Islands. Between teasing Jim, eating Judy's fresh baked bread and gathering on Butterfly for songfests, we had found some very good friends as we started cruising.

Another of Judy's worries was whether she could take the stress and strain of sailing. So far, she has done well. I cannot think of a much worse experience than the trip to Bermuda. Well, a hurricane would be worse I suppose, but I do not plan to sail through a hurricane. Why can not all sailing be like these last few days?

The banana companies, who promised that all West Indians who came to work would be provided with their own church (Anglican or British Methodist), English schools, and a decent burial, had started the church in Honduras. In the late fifties, there was a great strike and the fruit companies took back their promise. The Episcopal Church took over the churches as a mission.

I was to have a difficult mission, according to the bishop.

"Ames," he said, "I am sending you to Puerto Cortes to do a specific job. You are going to have to change the language of the congregation from English to Spanish. The women speak mostly English and the men and children speak mostly Spanish. If we don't make this change, the church will die."

I did not know how difficult the job would be until I discovered most of those attending church were women. We had three adult male members: a thirty-year-old, a fifty eight-year-old and a seventy two-year-old. There were no children over the age of sixteen.

In addition to getting to know the new congregation, I had great difficulty understanding and adjusting to the culture of the north coast of Honduras. One day as our family was sitting down to eat, I asked my daughter Debra, then about seven years old, what she had done that day.

"I played in the house with a dead man."

"Tell me that again."

"My friend Marta and I went to a house to play. There was a dead man there."

"There had been a death in the family."

"Yeah. There was a dead man lying on the bed. We had cookies and a lot of fun."

My daughter did not usually tell stories, but this sounded a bit strange. After dinner, I walked down the street where she had been playing. One house had what looked like a party going on. They invited me in, and there on a bed was a dead man, just as she had said.

They do not have funeral parlors in Puerto Cortes. The women wash the body and place cotton in the mouth and a bowl of salt on the stomach. Then they decorate the room with paper flowers. People come and go all day to give condolences and to gossip. They bring food and drinks, which everyone shares. There is very little weeping.

Out in back, the men build a coffin out of pine. It is a simple affair, just a box for the corpse to fit in. The women may pad the inside if they can afford the material. After the men build the coffin, it is varnished, and while waiting for the varnish to dry, they play cards and drink great quantities of rum. When the varnish is dry, the men add the handles, if the family can afford to rent them. After drinking enough "spiritual fortification," one of the men goes out to the cemetery to dig the grave.

The children have no fear of death. They usually play in the house and the room of the deceased. Their natural curiosity leads them to touch the body. The women chase them out if they get too rowdy, but the men usually chase them back in.

Having a funeral in such a culture is interesting, as no two are ever the same. There is only one common denominator: they all start later than scheduled.

The funeral procession starts from the house. The men, still tipsy from the rum, place the coffin on their shoulders and march to the church. The other mourners follow the casket as the pall bearers weave down the street. When the service is over, they take the casket to the nearest train tracks, where the funeral train waits.

The train consists of a steam engine, tender, a flat car on which the coffin is placed, and an ornate black and green funeral car. The train is necessary since it is the only way to get to the cemetery. After the funeral party is aboard, the train backs through town and others who want to go to the cemetery get on. Vendors who sell tacos, sandwiches, ice cream, and cokes also board. It is a great party.

When the funeral train leaves the city limits, the engineer blows his whistle in such a mournful manner that it made the hair stand right up on my head the first time I heard it. This is the signal for the mourning to begin. The women scream and faint, the men groan, and everyone weeps. Eventually the train chugs to a stop at the cemetery and the passengers and coffin are unloaded.

After the gravesite is found, the grave itself has to be widened or lengthened. It generally also has to be bailed. I had one funeral for a rather heavyset elderly woman. The grave was dug at the bottom of the hill and was full of water when we got there.

"Start bailing," I said to my acolyte Pepe. He bailed and bailed, but the water level did not go down much.

"What should we do?" I asked the family of the deceased. "Dig another grave?"

By that time it was getting dark.

"No," they answered. "There isn't enough time. Put her in."

I figured that since she was so heavy she would probably sink, so we lowered the casket in.

I opened my prayer book and continued the service. "Ashes to ashes and dust to . . ."

Blurp . . . up bobbed the casket like a submarine surfacing after a long underwater voyage.

I stood there mesmerized as it bobbed on top of the water. They never taught me what to do in a situation like this in seminary.

When in doubt, sing a hymn.

"Let's all sing 'Rock of Ages.'"

As they began to sing, I told Pepe to cut a couple of six-foot bamboo poles.

We were finishing the hymn when Pepe returned.

"Shove her down," I said in a low voice.

"What Padre?" Pepe asked hesitantly.

"Take a pole and push the casket down," I ordered in a louder voice.

Pepe and another fellow took the poles and pushed the casket to the bottom, and then stood back.

I flipped to the page and started, "Ashes to ashes and . . .

"Bloop . . . up she came again.

"Push her down again," I commanded Pepe and the other man. It was getting too dark to keep this up.

"This time hold her down."

And so, we finished the service.

Sometimes the service at grave side gets held up for other reasons, like forgetting the screw driver needed to remove the rented handles and having to send to town for one. Or not remembering which end of the casket the head is at:

"Got to have the head to the East, Padre, can't put the man in the ground backward. How can he find de way to heaven? He go backward, mon!"

This means opening the casket to check which end has the head. On one occasion, the grave collapsed, causing the pallbearer, casket without lid and body to fall into the grave. This led to screaming and shouting, fainting, and even fist fights.

"The duppies got me! The duppies got me!" screamed the man in the grave with the coffin and dead man on top of him. "Duppies" are ghosts.

Meanwhile, there was a discussion.

"Why didn't you make that mark right on the head?"

"I did make the . . . you see it right there."

"I do see it there . . . . but the lid not on right."

"I didn't put dat lid on, man."

"Who put dat lid on I goin' punch him for puttin' that lid on like dat."

After the man, body and coffin were extracted from the grave and sorted out, the service continued with only the coffin, with the body inside it, in the grave.

After the service it takes time to gather the mourners, who have wandered off all over the cemetery looking for where Tía Maria, Tío Gonzalez, or brother George is buried. Until all the people are on board, the train will not leave. I do not think I had one funeral that took less than seven hours.

I really was concerned with building my little congregation. I visited the homes of the congregation. The priest before me had made up nice cards with information about each family.

Gonzales, Guadalupe de	Children: María	age 1
Barrio Laguna	José	age 2
	Juan	age 3
	Guillermo	age 5
	Anna	age 7

Seemed simple enough. Just go to the Laguna district and find Mrs. Gonzalez and the children.

Barrio Laguna had about two thousand inhabitants and none of whom I spoke with had heard of Mrs. Guadalupe Gonzales. I spent a week without much success trying to track down my parishioners. The following Sunday I asked a long-standing member of the congregation about Mrs. Gonzales.

"Mrs. Holston," I said, "what happened to the Gonzales family? I could not find them last week. Have they moved?"

"We don't have a Gonzales family here, Father."

"Sure we do. I have their card right here. Guadalupe Gonzales in Barrio Laguna."

"Oh, that's not the Gonzales family," she said.

"It's not?"

"Oh no, Father, Mrs. Gonzales is not Mrs. Gonzales. She's Miss Lopez . . . Guadalupe Lopez. They live by the tracks in Laguna."

"But the card says Gonzales."

In a whispered voice, although no one else was around, she said, "But they are not married, Father. He doesn't even live there. However, the children are his. That's why the card is written so."

I had difficulty also getting acolytes together. I asked some of the churchwomen about prospects.

"Mrs. Vallasquez," I asked, "who do you think would make a good acolyte?"

"Well, now Father," she replied, "I think Juan Estiban would do well. Tell you what, Father . . . why don't you ask Mrs. Valle?"

"Good morning, Mrs. Valle," I said later that morning. "Do you know a boy who would be a help to me during services?"

"The boy for you is Pedro Gutierrez," she said energetically. "I think Mrs. Jimenez might know of someone also."

Later in the week, I ran across Mrs. Jimenez.

"Do you know a boy who would make a good acolyte?"

"Sure I do, Padre. There is a boy on my street by the name of Pepe who is an Anglican. He'd be glad to help."

At the next vestry meeting, I was proud to announce I had three possible boys for acolytes: Juan Estiban, Pedro Gutierrez, and Pepe.

There were smiles on the faces of the vestry.

Mrs. Zuniga said, "I am sorry Father, you have only one boy there."

"What do you mean? I have Juan, Pedro, and Pepe."

"These are all the same boy," said Mr. Salinas.

"Please explain," I said, trying to understand what was happening.

"Well now, Padre," she said carefully, "Juan Estiban is the name the boy's father's relatives call him. Pedro Gutierrez is what his mother's relatives call him as his mother and father never really got married in church. Pepe is what his young friends call him. So you see, Padre, you really have only one acolyte."

It was hard because I had two other congregations to take care of, the English speaking one in San Pedro and Trinity Church in Tela. After two years, there still were not many men in the congregation. I was at least keeping many of the boys past the age of sixteen, but I was impatient. I wanted to have adult men in the congregation and had no idea how to reach them. I had tried getting involved in community organizations, radio programs, developing co-operatives, and talking with them individually.

At the request of one of my few churchmen, a taxi driver, I helped start a co-operative for the town's taxies. Later I was requested to do the same for the local bus company. We were able to put a competing bus company out of business with our new buses and the people's dislike for the owner of the new bus company—the president's brother.

During my third year in Puerto Cortes, the American Military Attaché, Coronel Smith, in Tegucigalpa sent me a letter requesting that I come up for a visit and perhaps play some golf. Since this man was an Episcopalian attending the church Archdeacon Hurly was in charge of, I decided to go.

We went to a golf course that was more vertical then horizontal. A three hundred yards hole was one hundred yards horizontal and two hundred yards vertical. After playing golf we sat at the club's patio and had lunch. While we were eating, a group of men came in and sat at a nearby table.

"That is the president and his people," Coronel Smith said nodding towards the new comers. "Do you want to meet the president?"

"Sure," I replied. We went over to the table and the Coronel introduced me to the president. The man looked at me and asked,

"Are you the priest from Puerto Cortes?"

"Yes sir."

"You need to stick with religion and keep your nose out of co-operatives. If you don't I will not be responsible for what happens."

With this, I was dismissed. I had been brought to Tegucigalpa for the President of Honduras to deliver his message in person!

Not long after this, I started to help start a fishing co-operative. Fish were sold in the market on Fridays and any left over were thrown away. Meanwhile, just six miles inland people needed a source of protein. The co-operative was to freeze the fish they caught and truck them to the many towns near the coast.

Many lobsters were also caught. An American owned company would buy them for fifty cents per lobster no matter what the size. We changed that price to fifty cents per pound. Evidently, they complained to the president about this change in prices.

On New Years Eve of 1966, five shots were fired at the rectory. None hurt us because the house was built out of cement block. Besides, I thought they were just trying to scare us. They sure scared Judy! I would not know how much until the following fall.

Then a strange thing happened.

It started when we were expecting our third child. The baby was due right after Christmas. Christmas came and the day after our maid quit. She stayed to get her Christmas present, but did not want to take care of diapers, so she just quit without telling us.

I took a week off and took Judy and the girls to San Pedro where the hospital was, and we all waited at a friend's house for the baby to arrive. After a couple of false labors, I left Judy in the care of some English speaking parishioners and took the girls back with me to Puerto Cortes.

In two days' time, I had all the clothes dirty and there was no food in the house. It was all I could do to keep enough water boiled and filtered so we had something to drink. I was desperate for help and put the word out I needed a maid in a hurry.

"Buenos días," said the woman at the door. She was missing her front teeth, as were the majority of women over fifteen years old in Puerto Cortes, and was fairly heavy set.

"Can I help you?" I said in Spanish. "You are looking for a maid, yes?"

"Yes indeed." I replied. "I need one badly."

"I need a job," she said. "How much do you pay?"

"I pay forty Lempira a month." She looked clean and neat and I decided if she accepted the pay, I would hire her.

"I would like to work. Can you show me the work?"

I showed her around the shambles and introduced her to the children.

"There is much work to be done," she said.

I had a brilliant idea. "Perhaps I could hire someone else to help you. Do you know anyone else who would like to work here?"

"Oh yes, I have a cousin. I'll ask her."

Soon I had two maids. One came in at five-thirty in the morning when I started Mass and worked until six in the evening. She shopped in the market and made breakfast and lunch. At ten the second maid came and did washing and cleaning, made dinner and baby—sat the girls while I had church meetings in the evenings.

The following Sunday there were twenty new men in the church. I could not believe it. I must have done something right, but I did not know what it was.

The next week Judy finally gave birth to Laura, our third daughter, and on Friday I went to San Pedro Sula to bring them home. When we arrived back home the maids were missing and the girls had been taken over to their friend's house to play. Debra told me the women had said they would come back for their pay later. They had quit.

The next Sunday men appeared in church again. I was ecstatic. After the service, I cornered the only person on the vestry who would be honest with me, Miss Mary Ann Serrato, a sixty plus year old grey haired woman who stood five feet in her shoes. She was a nurse.

"Miss Mary Ann," I asked, "what induced all these men to come to church? What did I do?"

"Oh Father, I can't tell you."

"Come now, Miss Mary Ann, please tell me. You know I've tried so hard to get more men to come. What did I do right?"

"Well Father . . . these men, you know . . . You sure you want me to tell you dis?" She pursed her lips but there was a smile in the corner of her eyes." I nodded yes.

"These men . . . they come to church to see the priest who hired not just one, but two prostitutes when his wife was gone. They think you are some macho!" she said with a chuckle and a grin.

I had hired two of the most notorious prostitutes in town to be my maids. I never tried to explain the situation and later two of the men became staunch members of the church.

CHAPTER EIGHTEEN

"Judy, I think it's time to raise the main," I said, just as she was getting ready to come on watch.

"Why?"

"I think we would make better time with the main up."

"We're doing all right now, aren't we? How fast are we going?" She is always suspicious that I want to go as fast as possible. She is correct, but she always wants to go as slow as possible.

"We're doing five knots, but I'm worried about our arrival in the islands." I had been spending a lot of time on my watch trying to figure out our arrival time. This was our fifth day at sea and we were only 350 miles from our landfall.

"As I figure it," I continued, "at this speed we will arrive off the islands in late afternoon or maybe even after dark." The "after dark" always gets Judy, as she does not like sailing after dark. I do not either, not if there is land around.

"Well," she said as usual, "do what you want."

I put the main up with a reef in it. The boat stopped its jogging and began to surge along at between six to seven knots. We scooted along with an easy motion, dodging a few small squalls. Now we were going too fast. Even though I had shortened sail during the night, my calculations told me we would make landfall at three the next morning. That evening I took the main down, but the wind piped up and we continued at six knots. At dusk we could see the loom of the lights of St. Thomas . . . or Tortola . . . or somewhere.

Someone once told me that the sign of a good navigator is silence. If silence is not possible, then never tell the absolute truth. If someone asks, "Where are we?" the good navigator points to a spot on the chart (any spot will do) and says with confidence, "We are right here." Of course, no one can be that accurate, even with GPS.

When we saw the loom of the lights, Judy asked, "Where is that light coming from?"

"St. Thomas, of course," I said, crossing my fingers behind my back.

When I am near land, I cannot sleep. When I do lie down to rest, I visualize reefs with huge waves breaking over them, or sand banks just deep enough to catch our keel, or the one jagged rock that comes within two feet of the surface even if we're in ten fathoms of water. I just cannot sleep.

So tonight, I am bouncing up on deck, checking DR and GPS, and Judy keeps chasing me back to bed.

"You need to rest for the morning," she scolds.

"All right," I respond, as I head back to my bunk. Soon the reality on deck is much better than the visions I see as I try to sleep. I go back out on deck.

"There are some more lights over there," says Judy.

I look where she is pointing. It looks like a mountain of pinpoint lights. I take a bearing on them and duck below. *Must be Tortola,* I think. I look out again. *God they look close,* I say to myself. If I said it aloud, Judy might panic. I take another GPS position and plot it on the chart. According to this we are still thirty miles off Tortola.

By four the next morning I had reefed the mizzen and we are still doing 6 knots. I strain my eyes looking for land. Tortola's lights are real close, but the GPS says we are very far away. I go and look at the chart again.

"*Shark Shoals,*" I mumble. *It is still safe. More than ten fathoms. Oh, oh, here is another. Red Fish bank . . . no, it is OK . . . more than ten fathoms also. But what about the wave action? Out here, we are in one thousand fathoms. What will it be like over those shoals? Will the waves build?*"

Back up on deck. There is a faint light on the horizon to the east. I want the sun to come up in the south today so that the islands will be back lighted. However, the sun refuses and daylight slowly increases to the point where I can see the outlines and finally the islands themselves.

"Land-ho!" I cry with great joy. "Jost Van Dyke dead ahead!"

"You're a little late for that, aren't you Ames?" says Judy.

"We've been able to see the lights all night."

"Yeah, but now I know where we are!" Judy frowns and I kick myself.

When will I ever learn to keep my mouth shut?

The wind picks up as we near Jost Van Dyke and we romp along at six and a half knots. The islands are beautiful as we wind through them and head toward the island of St. John.

We drop the sails off the entrance to Cruise Bay and motor in to anchor. All of a sudden, we feel closed in. There seem to be hundreds of boats at anchor. We wander through the anchorage, trying to find a spot to drop the hook and relax.

"Hey! Butterfly!" someone calls. There waving at us frantically is Donna on Sea Level, which had departed Bermuda several weeks before us. Donna points toward the entrance and tells us that a boat had been anchored there earlier. We drop the hook. Donna and David come over in their dingy.

"We'll come back in about an hour and take you to customs. Then we'll have a big lunch at our boat, if you want."

"That's great," Judy says.

"I'll bring the champagne," I added. Some friends had given us a bottle of champagne before we left Annapolis. It only took a few minutes to clear customs and then we had lunch.

I was very grateful for the reception Donna and David had given us, but I was also very sleepy. It had taken seven days, two hours and three minutes to make 961 miles. Our average speed was 5.7 knots, which is not a bad passage for the old girl.

We went back to the boat, took off our clothes, went to bed and slept twelve hours straight.

After three years in Honduras, the church gave us a three-month sabbatical back to the U.S. This was a hectic time, flying the three children back and then visiting, visiting, visiting.

Before we left on this furlough, I talked with Judy about staying for three more years. This was the time to advise the Mission Society whether we wanted to return home for good, or planned to stay for another three years.

"Whatever you want, honey," was always her answer. I should have been more aware of what she was saying, but at the time I was having so much fun being a missionary and having so many adventures that I just heard what I wanted to hear. Looking back on this statement several months later, the translation would have been, "No, I don't want to stay, but I know you like it here and I'll try to stay if I have to."

When we returned from our trip back to the states I began to notice that Judy was acting strangely. We were driving home from the airport and I got behind a huge truck.

"What's in that truck?" Judy asked me.

"I don't know. Looks like boxes. No, they're caskets . . . baby caskets."

Judy started to cry.

I knew she was thinking about the high mortality rate of babies in Honduras, and the fact that our youngest was only eight months old. Women in Puerto Cortes, when asked about the number of children they had, would respond saying something like, "I have ten children. Three living, seven dead." They always listed both the living and the dead, and the dead usually outnumbered the living.

Health care in Honduras was very bad. Puerto Cortes, the third largest city in the country, had one doctor, and he worked only for the incoming ships. In addition, there were a couple of mid-wives and Miss Serrato, the nurse.

A few days later, Judy started to cry and did not stop for three days.

"What's wrong, honey?"

"I don't know."

"There must be something bothering you," I said as I cuddled her in my arms, "or you wouldn't be crying." Then it began to dawn on me. I did not want to test my idea, but I thought I had better.

"You . . . you didn't want to come back?"

Silence . . . . sniffles.

"You don't want to stay here?"

Silence . . . . more sniffles.

"You don't like it here?"

"I . . . I want to go home."

Now what do I do? I thought.

I had promised to stay for three more years. I had promised the congregation, which was always expecting me to leave since all the previous priests had always left, that I would not desert them. I had so many things I wanted to do here. We had almost all the money we needed for the hospital, the fishing co-operative was just getting organized, and we were about to get another missionary for San Pedro Sula, which would give me more time to work in Cortes. I did not want to go back.

I was not ready.

"What do you want me to do?" I asked.

"I don't know . . . I just want to go home. I'm sorry, Ames. I just don't like it here. The maids steal my things. People shoot at our house. I worry about our children all the time. I don't have any friends. Half the time you're off running all over the place. I hate it . . . . hate it!"

I felt very angry, but I love Judy very much. I called the bishop and he came the following week to talk with us. He saw that Judy could not stay in Puerto Cortes and asked me if I would take over an English-speaking congregation, which might make it easier for her. I refused. I thought it would be better for us to return home. We bought the airline tickets that afternoon and made plans to move out a month later.

I felt like a whipped puppy.

When I announced we were leaving, the congregation looked at one another. I had betrayed their trust. I was doing what all the others had done before: leave them.

"Every time we get to trust our minister," said one parishioner, "he leaves, and then the church falls apart."

I could not say, "*It's Judy's fault! If it were not for her I'd stay.*" I just had to swallow my anger and tell them "We just have to go."

"*Oh God,*" I prayed, "*I do not want to go.*"

Judy, meanwhile, was feeling a lot of guilt. She knew I loved the work and wanted to stay, but she had reached her limit. We sold the boat, packed up our meager belongings and boarded the airplane back to the States.

We arrived back in San Francisco with me angry and Judy feeling guilty.

I had visited the bishop while on furlough and he had assured me, "Anytime you are ready to come home, Ames, we have a place for you." I had worked with his son when I was in seminary and he had supervised me when I started a mission for him in La Honda, California. Now he did not know me.

"Didn't Bishop Richards write you about me?"

"Oh, yes, he had glowing things to say about you."

"Can't you help me find a position here?"

"I don't really know you. Be patient and we will see. Meanwhile, it might be good for you to check with the Bishop of Northern California."

"But San Francisco is my home. I would like to stay here."

"We all do what we have to do. Well," he said, as he got up and reached out his hand, "it's been nice seeing you."

I started to job hunt.

After a few months getting no results (the Episcopal Church thinks anyone who has been a missionary is a maverick and suspect), a seminary classmate, Don Ball, called me. He was a chaplain in the New York State Prison System. Don suggested I come out and apply for the job of guidance counselor at his prison. *Well, why not!* I thought.

I flew out to New York and boarded a bus to Ellenville. It was a miserable December day. Cold and wet and grey which matched my general mood. Don took me to apply for the job and I talked to the Personnel Director.

"You would be helping prepare these men for when they return to the street-guiding them toward getting an occupation or education. Helping them untangle their family problems and making adjustments while in prison."

It sounded good to me. "How many men would I have on my case load?" I asked.

"Oh, we have four guidance counselor positions here, and 2,500 men. That means you would have a little over 600 on your case load."

"It doesn't seem to me I would have time to do much counseling," I said.

"Well, you've got to remember these men will be here for awhile. None has less than a twenty year sentence."

I decided it was not for me.

That evening I called the Archdeacon for the Diocese of New York, asked for an appointment and took the bus to New York City.

"I have a parish that is looking for an assistant. The priest is overworked and his vestry wants to get him some help. With your background and experience you would be just right." The Archdeacon picked up the phone and made an appointment for me to see the rector and vestry that evening.

I got on the bus again and, as I made the two-hour trip, found I was becoming excited. Perhaps I could land this job and start over again. Later I could move back to California as a rector. It started to snow before I arrived in Middletown.

It was a bad omen.

"What we need here," said Father Carl, "is someone who can help me out. Someone who can preach, organize the church school, work with the youth, and make visitations to the hospital and parishioners."

"That sounds just great to me," I said with enthusiasm. "I enjoy preaching, church school, and I especially enjoy working with youth."

"We don't have much money," said a vestryman. "We'd have to start you out on entrance pay."

"I suppose we can manage on that for a year, but please remember I have three years experience," I replied.

"As a missionary," the vestryman said in a demeaning voice.

My face began to burn. "You will pay our moving expenses from California, of course."

"I don't think we can do that," snapped the vestryman.

"Well, thank you all," I said as I got up to leave.

"One moment," said Fr. Carl. To the vestryman he said, "Jim, it's usual to pay for the moving expenses."

"Well, all right, but keep them down."

They showed me the house we would live in. It was an old farmhouse in the back of a large estate with two bedrooms and a bathroom (that was accessible only through the larger bedroom) upstairs, and a kitchen and living room downstairs.

"We could just barely fit into this," I said to Fr. Carl.

"Oh don't worry, this will only be temporary. The church is buying a new rectory next year and you can move into the old one where we live now."

I called Judy later that night and we decided to take it. I flew back to San Francisco, loaded up our little car, and started for New York. It would be like a vacation traveling across country-although we would have to "keep the expenses down."

CHAPTER NINETEEN

We quickly tired of Cruise Bay. We felt closed in by all the boats at anchor and were constantly bounced and jounced by the huge wakes of the ferries, which came into the harbor at full speed. Their wakes would often be so big they would break on the deck.

"I told you so," I said with disgust to Judy.

"What?"

"I told you it would be like this."

"Now Ames don't start that again." Judy had that frown on her face that told me she was tired of my complaining.

"No, Judy, I mean it. Twenty years ago when we decided to go cruising after retirement, I knew it would be so crowded they would need policemen a hundred miles offshore to direct traffic. I can't stand this."

"Well, let's go then," she said, without enthusiasm. "Let's go to town, buy some groceries and leave."

"Butterfly, Sea Level" squawked our radio.

"You guys want to go to Francis Bay? We're leaving for there now."

"That's great," I replied. "We were just getting ready to leave ourselves. We've had about all we can take of Cruise Harbor."

"Where's Francis Bay?" Judy began stowing things.

"Just around the corner not more than a couple of miles." The Virgin Islands are not at all what I had expected. I guess I was looking for lush palm-lined islands. What I found looked more like a series of green Catalina Islands, mountainous and covered with scrub trees and cactus. They were beautiful, but not what I had expected.

As we approached Francis Bay, I could see the sandy beach and even some palm trees lining the shore. *This is more like it,* I thought.

"Ames, isn't that green water just ahead of us?"

We had read you could tell the depth of the water by its color: blue was deep; dark green, shallower; light green, very shallow; and white, you are aground. Ahead was what looked light green. I cut the throttle and put the boat in neutral. We glided over the area and the depth sounder read 35 feet. I felt foolish in my near panic.

As we came into the anchorage Judy shouted, "There they are! There's Nona Rosa!"

"And there's Ty Dewi," I added. The community, which had started at Beaufort, was beginning to reunite.

For the next day and a half we talked and compared passage notes with our friends, swam, snorkeled, and generally rested up from our passage. It seemed to take forever to regain our energy. We just wanted to relax and do nothing.

At last, with great reluctance, we pulled anchor and headed for Charlotte Amalee on St. Thomas. It was only about a fifteen-mile trip to the huge anchorage in front of the city.

"Look at this!" I called to Judy as we entered the bay. She had gone below for something. "You gotta see this."

"There must be five hundred boats anchored here!" she yelled with excitement, as she surveyed the scene after climbing up into the cockpit.

"On top of that, there are two cruise ships at anchor besides the four at that dock on the right," I said somewhat despondently.

"It doesn't look like we're going to get lonely out here."

After we found a place to squeeze in and anchor, we went ashore. The town was dirty and smelly. The sewers ran under the sidewalks and in many places the sidewalk had broken through and you could see raw sewage running down toward the bay.

We spent the next few days going to the post office for mail, hunting down a masthead anchor light to replace the one we lost on the way to Bermuda, finding out that the masthead wind unit was too expensive for us to buy now, buying groceries, and calling our family.

We did receive good news. Our car, which we had left with a broker in Virginia to sell, had been sold. This meant we had three hundred dollars more a month which we could save to pay for the next haul out and the insurance that came due the following November.

Two days before Christmas, a storm hit. Winds gusting to fifty miles an hour whipped up the harbor. It would not have been so bad, but the winds would stop, shift one hundred-twenty degrees and blast away again at thirty to fifty miles an hour. Boats were swinging on their hooks, some changing to the wind almost immediately and others swinging slowly.

We discovered this was not the time to be anchored in front of a boat with a rope anchor rode. The boat behind us would stretch out on its rode until the line was half its normal diameter and then, when the wind stopped, shoot forward as if shot out of a rubber band. I looked out and saw the boat pass us, doing three or four knots. It was time to re-anchor.

We hauled anchor in the gusty wind and found a likely looking spot behind other anchored boats. We settled in for the night after deciding to stand four-hour anchor watches. As I sat out in the cockpit, I watched gas cans, life preservers, boat poles, awnings, and even a dingy blow past. I also noticed a boat off Hassel Island, to leeward of us, picking things out of the water. I expected there would be a huge flea market over there after the storm.

At about two in the morning, the pilot boat for the bay came over and told us we would have to move as they were going to re-anchor one of the cruise ships. (We found out later it had dragged its two anchors across the harbor.)

We pulled our hook again and re-anchored closer in. Soon we began to drag, so we pulled it up once more and set it in another spot a little further out into the anchorage. There is nothing like anchoring four times in fifty-knot winds.

The next day the wind blew most of the day, but it had lost some of its fierceness. By evening things were calm again.

Just before this storm, Ty Dewi had come into the harbor and we had made plans to attend the Christmas service at the Anglican Cathedral on Christmas Eve together. Ty Dewi is owned and single-handed by David Jenkins, another Episcopalian priest who had gone into a non-parochial ministry at a university and is now retired. David picked us up in his dingy and we went to the cathedral midnight service. It felt wonderful worshiping with this rather strange congregation. The choir sounded beautiful and there was a trombone and tuba to augment the organ.

We did not get home until almost two in the morning, but we cranked up the portable generator, turned on our little Christmas tree's lights, and listened to a few Christmas carols on the stereo. I went outside and took a video of the harbor, which was as beautiful as a Christmas tree itself. Absolutely bushed, we went to bed.

We were awakened at five by a traditional contest of choirs on shore, but we forced ourselves to sleep until nine. Then we quickly hauled anchor and headed for Francis Bay where we were to gather with Nona Rosa, Ty Dewi, Sylmiril, and Sea Level for Christmas dinner. The dinner, which eventually was held on two different boats since so many other boats showed up, was turkey and all the trimmings. It was great being with all our friends.

The next day a group gathered with their instruments to sing sea songs. Judy played guitar; Jim, mandolin (with only half its strings); Dave on electric bass (powered through his stereo somehow); and me on banjo and concertina. We rocked the bay with "What shall we do with a drunken sailor?"

In the morning, Sea Level left to go on down island, Nona Rosa left to visit the British Virgin Islands for a few weeks, and Sylmiril and Ty Dewi returned to St. Thomas. All of a sudden, Francis Bay became very lonely.

We hung around the bay for a day and then moved to Leinster Bay, where we stayed through a quiet New Year's Day.

I was very angry with Judy. I had been since we left Honduras. I tried to hide it, but it slipped out every now and then. Judy was feeling guilty about making me leave and I wanted her to stay that way. This was her punishment.

My anger also made the bad situation in Middletown even worse. After driving ten days through ice and snow to reach our new home, I was greeted by Fr. Carl.

"We didn't expect you today," he said.

"I said I'd be here on the tenth," I replied.

"Well, with the weather being so bad, we didn't expect you yet."

"Can we get in our house?"

"It's not ready yet, but I suspect that Judy would like to see it."

It was freezing and dreary in the house. The toilet was broken and had leaked allover the kitchen table and frozen there.

"Like I said, it's not ready yet."

"When will it be ready?" I asked.

"Maybe in a few days, depends upon the weather. I'll get someone to turn on the heat."

Our welcome had been as cold as our "new house."

My friend Don lived about twenty miles from Middletown and he had a large house, so I called him and he said we could come over for a few days.

Three days later, we were informed that our house was ready. From the start, Fr. Carl and I did not get along. He wanted me to work exclusively with the church school, and did not want me to preach, celebrate Holy Communion, or even visit parishioners. I had no office, desk, or telephone at first. His paranoia included opening my mail. My life seemed to have reached the bottom of the pit.

CHAPTER TWENTY

I stood on the aft deck with a cup of coffee in my hand. Coffee tastes the best standing here, watching the sun come up over the horizon. First, the sky lightens and the clouds turn pink, then red, and maybe even orange. The water is still, disturbed only by a ripple as a light breath of air passes over its surface. Overhead the frigate birds begin their cruising on the air currents in search of fish. They are majestic creatures with their huge wingspan. Every so often a fish breaks the surface of the water as he tries to get away from the bigger fish that's chasing him.

There are only about ten sailboats anchored here. *The mirrored reflections would make a great watercolor,* I think. Then I notice that on three or four of them other men like myself are standing, watching, sipping their coffee and enjoying the morning. Every so often one walks to the toe rail and proceeds to relieve himself over the rail.

Why is it that men, when they get to sea, have this compelling need to piss over the side? At home they use the bathroom. At dock they use the head or restroom facilities on shore. What makes it so different underway or at anchor?

One by one, the males come up on deck and stretch, yawn, and then pee over the side. I know because I observe this while relieving myself over the taffrail.

I wonder if it is a left over from our early days. Dogs, cats and other animals mark their territory by urinating. Perhaps that is what we are doing. We could be trying to say to other males, "Hey, Ames has been here. Keep away or be prepared to fight."

Who we expect to come sniffing by?

Perhaps it is just a need for freedom from the social constraints of civilization. We may be really saying, "To hell with the rules and customs of society. I will piss here if I want to. Damn society!"

While I was waiting in line to use a unisex restroom in St. Thomas, two local women waiting behind me were philosophizing.

"I don't understand how the mens get away with it."

"What chu talken' about, hon?"

"Why mens can just go up some alley and piss on a wall. People still say they's gentlemen. Now, if we went up an ally and pulled up our skirts, they'd think we was bad womens."

"That's right, hon. I don't see how the mens can do it like that and we have to wait in line fidgetin' an' dancing."

I was not sure if they were telling me to go find an alley and get out of their way or not. I did let them go ahead of me, even though I was about to burst a gut.

We are anchored in Ensenada Honda, Culebra Island, Puerto Rico. This is a beautiful bay that is almost land-locked. We came here to rest after six weeks of St. Thomas.

We had moved our base of operations at Charlotte Amalee to Honeymoon Bay off Water Island in St. Thomas, which is only a short dingy ride from the city. Gathered there were Nona Rosa, Sylmiril, Ty Dewi, Queen of Hearts, and Blue Ribbon, all of whom started out from the States with us. We began having Sunday services on our boat and would have up to fourteen people come to worship. Then there were great gatherings to sing sea songs or just talk about sailing.

However, the anchorage was crowded. As long as the wind blew all the boats lined up nicely, but when it stopped, as it frequently did in the early morning, one's neighboring boat might come "knocking" on your boat. Thus, we had motored the 25 miles to Culebra over a calm sea.

My life in Middletown did not get any better in the Spring. I did all sorts of things to try to raise my battered ego. I painted oil paintings . . . they were not so good. I completed my Symphony for Band and even got it played by the local concert band . . . it was not so good. I wrote and conducted an Oratorio for Whitsunday . . . it was not so good. I made model ships in the freezing cold of the attic . . . they were not so bad.

After being in Middletown a year and a half, an event took place that was to change our lives. One Friday afternoon I received a phone call.

"Hey, Ames," said a strange voice.

"Yes," I said cautiously, as I tried fruitlessly to recognize this voice.

"This is Don . . . Don Garvey, you remember me from San Francisco."

I vaguely remembered Don Garvey. He had graduated from my seminary a few years earlier than I and had been in charge of a mission in San Francisco. We knew each other, but were just acquaintances.

"Oh, hi Don." I was surprised to hear from him.

"Ames, I need a favor."

"What can I do for you?" I asked.

"I just arrived in town, and seem to have forgotten to pack a clerical collar. I'm due for a press conference tomorrow and I need to borrow a collar."

"Sure," I said. "I'll be glad to loan you a collar. Come on over."

We opened the gallon bottle of wine Don had brought, sat at the kitchen table, and talked.

"I've left the active ministry," Don said. "You know I have a background in police work."

"Yes," I said, vaguely remembering his saying something like that. "Why did you leave the parish ministry?"

"I got divorced and just did not think I could continue in parish work. I'm doing security work for Woodstock now."

"You mean you are working for the town of Woodstock?"

"Not the town," he said with a smile, "The rock festival."

"Oh that sounds interesting." I poured us another glass of wine.

"It's going to be the biggest thing to hit this area. We are expecting twenty thousand people. We're going to hold it right here in the Township of Wallkill."

"This is the first I've heard of it."

"We're going to announce it at a press conference tomorrow." He poured us another glass of wine. He continued, "We're going to have the Jefferson Air Plane, Jimmy Hendricks, Janis Joplin, Blood Sweat and Tears, everybody. It is going to be three days of 'Peace and Love.' That's our motto."

"Sounds like great fun, but I suspect you'll have some trouble with the town fathers here. They are a conservative group."

"Yeah, we know that. That's why I'm going to wear my collar tomorrow at the press conference."

I poured us another glass. I was feeling pretty good. I could tell because my nose and lips were numb. I was visualizing twenty thousand young people at this rock festival. There might be some need for a ministry there. I was feeling sure I was being called by the spirit (though I did not know whether it was the Holy Spirit or the bottled spirit) to minister to these young people.

"Don, have they considered having a ministry at the festival? You know, a chaplain to work with any pastoral problems which might come up, hold services on Sunday and organize volunteer clergy, that kind of thing."

"Hey, that's a thought! It might be a good idea. We could get you a trailer for an office, and a phone. That sounds great!" *The same spirit was moving him that was moving me.*

"Wait a minute! I didn't say I would do it!" The thought scared me.

"Sure, you're the one. You'd be good at it. What a great idea! I'll have to contact the promoters and see if they'll go along with it. I'll let you know next week."

We finished the bottle of wine as Don told me about the security arrangements. They planned to hire the off duty New York police. The Hog Farm Commune was coming to help with any "freak outs" they might have. The Grateful Dead would be there. They even planned to hire the "Up the Wall M-F'ers," a group that had created a riot at a prior rock festival, as part of the security team. There would be a meditation area,

"A great place to hold services," Don said his hands waving in the air attempting to define unseen objects, "with natural wood sculptures."

When Don left my head was whirling with ideas for ministry at the festival, as well as with the vapors of all the wine I had drunk. I had not been this excited since Honduras. This could certainly be a mission for me.

By Thursday of the following week, I was beginning to hope Don would not call back. The announcement of the impending Rock Festival had turned the town upside down.

"We don't want any of those long haired hippies in our community," said some.

"We don't want our children listening to that kind of music."

"It's not just the music. You'll see, they'll teach our kids to smoke pot and take drugs," a few of the staunchest conservatives predicted to anyone who would listen. And so it went around the church. Since the church pretty much ran the township, I knew the festival and Don were in for hard times.

What I could not understand was the ignorance the parents had regarding their children. They all listened to "that kind of music" all their waking hours and they knew plenty about drugs. It was plain to see that the parents who yelled the loudest knew the least about their kids.

Laws were introduced in the Town Council to forbid a rock festival. I knew if Don ever called back, I would have to make a decision. If I decided to take the mission, I would probably have to resign my job in the parish.

"I know you've been unhappy here," said Judy. "Maybe it would be best to quit anyway."

"Do you really mean that?" I asked.

I knew she had been happy in the little house on the huge estate. I had to make sure. "Or are you just saying that?"

"I really mean it. You do what you feel best."

I had heard that before. "I really need to know your feelings."

"What would we do after the festival? Where would you work?"

"I don't know." I said. "I might have to get a secular job. I could always work in a gas station, I guess."

"Well, we don't even know if they will ask you to work at the festival or if the church would ask for your resignation. Let's wait and see."

A few days after this conversation, Don Garvey called and said the promoters thought we had a great idea. They would provide a trailer and pay me seventy-five dollars a day. I should keep track of any time I spent before the festival and they would pay by an hourly rate of five dollars an hour. That was excellent pay in those days, when I made only five hundred a month. More than this, I would be a missionary again. I said I would do it.

I told Judy and she seemed a little nervous.

"We'll keep this quiet for awhile, as I will have nothing to do for a few months," I decided.

During the next two months, the Town Council turned the heat up on the festival. They passed a law outlawing rock festivals but a court ordered an injunction on the grounds of freedom of speech. The council eventually passed a law that prohibited any function if the noise of said function would escape its boundaries. However, the law exempted the racecar track on the other side of town.

It seemed unconstitutional to me, and even some of the town fathers thought it wouldn't stand up in court.

"It doesn't matter though," they said. "It will take them until next year to fight this one."

Sure enough, the lower court upheld the law, and Woodstock was forced to move just months before the festival.

]I started rounding up volunteer ministers, Catholic priests, and rabbis to hold services during the festival and to help in counseling. It was difficult to find ministers who would help.

"I'd like to help," said one minister, "But it would mean I'd have to resign my congregation. They are dead set against it, you know. No, I'm sorry, but I can't help you."

After a month of calling and talking, I was able to find a few brave souls with a vision of mission. A young Lutheran, several monks from the Episcopal Order of the Holy Cross (a monastic order), a Baptist choir that was to come and put on a rock service, one brave Catholic priest, and the only Reformed Jewish rabbi in the Catskills.

A month before the festival, I went in to see Fr. Carl. After a brief argument, I resigned.

The next few weeks were hectic. I ran around attempting to find work and wrapping up my business in town. By August 1, Fr. Carl still had not announced my resignation. This made it very difficult to talk with the friends I had made, so I found myself withdrawing from them. As for finding a job after the festival, it seemed hopeless.

In those days one did not find a church; the church found you. There was not enough time for this system to work for me. I was going to be out of work in a month with five mouths to feed. I gave up trying to find a job, thinking that something would happen somehow.

The Monday before the festival I kissed Judy and told her I was going to drop by the site to be sure my trailer was set up and everything was ready.

When I arrived, I found the place jammed with people. I stopped by the security trailer (the center of three trailers) and Don took me to my office. It was not really a whole trailer, but an office at the end of the mobile building that housed the First Aid Clinic. It was not bad and had plenty of room for counseling. Across the end was a built-in table. I carried a few boxes of materials in from the car and straightened up some. Before I finished there was a knock on my door.

A young girl was standing in the doorway with tears running down her face.

"Are you a minister?" she asked.

"Yes." I was wearing blue jeans, black shirt and a collar. "What can I do for you?"

"My . . . my boy friend . . ." She broke into sobs and threw her arms about me. "He doesn't want me any more."

Your boyfriend and you have split up?"

"Yeah . . . He split."

I disengaged her arms and led her to the only chair. I sat on the edge of the table.

"Tell me about it."

It was a long story. They had been going together for two years since she had run away from home to "join the hippies." She had found Johnny and he took good care of her. Recently he had begun to act strange and mean. Last night he just got up from their bedroll and told her he was leaving her for good.

"I'm so frightened. I don't know what I'm gonna do."

"What would you like to do?"

"I want to go home . . . but they're mad with me. They won't let me come back home. I know that."

"Why don't we call them and ask?"

"We can do that?"

"Sure." I picked up the phone, called the girl's home, and talked to her mother.

"Oh my God!" her mother said after I had explained the purpose of the call. "Is she OK? We've been worried sick about her."

"She's fine, just fine. Would you like to talk to her?"

"Oh please, yes please."

They talked for a few minutes and arranged for bus tickets to be sent to the bus station in a nearby town. After she had gathered her belongings, I helped her find a ride to town.

This was the first of many sessions that lasted into the night. There were already twenty thousand people at the festival, and it had not even opened. They were camped allover the place. Many of them needed help and when they found a chaplain was present, they went in search of me. By eleven that night, I was cold, hungry and exhausted. I called Judy and told her I was not coming home, curled up on the table and fell fast asleep.

Bang! . . . Bang! . . . Bang, bang, bang!!

I woke up to a pounding at my office door. I was stiff and a bit disoriented as to what I was doing sleeping on a table.

Bang . . . Bang!

"I'm coming!" I yelled, not too politely, as I climbed down from the table and opened the door. A young man of about twenty jumped through the doorway. I stepped back quickly, because he had an axe in one hand and a hunting knife in the other.

"I'm gonna kill you!" he shouted. He had some friends outside the door who were trying to calm him. "I'm gonna kill you right now!"

I was at a loss for words. I was facing real death. I was going to die within minutes. I hoped it would not be too painful.

"What's your name?" I asked, as I struggled to keep calm, at least on the outside.

"Jim," he said, slightly lowering the axe, which was hovering over my head.

"Where are you from, Jim?" *Keep him talking,* I thought. *Maybe he will forget about killing me.*

"From Ohio . . . I'm gonna kill you!" he shouted, and the axe went up again. "I hurt . . . hurt!"

"Where do you hurt, Jim?" I asked.

"Allover . . . I hurt allover!" I noticed tears running down his face.

The interconnecting door to the clinic opened and the doctor came in.

"Don't come near me. I'll kill him!" Jim shouted.

"What's your name?" the doctor said gently.

"I told you it was Jim!"

"Jim's in a lot of pain," I said to the doctor.

"We can help you, Jim," said the doctor. He held out a little cup with a pill in it. "Take this pill."

"No more pills! They're killing me . . . no more pills."

"This one's all right. It won't kill you. It will take the pain away." He held out the little cup toward Jim.

Jim looked at the cup and finally he slowly laid down the knife and took the cup. The axe stayed steady over my head.

"Wait a minute," the doctor said, and left the room.

I felt deserted. The doctor's being there was a comfort . . . a ray of hope that maybe I would not die today.

The doctor came back with another cup in his hand.

"Here's some water to take the pill with." He offered the cup to Jim.

"Ahhh!" he screamed. "You're trying to kill me! The pill will kill me!"

"No Jim," said the doctor, "The pill will take away your pain."

"Listen to the doctor," I said. "He's trying to help you."

The doctor offered the cup again. "Here Jim . . . take your pill."

Slowly . . . ever so slowly . . . the axe descended to Jim's side and dropped. Before it hit the floor, one of his friends took it out the door. Jim took the cup of water. He looked me straight in the eye and said, "This won't kill me?"

"No," I replied.

He put the pill in his mouth and took a sip of water.

"Ahhhhhhhh . . . !!" He screamed in agony and dropped onto the floor.

"He's dead!" I vacillated between relief and feeling betrayed by the doctor.

"He'll be all right," the doctor replied calmly. "Welcome to Woodstock."

CHAPTER TWENTY-ONE

Culebra is a fine harbor, well protected with good holding for anchoring. This is a quiet place, except for the occasional airplane, which takes off over the harbor at masthead height. The village nearby is a sleepy little town with a few stores and one factory, which manufactures medical instruments. The biggest excitement in town is the ferry from nearby Fajardo, bringing the fruit and vegetable truck to the island on Tuesday evening. The whole town comes down to the dock to wait and gossip.

We had only planned to stay for a week, but the week became two weeks as we settled into the lazy life. Some of the boats we had left Beaufort with were here. There were sundown gatherings and our usual mornings of working on the teak, which was improving little by little. Exploring the island on our bikes was a special treat, especially when we would find a beautiful sandy beach.

I awoke one night hearing a huge crash. I found Judy passed out on the sole of the saloon. She seemed all right, but the next day I took her to the doctor. He said that the Vegas nerve had been stimulated by a glass of cold water she drank just before fainting.

On the way back to the boat, we stopped our dingy in the bay to talk to the crew of Sea Wolf. Judy told her what had happened and she replied, "That happened a couple of times to me. I just don't worry about it anymore."

"You'll worry about it," I told Judy. "What do you mean?"

"No more cold drinks in the night for you. My heart can't stand it!"

"Do you know where I can get a cup of coffee?" I asked the doctor who had just saved my life at Woodstock.

"Sure. We have some on my side. Come through here."

We drank coffee and I received my first lesson in dealing with people overdosing on drugs.

"How does one help someone like Jim?" I asked. "I really don't know much about the effects of drugs."

"The guy we just dealt with had been mistreating his body so badly that there was no reality left, just paranoia. Luckily, you did the right thing in talking to him. It was really touch and go."

"Yeah, I said a few prayers. But what is the best thing to do?"

"Find out what their name is and use it in every sentence. If you can touch them, hold their hand or arm, it helps. These things help focus them on whatever reality they have left."

"What will the Hog Farm do with him?" The Hog Farm is a commune from California, which was at the festival to help with drug overdoses.

"Oh, they'll continue touching him and talking with him until the poisons are out of his system. He'll be OK."

I was to use his advice many times before the festival even opened.

It was night and had just rained. The cold rain and warm ground made a fog develop, a thick fog. Out of the fog a young man stumbled into the clearing between the trailers.

"Help me! Help me," he cried in a weak voice.

"What can I do for you? Are you hurt?"

"They're after me. They're crawling allover me." I went over to him and took his arm.

"What's your name?"

"What?"

"What is your name? What can I call you?"

"Bart . . . my name is Bart." He seemed to calm down a little.

"Where are you headed, Bart?"

"Don't know . . . I was walking and they started following me."

He pulled his arm away and started hitting his legs. "They're all over me!"

Gently I took his arm again. Here was another case for the Hog Farm, but it was a long way from the trailers to their tents. I would have to cross the Meditation area where sculptures were arraigned in an artful way to promote meditation. It would be hard to do in the fog.

"Let's go for a walk."

"I can't. They'll follow me."

"It's OK," I said.

"You promise?"

"I'll not let them bother you. I promise. Let's go." The fog swirled around us as we climbed the hill where the Meditation Garden was located. The benches and art forms came out of the fog like monsters. I was becoming paranoid too. Bart slipped and fell.

"They've got me! They've got me! You promised!" He yelled at the top of his lungs.

Bart had completely disappeared. The fog was so thick I could only tell where he was by the sound of his voice. Moreover, that sound came from below my feet. *How did he get underground?*

"Ahhhhhh. Help me, preacher!"

Then I understood what had happened. In the meditation area, they had dug a conversation pit. Bart had obviously fallen into it and I was about one-step from falling in myself. I carefully climbed into the pit and found him, took his arm again and he settled down.

"Don't leave me again. You promised!"

"I'm sorry, Bart. Let us climb out of here and get going. I know of a great place where we can rest in safety."

I was having trouble getting my bearings in the dense fog, but for a second it lifted and I was able to see the path. Now we went downhill through the trees. Every time I stopped talking, Bart would begin to go off the deep end. After what seemed like an hour, reached the Hog Farm and they took Bart off my hands.

I went into the main tent of the Hog Farm group and loaded my pockets with farina—my main sustenance for almost a week. The Hog Farm people had plenty of farina and anyone could come and get it. I had farina with raisins, the best. Dry farina. Wet farina, both hot and cold. I was able to come across a bologna sandwich a few times. If ever there was a miracle of feeding, it took place at Woodstock.

The papers headlined the festival with two banners: ALL ON DRUGS AT WOODSTOCK or NO FOOD AT WOODSTOCK. The fact of the matter was that there were drugs at Woodstock, but not all were users. We figured that only twenty percent were using pills, and less than one percent were on heroin, but had no estimate of the numbers using marijuana. Of course, twenty percent of five hundred thousand is one hundred thousand, and that is a lot.

The "no food" was not true either. The several concessions at the festival ran out of food before the festival began and were not able to restock due to the huge traffic jams. However, many people there were camping and they did have food. They shared what they had with their neighbors so that no one went hungry.

There were many times when someone would come up to me, give me a hard roll with cheese and pour me a paper cup of wine. However, they were not doing this for just me; it was for everyone they saw until they ran out.

As we approached the weekend, my business picked up and I could hardly wait until my volunteers to arrive and spell me. There was a multitude of pastoral concerns: abortion, boy friends, girl friends, young people thrown out of their homes because of long hair, youth who wanted to go home but were afraid even to call their parents, and those who wanted encouragement about life, college and God.

Friday came and the festival officially began. Because it had been forced to move to this location at the last minute, there had not been enough time to build the chain link fence and there was no way short of a riot to remove those who had arrived early. Therefore, they did not try to collect tickets. The show went on, and it rained.

It rained off and on throughout the whole weekend. I remember spending a lot of time after the first night's show helping people who were lost. Those we were not able to get to their campsites, we housed in my trailer and at the Hog Farm. Eventually most found their way to their camp.

It was after one on Saturday morning that I happened to walk through the security trailer, which I usually did before going to bed. It was quiet except for an older woman who was sitting there. At first, I did not pay any attention to her, but then I heard sobs.

"Is someone helping you?" I asked her.

"No." Now the sobbing increased to near hysterics.

"What's the problem?"

"I have forty kids out there."

"Out where?"

"Out in the pasture with cows and other wild animals. I am so afraid for them." More sobbing. "I just don't know what to do."

"Start at the beginning. How did you get here?"

"I'm a social worker from Harlem. We thought it would be great to bring some of the kids out here in the country to hear the music. The bus dropped us off about three miles from the festival, and we got lost. Just after sunset I took the children into a pasture (more sobs) where I told them to stay until I got some help."

"Then you came here?"

"Yes, but I got lost in the dark (breaks down in tears). I don't . . . I don't know if I can find them now. They've never been in the country.

They are afraid. I am so worried. I came in here and the man said for me to sit down. I've been sitting here for an hour."

I went into the radio room and gathered some help from our peace corps (police) on motor scooters. They set out to find the kids with the social worker on the back of a scooter.

I took off for the Hog Farm to tell them they would be having company and to make some of their famous hot farina with raisins for the kids.

I started back home and was walking through the "Drug Store" (an area of the grounds dedicated to the selling of drugs). You could buy drugs here twenty-four hours a day and get your picture taken at the same time by the DEA. I was very tired as it was almost three in the morning. I walked over to a large tree and settled down to sleep.

What seemed like seconds later (it must have been an hour later), the bells and cymbals of a group of Hare Krishnas who wanted to discuss religion awakened me. We talked for a while and I told them I had to get some sleep and excused myself.

I stumbled down toward my trailer and, as I was passing through some parked trucks and cars, a thought came to me. If I returned to the office people could find me and wake me up again. I crawled under a phone company truck and went to sleep.

I awoke as someone grabbed my ankles and pulled me from under the truck.

"God dammit Father, that's no place to sleep. Jesus, you ought to know better!" The speaker was a large man with a full beard and leather jacket. I looked around and saw about a dozen men clad the same way.

"We've been lookin' allover for you. Jesus-f—kin'-Christ. What are you doin' sleepin' under that truck? You can get your f—kin' ass killed that way."

Trying to get my brains working I asked what they wanted with me.

"We're Hell's Angels and one of our women has got a problem. We need your help."

"All right," I said. What else was one going to say when faced with a gang of Hells Angels? "I'll be glad to talk with her. Where is she?"

"Come here, Mary Lou," the leader called. A thin young girl of maybe twenty years came out of the back of the group. She was plain looking and she wore a Hells Angel's Tee shirt and jeans. She carried a knap sack over one shoulder and it was clear she had been doing some crying.

"Will you all leave us alone for awhile so we can talk privately?" I asked the group.

The leader looked at me and then at the group as if asking if there were any objections. Then he got up and walked away and the rest followed him.

"How can I help you?" I asked.

"Well, my husband is in prison. He has been for a couple of years now." She was quiet for awhile.

"And . . . ?"

"Well, you see . . . it's this way. I'm pregnant and I don't know what to do."

"How long will your husband be locked up?" I asked.

"For ten more years, I guess. He might get a parole in five more. I'm not sure."

"What are you thinking about doing?"

"I don't know . . . maybe get an abortion. What do you think?"

"There must be other options."

"Well . . . I could keep the baby, but if I tell Norm I'm pregnant he'll kill me."

"Anything else?" I prompted.

"I could get divorced," she said in a quiet voice. "Then the father of the baby and I could get married."

"What do you think about that last option?"

She thought a minute then in a very low voice said, "I think that's what I really want to do. I never did love Norm. I was afraid of him all the time. Bud, the baby's father, he's so sweet and kind to me."

"That sounds like a good decision to me."

After a minute of silence she got up, said thanks and gave me a kiss on the cheek. Then she left.

I looked around and saw that dawn was beginning to fill the sky. Birds began to sing and the eastern horizon felt the warming of the first red glow of the sun. I got up off the ground and stretched my aching bones.

I wonder what happened with the kids, I thought as I walked to the security trailer.

"What's happening with those children from Harlem?" I asked the man in communications.

"They're on their way. Should be here in fifteen minutes. It looks like its going to rain. Too bad."

I went over to the Hog Farm to see if everything was ready. They were making rain ponchos. They had taken heavy plastic sheeting and cut it into strips with holes that would fit over the children's heads.

"It might not do much, but at least it will keep them a little warmer and keep the rain off," said a woman from the commune.

It started to rain . . . heavily.

I grabbed a stack of "ponchos" and took off, meanwhile mumbling about whose stupid idea it was to bring these kids out here. A few others also ran down the road loaded down with ponchos. We met the kids trudging up the muddy road, looking like a lot of drowned cats. In the lead of the procession was the social worker.

We quickly passed around the ponchos. The youngsters were exhausted and crying. A few of them were beginning to see this experience as a wild adventure.

"Wow," said a twelve-year-old Afro-American girl. "Did you hear those tigers growling last night? I was afraid we'd all be eaten by them!"

"There weren't no tigers there," said a young boy walking next to her.

"Them was deers. I could see their horns. These deers had two horns. I could see them."

"Oh yeah?" said the girl, "Deers don't growl!"

"Oh you don't know nothing. The deers weren't growling. They were making a sound like: 'moo'."

Soon we got the band of weary travelers to the Hog Farm where the girls went into one tent and the boys into another. The commune dried them off and bedded them down, and then members of the commune went out and stood in the rain because there was not enough room for both the kids and the adults in the tents.

Soon a steaming kettle of farina with raisins was sent in to the kids. I went over to where they were cooking the stuff and begged a cupful for myself.

It tasted wonderful.

CHAPTER TWENTY-TWO

"I think I goofed." Butterfly hit a large wave and shuddered to a stop.

"This is miserable," she agreed as the boat picked up some speed, only to hit another wave and shudder. "It looks like we made a bad choice."

We were heading back to Water Island and Honeymoon Bay from Culebra. For days the wind had been blowing twenty to twenty-five knots out of the east and south-east. This morning was beautiful when I got up at six. The weather report seemed great. Only I had forgotten that the waves would still be coming in after the weeklong blow. That was my "goof," and now we were paying for it. After we cleared the channel through the reefs, the choppy six to eight foot waves built up on our course line. We had just the main up and were under engine. We had to go about a mile on a course that was directly into the waves and they were beating us to death.

All of a sudden, the engine began to increase its rpm's dramatically. Then it quit.

In the silence, my stomach turned over. I knew the symptoms. The fuel tank had clogged its exit port again. On our port side we had reefs about hundred yards away, and to starboard there were shallows that would cause the seas to be even worse.

I let the boat fall off to starboard and Judy got up the jib. When we were under control, I headed below to clear the fuel line.

This can be an interesting project when one is at dock or in a quiet anchorage, but at sea, in a chop of large waves, it is absolutely miserable. To top it off the engine was hot, having run for an hour.

I got the fuel line on the intake of the fuel filter disconnected and with all my breath (while burning my chin on the engine) blew through the line. It took four of these huffs and puffs to clear the line. *I have to get this fixed someday,* I thought, as I prepared to bleed the fuel line. In the process, I burned my forehead on the water reserve tank.

"Oh shit!" I cried.

"What's the matter now?" asked Judy in her panic voice.

"Nothing, I just burned myself."

"Oh, that's good," she said, much relieved, "I thought something bad had happened to the engine."

With Judy turning over the engine, I was able to clear the last of the air from the injectors and the engine roared to life again.

"Shut it down," I called up to Judy after a few minutes. "We'll save it for an emergency."

I went on deck and we tacked to the north, which was as close to the wind as I could get and make some headway. The wind was too light. It took us five minutes getting up to five knots or so and then a large wave dropped our speed to one. To get going anew we fell off downwind a little and started the process over again. A little more wind would have helped.

There were reefs to the northeast of us. *Would we clear them?* We hardened up the sails when we could, and barely inched past them. I was ready to jump for the starter switch, but held off. I think I was afraid the engine would not work and we would be in real trouble. It was better not to know.

For hours we sailed to the north and north-east, until we were in the middle of the Virgin Passage. We kept taking bearings on Sail Rock, which lies on the eastern edge of the passage, but we seemed to be creeping toward it. Then we spotted a tanker coming in from the Atlantic, right at us.

"I'll have to start the engine and tack," I said.

"Do we have to start the engine?" asked Judy nervously.

"Yeah, we can't tack in this chop. We'll go in irons."

I took a deep breath, said a prayer, and then turned the key. The engine roared to life and we motored through the tack.

We made it just in time. I looked up and the tanker was less than a hundred yards off our port. We had cut that a little close.

"Shall I turn the engine off?"

"No," I said, "let's see if we can motor-sail a bit." Under engine we could make about three knots to the south-east.

"It's getting late," said Judy. What she was really saying was that in a few hours it would be dark, which would make it difficult to get into the anchorage.

"Don't worry," I said. "I can get us in." I felt I could as it was straight forward, but I did not like the prospect.

Slowly, very slowly we tacked and motor-sailed until we got into the lee of St. Thomas, where we took down the jib and headed straight for

Water Island. There are a couple of islands there with a reef lying to the north of them. I wanted to get past them before dark, but it was already six and the sun was setting. Worse than that, the tide was going out and we had a depth of seven and a half feet.

I put more throttle to the engine. Judy looked at me with fear in her eyes.

"That was me," I said.

"I thought the engine was stopping again. Are we going to make it in before dark?"

"No problem," I replied, but I was wondering if we could get past the reef in time.

Suddenly, it was night as is usual in the tropics, which have very little twilight. I watched the depth sounder.

"50 . . . 40 . . . 27 . . . 23 . . . 28 . . . 14" it read.

"O lord," I prayed, "let us get over this reef."

"14 . . . 13 . . . 8(!) . . . 12 . . . 14 . . . 18 . . . 19 . . . 20 . . . 21 . . . 23"

"Thank you Lord!" I exclaimed.

"What?" Judy looked at me, obviously in her frightened stage.

"Nothing."

I could make out the lights near Honeymoon and some of the lights of the boats in the harbor. Although getting in the harbor was easy, we had to anchor three times to get it to hold. It was seven, and we were very tired. It had taken us over ten hours to cover twenty-two miles!

I had goofed.

I grabbed a couple of hours sleep, this time in the back seat of my car, and then went to check on what was happening with the kids from Harlem who had been stranded at the rock festival. They had been taken by bus back to New York City.

"Chaplain . . . Chaplain . . . Control," squawked my radio.

"Go ahead, Control."

"We got a rabbi on the phone for you." Security was looking for me.

I glanced at my watch. It was ten-thirty. We had scheduled a Jewish service at 11 a.m. I rushed to the phone.

"Hello, Rabbi."

"Oh Chaplain, how is it out there?"

"Just fine. When are you expecting to get here?"

"I have bad news. We can't get there. The road is completely blocked. I spent an hour trying, but only got about a mile. Not to worry. We have our hands full here."

"Is that so?" I was feeling disappointed that we would have no Jewish service.

"You won't believe this. I don't believe it myself. Monticello is filled with kids who can't get to the festival and they can't get a bus because there's not enough room. The Catholic Church is letting them sleep in the school and parish hall, but they don't have the funds to feed them."

"Sounds like a mess."

"It is. It is. But here is the best part," he chuckled. "In our temple ovens we are baking ham! Yes, ham. Can you believe! We couldn't find any other meat, so our women bake ham and apple pie and take it over to the Catholics so the kids can eat. Will you believe? I never thought Jews and Catholics could get together over anything. Now here we are baking ham for people at the Catholic church!"

"Keep up the good work. So long."

"So long, and shalom!"

"Chaplain Ames, Control," went the radio.

"Go again."

"This is Don. We need you down by the stage. Someone is trying to jump off the scaffolding."

I ran down to the stage, which had about five stories of scaffolding packed with speakers. Up on the top was a young man hanging by a hand and a foot to a scaffold. I was trying to make up my mind whether to try to go up to where he was when I saw someone was already up there talking to him. I waited down below in case he fell or jumped. After a few minutes, they talked the man back in and brought him down. I helped escort him to the Hog Farm as he was freaking out something awful.

I went into security to tell Don what had happened.

"By the way, Ames," he said, "we have another problem."

"What's that?"

"For some reason the Legal Aid people and the Social Workers did not show up this morning and we have the feeling they're not coming back. The colleges that supported them did not like the publicity we were getting. Could you take over their trailer and see what you can do there?"

"Sure, I'll give it a try."

There had been a trailer assigned to some student lawyers with a professor in charge to handle any legal problems those attending the festival might encounter. Social service had the same setup. Evidently, both groups had withdrawn for the same reason.

As I could not do any legal work, I attempted to try to handle the social work calls that came in. The phone would ring about every ten minutes with parents looking for their children. I made a list and delivered copies to the main stage, the Grateful Dead auxiliary stage, and the Hog Farm, in the hope that some of these people could be found and brought back into their families.

That evening one or two came drifting in, saying they had heard that someone was looking for them. Sometimes I had to talk long and hard to get them to contact their parents, but most of them ended up calling and a few decided to go home after the festival.

Some parents were not interested, even if their son or daughter had been injured.

"Hello, Mr. Doe, this is Chaplain Ames and I'm calling you from the Woodstock Festival."

"Yeah? What do you want?"

"Your daughter Mary is here and she has broken her arm. We have given her medical attention and she's doing fine. Would you like to talk to her?"

"Hell no! She's nothing but a slut and I don't care if we ever see her again."

"Please, Mr. Doe, it would be good for you and her to talk."

"The only message I have for her is 'go to hell!'"

Towards late afternoon, I began to wonder if the Catholic priest was going to show for the Mass I had planned for six in the Meditation Center. I decided to call him.

"Oh, I don't think I can get there. The roads are all jammed."

"Don't worry," I said. "Can you get to the Monticello Airport?"

"I think I can get there."

"Go there at five and I'll have a helicopter pick you up."

"That's great! See you in awhile."

I went over and asked Don to send a small helicopter to pick up the priest. We had developed what was called the Woodstock Air Force. There were several helicopters to bring in food, musical groups, medical supplies and whatever. The cow pasture across the street from the trailer area had become our airport and the security trailer was the control tower.

At five-fifteen, I went over to the "airport" and met the priest. He was a gray-haired man in his sixties and carried a suitcase. I took him to my trailer so he could freshen up before mass.

"I'm sorry I can't have a mass tonight," he said.

"Why not?"

"I didn't bring my mass things."

"What's in the suit case? I thought your equipment was in there."

"No. I heard there was no food here so I picked things out of my cupboard to bring." He opened his suitcase and there neatly stacked, were cans of string beans, carrots, pork and beans, etc. My heart went out to this man who was trying to help.

"Well, it doesn't matter. I can find a glass and a plate. There is enough bread and wine also. It won't take me a minute to gather it."

"Oh no. I couldn't! Not without my communion equipment and vestments. I had to make a decision: the vestments or food. I brought the food."

Although I tried to see things his way, I found it very hard. It would not have bothered me to have communion out of a paper cup and plate. However, I was not an elderly, conservative Catholic priest. I took him to the conversation circle in the Meditation area where there were about thirty Catholics waiting for the mass. We sat down and I asked the priest to give us at least his sermon and a prayer. As he talked, more and more people gathered around until there must have been at least a hundred. After the sermon, they began to question him about the meaning of what he had said.

After the service, I got the priest away by helicopter. By then the evening performances were well under way and I was very tired.

I had arranged to go home on Sunday morning since I was to conduct the eight o'clock service at the church in Middletown. Leaving the festival grounds was like a James Bond spy thriller. I was to leave with members of the "Peace Corps," which were really New York City Police moonlighting against department orders. The hiring of off duty NYC police had interesting ramifications. They were all retrained in "peaceful" peacekeeping. They were not allowed weapons and all carried plastic handcuffs. Their uniform was a red and white T-shirt which said "Peace Corps" and blue jeans. In order to preserve their anonymity, they were paid in cash, and came and went in the dead of night by special bus routes.

I was to leave on such a bus. I was taken by motorcycle to the edge of the grounds about one thirty Sunday morning. I climbed on the bus and, after a ride of about an hour, was dropped off at a crossroad about twenty miles from my house. Judy was waiting there to meet me. She drove me home and I jumped into a hot bath, the first I had been able to have for a week. Then to bed. A real bed. It was three-thirty in the morning before I got to bed looking for at least four hours uninterrupted sleep before church.

It was not to be. At five-thirty Judy got a call from the festival. There had been a death; a young man had overdosed on heroin. They had flown him to the Middletown hospital, but he had died en route.

I got up and somehow drove to the hospital. The festival people had called the family and they were on the way. I spent some time with a friend who had been with the young man and then an hour later his parents came. I just had enough time to get to the church after counseling with them.

I am not sure how I made it through the service.

It was the first one I had been allowed to have by myself in two years. Fr. Carl was on vacation and he still had not announced my resignation, which would be in effect in two weeks. As I greeted the people at the door, they assured me they knew all about the bad things happening at Woodstock. I was too tired to tell them what I felt about it. Several did say they thought it great that I was ministering there.

When I got home, Judy said that Woodstock had called and a helicopter would land in our yard in half an hour to pick me up.

I groaned. I was tired and burnt out. I also knew that the powers of the church would explode if a helicopter landed in our yard. I called the festival.

"Hello, Don?"

"Yes."

"It's Ames. No helicopter on the lawn. I mean it."

"But we need you in a hurry."

"What's the problem?"

"We have some trouble at the airport."

"I'll drive to the airport then. I'll be there in an hour."

"Make it faster if you can."

I gobbled down the eggs and bacon Judy had fixed, grabbed the toast and coffee, and went to the car. She drove me to the airport while I ate.

"What's happening out there?" She had read the newspapers and had been concerned for me.

"It's not as bad as the newspapers say, Hon."

"But what's going on?"

"Sweetheart, I am so tired I can't talk about it now. I'll tell you about it when it's over." I kissed her goodbye and made my way to the tiny airport.

On one side of the little building was a giant "Huey" helicopter. I went inside the office.

"Chaplain. Glad you made it", said a man I had never met before.

"What's going on?"

"We are having a problem with the Jefferson Airplane, the rock group. They want to jump out of the helicopter. The pilot won't take off unless someone is there to control them. Security says you are the man. They go on stage in an hour, so we have to hurry," He grabbed my arm and walked toward the helicopter. Inside were what I took to be the members of the Jefferson Airplane and the pilot. They looked to me to be stoned.

"You got to keep them quiet," said the pilot.

I turned to the group. They seemed quiet now. "Look," I told them, "we got to get to the festival so you can play. Let's cool it and go."

I turned to the pilot. "Shut the door and let's go."

He looked at me strangely. "There is no door. Just that webbing. That's the problem. They want to jump out."

"Let's get going anyway."

The helicopter took off and shortly after the drummer of the group went over to the doorway and leaned over the webbing.

"Ayyyeeee" he yelled over the sounds of the engine. "I can fly!"

"No you can't," I said. "Now, sit down."

"I can flyyyyy!" he cried as he leaned further out.

The other members of the group sat there with silly grins on their faces.

"I can flyyyy!" he yelled again. I went over and tried to pull him away from the doorway. He just pulled harder and kept yelling that it was cool and he could fly. He pulled me so hard I thought I was going to go flying with him. I became angry.

"Well," I said, "jump if you want to. I don't give a damn. Just try to fly and see what happens, but for God's sake don't fall on any of your fans down there!" I let go of him and sat down, disgusted. He stopped yelling, looked down, and with shaky knees came and sat down.

After the Jefferson Airplane was settled in the dressing area, I picked up my radio and went to the stage area to see what was happening. It was an awesome sight to see thousands upon thousands of people sitting together on a hillside.

I noticed that off in the distance there was a dark green storm cloud. *That's all we need here, a tornado or something,* I thought. I decided to stand on the hill behind the crowd just in case something happened.

Soon the cloud darkened the whole area, the wind blew and it began to rain. Heavy rain. I did not have an umbrella or even a rain coat, so I just stood there getting soaking wet. I felt someone put a raincoat over my shoulders. By the time I turned around, he had crawled into a nearby tent. Tears began to run down my face and mix with the raindrops. After the rain stopped, I found the young man who had given me the coat.

"Thanks for the coat," I said. "Why did you do it?"

"Oh, I don't know. I guess because I had a coat and you didn't."

I walked slowly to my now enlarged trailer, thinking about what the man had said. *Wouldn't it be wonderful if we all felt that way? I have something you don't. So you take what I have.*

When I arrived at my trailer it was packed with almost forty who were trying to get out of the rain. The phone was ringing as I entered.

"Hello," I said.

"This is Pastor Jones of the Baptist church. Is this Chaplain Ames?" Pastor Jones' group of young people was going to put on a folk-rock Protestant service.

"Sure is. Are you on your way?"

"No, there is too much traffic and we don't think we can get there."

"Don't worry. I'll send a helicopter for you."

"Oh, I don't think that will do."

"Why not?" I already knew what he was going to say.

"Well the parents . . . you know."

"They don't want you to come?"

"Yes, I guess that's it."

"All right." I slammed the receiver down. The tears that had started when the man had given me his coat now burst forth in a mighty stream.

"Hey, Padre," said one of the young people in the trailer. He was in his early twenties, had long blond hair, and wore blue jeans and a Pendleton plaid shirt. Hippy beads adorned his neck. "What's wrong?"

"Everything's wrong! The Jewish service was canceled because of the traffic, the Catholic priest didn't bring his stuff so we couldn't have a mass, and now the Baptists can't come because the parents are afraid. Here I am trying to do the work of ten people and I can't do it. I just can't do it."

"Be cool Father," said another person. "Don't worry. We'll help you out. We can be your runners. Heck, I don't care to see any of these groups until Blood Sweat and Tears comes on. We'll all help." He turned to the others. "Right?"

Most of them nodded agreement.

"And Father, don't worry about the services," a young woman said. "We've had our wine and we've had our bread. Hey, this whole thing is sacramental."

CHAPTER TWENTY-THREE

It took a week to repair the damage from our twenty-mile trip from Culebra to Honeymoon Bay. The slides in the reefing line, which I had installed on the main before leaving Annapolis in order to make reefing easier, had come off their attachments. It was not a hard job to lash the slides on with marlin, but it took some time.

The main halyard winch and halyard stop had pulled out of the mast. I suppose the stop went first, putting pressure on the winch. Having a wooden mast has its drawbacks. I took a hammer and straightened the stop, drilled out the holes for the stop and winch, epoxied some dowels into the holes and reattached the stop and winch.

These small jobs took a week, and meanwhile I was eager to leave. One reaches a point when it is time to go, and I had reached that point some months before. I did not like St. Thomas, but my friends had been here so we had stayed. Now it was time to go.

Early the next morning, we hoisted our dingy onto the davits and hauled up the anchor. We had a lovely fast sail to Jost Van Dyke Island, which is part of the British Virgin Islands. The anchorage at Jost Van Dyke was nearly empty when we arrived just before noon. It took several attempts at anchoring before we felt the anchor was truly secure. The test we use to determine this is running the engine in reverse at fifteen hundred rpm until the prop wash reaches the bow. If the anchor does not drag, then it's not likely to drag in a blow.

We went ashore to clear customs and see some of the island. The whole beachfront is given over to restaurants, the most famous of which is "Foxie's." We headed there for lunch and found something a little different from what we were expecting.

Foxie's is a restaurant/bar with a dirt floor, a thatched palm roof, and a few long picnic tables. One area has a dance floor. Foxy himself sits around playing guitar and singing songs. We ordered hamburgers and drinks and looked around. It was obvious we had not come at the busy time of day. There were a few people sitting around, drinking beer and eating sandwiches, but overall it was rather quiet.

There were a couple of men sitting with their beers and a woman sat down to join them.

"Hi there," she said.

"Hi, you want a beer?"

"Sure," she said. "You guys chartering?"

"No, we're just cruising around."

She looked around the place disdainfully and asked, "Is this all there is?"

"What do you mean?"

"I mean, is this all there is to do? Doesn't it get any more exciting and fun than this?"

"Ah . . . no," said one of the men, leaning back in his chair. "This is about it." He took another swig of beer and added, "But it sure beats working!"

From three-thirty on, the charter boats piled into the anchorage while I watched their anchoring techniques. They would come roaring in, drop the anchor, get into the dingy and head for shore. Very few of them set their anchors. One came in across the wind and dropped his anchor directly ahead of us. He was amazed to find his boat coming down on ours when it swung to the wind.

Anchoring is somewhat like sex. You really do not want other people watching you while you are doing it. However, how you anchor tells other boaters what kind of sailor you are.

One kind of anchorer is the "screamer." He stands at the wheel, screams, and yells at his crew on the bow. He does this because he does not have the vaguest notion of how to anchor.

There is also the reverse screamer, who stands at the bow and yells at his crew at the wheel.

Next, there is the "do-it-yourselfer." He does not let his crew do anything because he does not trust her, him, or them. He must have a history of running track, because he sprints up to the bow . . . then back to the wheel . . . up to the bow . . . back to the wheel.

Then there is the Frenchman. He plows through the anchorage at five knots and drops his anchor. When the boat comes to the end of the anchor line it swings madly around, just missing the boat behind it. Then the captain and crew hop into the dingy and are away. You will notice I said his boat just misses the boat behind him. This is because there is always a boat just behind a Frenchman. If there is only one boat in a harbor, a Frenchman will anchor just in front of it, allowing about six inches of swinging room between the two boats. I have even had a French boat who was anchored next to me pick up his anchor and re-anchor right in front of me. It does no good to yell, because they simply shrug their shoulders.

One sailing couple we know was so impressed by the French way of anchoring they even bought a French anchor.

"They anchor so quickly," he said. "I just had to have one of those anchors."

"Have you noticed how many French boats drag their anchors all through the anchorage?" I asked.

He blushed and said, "Well, yes, that's why we still use our old anchor."

There is nothing wrong with French anchors. The problem lies in the French method of anchoring.

Friday Nona Rosa arrived. It was always exciting to see them come into an anchorage-first, because we enjoyed their company so much, and second, because there was the perennial sword fight raging between the younger boys. Their wooden swords, dripping with painted blood, clashed up and down the deck as the pirates fought for control of the vessel and the treasure.

Saturday we sailed for Norman Island with Nona Rosa. Norman Island is a nice little island where pirate treasure was found a few years before. There are caves there near Treasure Point where you can snorkel. Most all the charters anchor in a bay named The Bight, but we elected to try to get away from the charterers by anchoring in Benures Bay. This is a deep bay and one has to anchor in fifty feet of water; therefore, it is not one of the recommended charter anchorages. We dropped anchor in forty-eight feet of water so clear we could see the anchor on the bottom and watch it dig in. We put out two hundred-fifty feet of chain and settled in for the night.

Toward evening, a charter boat came into the bay and dropped his anchor with what looked like a short anchor line. He just let it go, tying off the end, and went swimming. *It must be nice* to *have such faith in your anchor,* I thought. I did not think his anchoring would hold up in a blow, and he might be dragged across the bay and onto the rocks.

The night was calm with hardly a breeze blowing. We felt so little wave action it was as if we were at dockside. I got up at dawn, made some coffee and went up on deck. Looking around the bay, I noticed that the charter boat had dragged her anchor clear to the other side of the bay. *Now how could that happen without wind or waves?* I thought.

Later that morning Jim from Nona Rosa came over. He had talked with the man on the charter boat and reported on their conversation.

"Hi there," said Jim, as he approached the boat. "I see you've dragged anchor."

"It looks that way." The charterer looked at his anchor line, removed his baseball cap and scratched his head.

"It's hard to drag on a calm night. How much line did you have out?"

"Oh, I put it all out," was the reply. "There must have been at least 100 feet." In this bay, anything less than two hundred and fifty feet could cause dragging.

There is a story going around about a conversation overheard on the VHF radio.

"Just Charters, Just Charters, this is Maribel."

"Go ahead Maribel, this is Just Charters."

"Could you bring us another anchor?"

"Why do you need another anchor? There were two of them on the boat when you left."

"Well we've anchored twice already, and we will want to anchor tonight."

I guess that cutting one's anchor line is easier than hauling it up, but . . .

The remainder of that Sunday afternoon at Woodstock went quickly. My team of about thirty helpers worked long and hard taking messages around and finding people whose families were looking for them.

In the middle of the afternoon, I needed a break and took a walk. My meandering brought me to the rock band, The Grateful Dead area. They had their own stage and managed the shows there. Some of the men invited me into their bus and we sat and talked for about an hour. The discussion centered on religion and philosophy. As I left, I had the feeling something was not right about the situation. It was not until I turned around to say goodbye that I noticed none of the women were wearing tops. They had painted their breasts with swirls and flowers. *Why had I not noticed that?* I thought. *I guess I really am tired!*

"Chaplain?" again the radio.

"Go ahead."

"We have a problem down behind the stage. It looks serious. Could you see what you can do?"

When I arrived on the dirt road that passed behind the stage, I saw there was a confrontation between two state police troopers and the Hell's Angels. The police officers had their hands on their gun holsters and the motorcycle gang looked ready to fight.

I walked in between them and asked, "What's the problem?"

"Those motherfucker pigs won't let us ride past 'em!" said the leader of the gang, shaking his fist at the police.

"They're not going anywhere," said the police officer, his face red with anger.

"Cool it," I said to both parties, "We're here for peace and love, not arguments."

"Yeah," said the motorcycle gang leader, clenching his fists. "If he'd let us pass there would be no trouble."

"Well, it's too dangerous for you to drive on this road. They're too many people crowded on it."

About this time, I heard the music of Blood Sweat and Tears begin on the stage. This was the only group I was interested in hearing and I was stuck trying to solve this problem. I was angry.

"Cool it, dammit!" Turning to the Hell's Angels I asked, "What's so damned important that you all have to leave now anyway?"

"Now Padre, if you weren't our friend I would have to take you out for talking to me like that."

"We'll see who clobbers who. You all are making me miss the only group I wanted to hear."

"Oh yeah," said the leader somewhat repentantly. "We're sorry. All we want to do is find some cigarettes. We haven't had a smoke in almost a day."

"Is that your problem?" asked the officer.

"We was just trying to go down the road and buy some fags. Maybe some beer too."

"Wait a minute." The officer went to the trunk of the squad car, opened it, and reached in. It was a tense moment for all. Everyone knew that police kept tear gas and other weapons in the trunk. When he straightened, he had a carton of cigarettes in his hand.

"I know how it is. Here." He handed the cigarettes to the gang leader and added, "Peace." Getting two more cartons out of the trunk he got into the car and drove slowly down the road, tossing packs of cigarettes to anyone who wanted one.

The Hell's Angels sat on their bikes with dazed expressions. They were too shocked to smoke. The leader got off his bike and walked over to me.

"This is the second time you've helped us. We really owe you," he said as he reached out and gave me a bear hug that just about broke my ribs.

Afterward I began thinking about what I had just seen. On several occasions the New York City Police (the festival's Peace Corps), the same ones who had been hitting these young people over the head during a riot a week earlier, were passing out cigarettes and candy bars. Moreover, these same youngsters, who had been rioting and rebelling against anything that was "establishment," were passing cold beer and cokes to the officers.

When I returned from Honduras, I had completely lost touch with what was happening in the U.S. The college students were having strikes, rioting, and picketing political conventions while the police reacted with more force than was needed. I did not understand nor like much of the music. I was worried about the future of the youth of our country.

Woodstock brought me closer to the real youth of the day. Most of them had high respect for what was right and no tolerance for the grey areas. I saw Woodstock as a turning point for young adults. They had battled the system up to this point, but they were not able to change it. I felt that something was going to happen. A change was in the air, and I had great hope for the country now. "Peace and love" was to become the new by-word for the 70's.

By Sunday evening, my gang of workers had dwindled some, but twenty of the "temporary" helpers were still working. Some time in the afternoon a large bag of farina mixed with almonds showed up in my office. What a treat!

Woodstock had kept the show on long past its closing time. The hill was dotted with flames from campfires where hot dogs roasted, and it looked like the lights of a city. I had been told that with four to five hundred thousand people at the festival, we were one of the largest cities in the U.S., and we had the fewest crimes. There was no rain and the stars were very bright. By midnight, things began to wind down. We had made close to three hundred contacts between parents and their children during the last fourteen hours and we all felt pretty good as we curled up to sleep in the trailer.

We awoke at dawn and my helpers asked if I would need them anymore. I thanked them for their help and most of them started their long journey home. I wished I had taken their names so I could have written each a letter thanking them for their unselfish help.

A few stayed with me, helping clean up the trailer. As we were working, a woman came in.

"I found this purse and I don't know what to do with it," she told me.

"That's fine," I said. "Leave it here."

I looked in the purse, hoping to find some identification. I found, in addition to identification, forty-eight dollars in cash and a couple of hundred in traveler's checks. I did not know what to do with it, so I decided to keep it in the office until someone came to claim it.

A little later, another person arrived with a lost wallet he had found. It had close to two hundred dollars cash in it. Soon word got around that we were now the "lost and found" department and all morning a steady stream of purses and wallets were brought in. Just for the heck of it I kept a running total of the cash we received. By the afternoon, we had almost five thousand dollars. Only five wallets brought in had been cleaned out. There were also some drugs found: uppers, downers, and marijuana mostly. These we burned in a garbage can.

The honesty of those attending the festival was astounding. My helpers said the value of the drugs we destroyed was higher than the cash we had found. Very few people came looking for their lost items. We packaged and mailed the purses, wallets, and their contents (with the exception of the drugs) back to their owners.

With a heavy weariness, I collected my stuff, went to my car and somehow drove home. It was evening when I arrived and Judy had dinner ready.

"What happened out there?" she asked. I knew she was curious because of all the news from the newspapers and radio broadcasts. But I was too tired.

"Oh, nothing much. It wasn't as bad as what the newspapers said."

"What about all the drugs?"

"Yes, there were some drugs, but not as much as what the papers said." I was feeling somewhat repetitive, defensive and for some reason irritated.

"I'm tired. I think I'll go to bed." Judy helped me get to bed and I was asleep immediately.

I slowly became aware that I was awake. Judy was in bed and I could see by the windows that it was still night. My body told me I was hungry. I started to get up. My movements woke Judy.

"Are you OK?" she asked, feeling my brow for a temperature. "Do you feel all right?"

"I'm fine. I'm just hungry," I said still groggy from sleep.

"I was worried about you."

"Why?"

"You've slept almost 24 hours!"

After eating, I tried to tell her about the festival and what had happened, but every time I tried, I would get tears in my eyes. I did not know it at the time, but I was suffering from exhaustion and post-traumatic shock.

The following few days were spent looking for a job since we were going to have to move somewhere in another week. With the help of a friend I found and was accepted into a Clinical Pastoral Education Program (a program that helps a pastor develop his counseling skills) at Lutheran Medical Center in Brooklyn, New York. I was to be a resident in the program and would make six thousand dollars for the year. It was something I had thought about for some time and felt it would give me a chance to evaluate myself and decide on the direction I wanted to go in my ministry.

I hired a couple of men and we loaded the U-Haul and made a trip to Brooklyn. When I returned that evening, I found Don Garvey waiting for me. I hoped he had brought the check for the eight hundred and seventy-five dollars that Woodstock owed me.

"I submitted the bill," he said, "but the festival went bankrupt. When the film and recordings are released they'll have some money, so check back in a few months."

I was very disappointed in this because I needed the money to pay for the move. We sat on the steps in silence thinking about our experiences at Woodstock.

"They're plowing it under," he said breaking the silence.

"What?"

"They're plowing the festival grounds. It looked as if a war had taken place there, so they're plowing it under."

I started laughing.

"What's so funny?"

"They are plowing everything under?"

"That's what I said."

"I can visualize an archeologist six centuries from now making a dig there. He picks up a wine bottle, then a coke bottle, a rusty thermos and maybe an old frying pan, a tent stake and maybe even a broken guitar with a rusty string on it."

He says, "It looks to be that we have discovered a new civilization. A city that was never listed on the ancient maps. This civilization," he will tell his students, "seems to have been based on drinking, music, and strange cultural ceremonies."

I doubled over laughing at my own vision. Don had begun to laugh also.

"And you know what?" Don asked, grinning.

"No. What?"

"He will be right!"

CHAPTER TWENTY-FOUR

After spending some time at Norman Island, we sailed over to the island of Tortola and Road Town. I had been having some problems with gout off and on since we left the U.S. Virgins and my medication was not helping much.

At Road Town, I went to shore and found a doctor who gave me a prescription. I sat in the town square enjoying the sun while Judy went to the drug store to get it filled. As I sat there, an old man in his seventies came up to two younger women.

"Where are you goin'?" he asked them.

"We've been shoppen'," one of the women replied.

"We're goin' home now," said the other. "Where you goin?'

"I'm going home with you," the old man said with a toothless smile.

"And just what do you plan to do when you comes home to my house?"

"You knows what I plans to do," he said, smiling even more.

"Oh no," said the woman, "I ain't goin' to be responsible for your death old man."

All three of them laughed and went their separate ways.

At Beef Island, we met up with Ty Dewi and Nona Rosa, and we all went on Ty Dewi to the island of Virgin Gorda to visit The Baths. The Baths are a pile of huge boulders lying along the beach, some of them big as a house. One can swim among them in the crystal clear water. Hiking over and around them is interesting.

That evening we all gathered on our boat and had a sea chantey songfest, which we thought would be our last one together as our gang was splitting up for other islands. After singing our rendition of Drunken Sailor, the boats in the anchorage responded with a round of applause. However, it was a sad time as we were not sure we would see our friends for a long time.

On the other hand, we were looking forward to seeing other friends down island. This is how the cruising life seems to go. You leave one set of friends only to find another waiting to welcome you to a new anchorage. If there are not any friends already there, there are generally many possibilities for new friendships while swinging to your anchor.

The sail to St. Martin across the Anagada Passage is dreaded by most cruisers, ourselves included. It is a seventy-mile bash to windward against good-sized waves and current. Most boats start this crossing at night when the wind and waves subside somewhat. We cleared customs at Spanish Town and headed out between Round Rock and Ginger Island into Anagada Passage.

We were lucky and had a good passage of only twenty-six hours. When we got in, our friends greeted us.

"How's the anchorage?" I asked Ron, skipper of Mariah.

"You've got to watch out for dragging. We had been here for two or three days and then one day we just started dragging."

"I think there is just a little bit of sand covering rock. The anchor doesn't hold well," Jim from Northern Girl added. "Oh, and don't leave your boat at night."

"Yes," Ron interjected. "They have a gang of thieves here. They sit in the parking lot where the dinghies land. People come in for a great French dinner and leave their dinghies and the thieves steal them."

"They have it easy," chimed in Jim. "These guys read the name of the boat on the dingy, steal it and go out to the yacht. Then they take everything of value and leave. They do not even have to worry about hurrying since they know the owners will be gone several hours to eat and then will have to find a way to get back to their boat. By the time they do get back the thieves are long gone."

Occasionally a cruiser will end up in an anchorage where there is a problem with crime. You hear about it from time to time on the Ham net or single side band. If it seems bad, you just skip that anchorage.

In St. Martin, we resigned ourselves to not going out at night for dinner and, just to be safe, Judy and I put our hard dingy in the water and trailed it behind our boat as a "decoy dingy." We hoped thieves would think we were on the boat even during the day when we were gone.

Making the move to Brooklyn was hard on the whole family. Since we were to live in a high cost area, Judy decided she would have to go to work. My mother came out from California to help care for our three children.

It was hard. It was hard on our oldest daughter Debra because she had to go to school in a huge city and be somewhat responsible for her younger sister. It was hard on Alaina, who had already experienced too many moves, and it was hard on Laura who missed her mother during the day. It was hard on my mother to give up her life for a year, and it was hard on Judy to go to work.

It was hard on me because I was going to have to go back to school where everything I did would be critiqued by a supervisor and peer group. Clinical Pastoral Education, I had heard, was the most difficult of programs, so I had very mixed feelings.

I was able to make contact with an Episcopal priest, rector of Christ Church Bay Ridge, who needed help and could pay for it I soon found myself working with the youth of Christ Church and having the eight o'clock service on Sunday mornings. Between this, my residency pay, and what Judy brought in, we were able to live.

I was involved in many interesting situations while serving as a chaplaincy resident at Lutheran Medical Center. My first ward assignment was the gynecological ward. Since most of the patients were Puerto Rican and spoke Spanish, it fell to me to translate from Spanish to English. The resident and intern doctors were mostly Korean, who spoke very little English. Consequently, there I was in the examining room with my clerical collar, attempting to translate from Spanish to broken English so the doctors could understand in Korean.

"What long we her?" asked the doctor, who was a woman in her late twenties.

She wants to *know what is wrong with the patient,* I decided and translated,

"Quí es la problema?"

"Me duele," responded the patient, a nineteen year old woman who was very embarrassed at having a priest in on the examination.

"¿Donde?" (Where?)

"Me duele . . . me duele aquí," she said as she pointed to her genitals.

"She has pain in her vaginal area," I told the doctor.

"Whoa pain?" said the doctor.

"In her vaginal area. Her genitals," I replied, pointing to my crotch.

The doctor smiled, "She no pain there. No can."

Now I am getting very embarrassed and frustrated.

"No," I said in a loud voice, "she says she has pain there." I pointed to the patient's genitals.

"Oh," said the doctor, who was getting embarrassed herself.

I also experimented in setting up a special chaplaincy for surgical patients, worked in a nursing home, set up a chaplaincy for an outpatient clinic, and did some counseling at a clinic for disturbed children. In all of this, I became more attuned to myself and the blocks I had to self-growth. I attempted to get more in touch with my anger and fear of failure, which I carried with me from the Mission District. I was so afraid of failing that I did everything I could to keep from being successful. They were interesting and painful days.

Spring rolled around sooner than expected. I picked up a CPE Quarterly Newsletter one evening while on night duty. There were many openings for hospital chaplains listed there, but I was not sure if I was really cut out to be a hospital chaplain. Just as one was getting to know a patient they would be released or worse, die. I had thought about a ministry to the mentally ill, but I really did not think I was equipped with the patience that ministry required. *Back to the parish? Well, perhaps.*

Then an advertisement in the newsletter struck me. The U.S. Bureau of Prisons was looking for a chaplain. My friend Don had seen to it that I preached at his New York state prison several times and I had also volunteered to do retreats at another state prison in Wallkill. I was not sure I was cut out to be a prison chaplain, even though Don insisted I was. I realized I was afraid of working in prison because I saw myself there behind the bars. I had heard that the federal prison system was one of the most advanced and innovative in the country. I was not really interested in prison work, but decided I could find out more about it.

I wrote a letter to the Council of Churches, who did the nominating for these positions, asking for information and an application. Two days after I sent the letter there was a postal workers' strike.

"Well," I told Judy, "I didn't think God wanted me to be a prison chaplain, and this proves it."

A day or so later I received a call from the National Council of Churches.

"Chaplain," they said, "we are sorry we could not send you an application because of the mail strike. We are going to hold some interviews on Thursday. Can you come over and interview?"

"Sure," I said, "I'll be glad to."

Even though I did not want the job, I thought it would be interesting to interview. I could be myself and they would not hire me. Anyway, I had heard there were two openings and forty applicants, not very good odds.

I put on my black suit and collar and arrived at the designated time. I was trying to look as Anglo Catholic (Episcopalian) as I could so that they would not want to nominate me.

I was escorted to a waiting room and told to wait. Forty-five minutes later, I was shown into another room and the interview began. I sat on one side of the table with ten chaplain-types on the other side. They were from various churches including Lutheran, Baptist, Presbyterian, Church of Christ and Assembly of God. They pounded questions at me:

"What would you do if an inmate wanted to give you a gift?"

"What if you saw two inmates fighting? What would you do?"

"What if you saw an officer beating up an inmate?"

"Can you work with other religions?"

"Do you feel you have to wear a clerical collar?"

On and on they went for an hour and a half. I answered with the first thing that carne into my mind. When I left the room, my head was splitting. I really did not care if I got the job, but I felt I had done the best I could to answer their questions honestly.

After another hour of waiting, they called me back in, and I was told that they were going to nominate me for one of the open positions. I would be the first Episcopalian to become a federal chaplain.

"We're very happy to have you on board," said the Chief of Chaplains as he shook my hand. "Would you please fill out an application before you leave?"

When I got home that night, I was elated, although I felt God had trapped me. My feelings surprised me and I had difficulty understanding them. I eventually got it sorted out.

I was still hurting from having to leave Honduras. Judy and I had worked out some of the anger, but it was still hanging around. I was a missionary at heart and the more I thought about prison work the more excited I became.

The next few months were busy with finishing my quarter of CPE and closing out with my peer group. They all thought I was nuts.

"Why do you want to work with psychopaths?" asked Sol, who later also became a Federal Prison chaplain. "You must be crazy!"

"Do you feel you can't do anything else?" asked Jim.

Being warned by a friend that the Bureau would never send a person where he wanted to go, I had to be very careful. There were two institutions open: Federal Correctional Institution, Milan, Michigan; and Federal

Correctional Institution, Tallahassee, Florida. I wanted to go to Florida, so I wrote a letter to the Chief of Chaplains requesting to be sent to Michigan.

He responded that the Bureau did not accept requests and I was subject to being assigned anywhere. I am sure that with this in mind he felt he could not assign me to Michigan, so I would have to be sent to Tallahassee.

I was on my way to becoming a bureaucrat.

CHAPTER TWENTY-FIVE

For my birthday, Judy decided my present would be a trip by ferry to Saba. This island is about thirty-five miles from St. Martin. To get there by ferry would be very expensive, but Judy had a plan.

"What we can do," she said, "is go look at condominiums."

"I don't understand," I said. "What do you mean 'look at condominiums'? How does that get us to Saba?"

Some condominiums here will pay seventy-five dollars if you go and listen to their sales pitch. We could hit a couple of them and we'd have enough to go to Saba."

It sounded like a plan to me, so we searched out one of these gold mines.

We had to listen to three sales pitches in order to make the trip. I wondered what kind of present this was that I had to work so hard to get.

The thirty-five mile ferry ride took only two hours. It should have been faster, but the starboard engine decided not to work. It sounded as if there was a block in the fuel line. It was a great feeling, knowing I was not the one who would have to crawl down into the hot engine room to clear the blockage. I just sat there with what Judy termed a "silly grin" on my face while the other passengers were being seasick and frightened out of their wits.

The island is beautiful and spectacular. It rises straight up out of the sea and its peak is lost in the clouds. We could have come here on Butterfly, but the water is too deep for anchoring. There are a few moorings available, and as the boat ran alongside the island, we saw that the moorings all had been taken. I was happy we had come by ferry.

A taxi dropped us off where a set of stairs led to the top of the mountain. It was hot and airless as we trudged up the steps to the top of the mountain that was Saba. We went through marvelous shades of green. These stairs had four or five paces between each. As we climbed, my breath got shorter and shorter and my legs began to ache.

"I think I'm too old for this," I told Judy between puffs of breath.

"Yeah," she said, "but isn't it breathtaking?"

"We've got to be there soon," I said. "I don't think I can make it much further."

As we climbed, the air became cooler and we found ourselves in the clouds. The condensation continually dripped from the trees and foliage around us. Soon we came to the top of the steps. The trail continued on, but started downhill.

"I declare this the top of the mountain!" I said.

"All right," Judy readily agreed. She must have been tired too because she always wants to continue to the end.

The trip down was a little faster but twice as far since we had to go to the bottom of the valley. There we found a sign:

> "THERE ARE 1080 STEPS TO THE TOP
> IF YOU HAVE HEART PROBLEMS,
> DO NOT ATTEMPT THIS CLIMB"

We made it back to Butterfly in good time, but for the next few days we couldn't move. Neither of us had ever been so tired.

After some difficulty, I found the Federal Correctional Institution at Tallahassee. I had arrived the evening before and was still tired from the drive. As I drove onto the grounds, I felt a lump growing rapidly in my stomach. *What would it be like working in a prison? Would I be able to handle working with those "psychopaths" as my CPE friend had described the inmates?* I felt like turning the car around and leaving.

Driving up the tree lined driveway to a formidable brick building, I thought about what one of my college professors had told me. He was a seasoned journalist and he gave the class this advice:

"Don't ever say you do not know how to do something. You have brains and you can learn how."

Repeating this to myself, I stopped the car at a little sign: "Report Here."

A voice from a small black box asked me,

"May I help you?"

"Yes," I replied, looking around to find the person speaking. There was no one.

"What is your business here?" asked the voice.

"I am the new Chaplain. Ames Swartsfager," I stated, trying to keep the nervousness out of my voice.

"OK. Park your car in the lot on the left, Chaplain Swatsberger, and go on inside."

I decided not to try to correct the voice's pronunciation of my name.

Parking the car, I walked to the front steps and through the door into a lobby. There was no one in the lobby so I went to the next door and pushed, but it did not open.

"Buzzzzz." The door opened. Standing about six feet from the door were two men. Without moving, they held out their right hands as if to shake my hand, but they were too far away for me to reach. As I took a step toward them and put my hand out, my feet slipped out from under me and I landed on my rear.

It must have been very funny. I was extremely embarrassed. The younger of the two men gave me a hand up.

"Hi, I'm John Kemp, the Associate Warden." He turned toward the other man, "And this is Mr. Jefferies, the Warden."

"We should have warned you," he continued. "They just finished washing the floor."

We went down the hallway to the Warden's office and after he sat behind a great desk, he said, "We're quite surprised to see you here today."

"You are? Why's that?"

"Oh, we weren't expecting you until much later."

"You sent me a letter telling me to report today." I was a bit confused.

"Not that I know of," said the Warden. "You can't start for a month yet."

I reached into my briefcase, wondering how I could have made such a mistake. I found the letter and read it again.

"Sir, it looks to me as if you asked me to report here on Monday, May 20. Is this your signature?"

He took the letter and read it.

"All I was saying was you could come down here on the twentieth to find a place to live. It's very hard to find houses here. You cannot start work until you find a place to live." He handed the letter back to me.

"I can't start until I find a place to live," I repeated, more for my benefit than for his.

"That's correct," he stated as he ushered me to the door. I was depressed and angry. *What I had gotten myself into?* I was determined to find a place to live that day.

I went to the local Episcopalian church and talked to the rector, who gave me the name of a parishioner who rented houses. By four that afternoon, I had rented a very nice house at less rent than we had paid in Brooklyn for an apartment. I moved out of the motel, unrolled my sleeping bag in the bedroom and was asleep by sunset.

At eight the next morning I went into the institution (without falling on my rear this time) and made my way to the Warden's office.

"You're back again." Warden Jefferies wrung his hands irritably. "I thought I told you. You can't go to work until you find a place to live."

"I have, sir." I handed him the address of my new home.

"There is no way you could find a house so fast." He slammed his hand on the desk "Give me the name and number of the landlord."

I did and he called her.

I could not believe this was happening. I was ready to quit before I began. After talking to the property owner for a minute, he hung up and said, "Well, I guess you're right. You can start work, Chaplain Swatfazzen."

"You can call me Chaplain Ames. Ames is much easier than my last name."

"It is Chaplain Swearbarger here," he said sternly.

"The correct pronunciation is Swarts-fager," I corrected.

The Associate Warden, who was sitting with us during this exchange, said, "I'll show the Chaplain around the institution."

As we left the office, he put his arm around me. "As far as I'm concerned, it's Chaplain Ames."

I later learned that the Warden had decided to save year-end money to balance his budget. My coming had ruined that plan. He directed his irritation over this toward me.

The sum total of my orientation and training to be a prison chaplain was an hour's tour of the facility. I was handed a set of keys and told not to lose them and to keep everything locked up.

The prison, The Federal Correctional Institution at Tallahassee, housed some eight hundred young adult offenders between the ages of eighteen and twenty-five. Most of them were there for stealing cars and taking them across state lines, but they were all determined to out do each other in toughness.

The prison was in good shape, but there was no chapel. The services were held in a very smelly very old auditorium that sat six hundred. There was no air conditioning. Four huge floor fans moved the hot air around the room. The noise from the fans was so loud I had to use an amplifier to be heard by the dozen or so inmates who showed up for services. I was beginning to wish I was in the state system where, it seemed to me, they had more respect for religion.

To make matters worse, the auditorium was over the kitchen and every Sunday they would have fried chicken. The smell of hot fat wafted up into the chapel. In addition, since the auditorium was used for movies on Saturday evenings, it was especially smelly after a "two sock" movie (a movie with semi-clad women in it. The inmates would masturbate into their socks).

With the heat and the smell, I could understand why no one wanted to come to the service. I didn't want to either. After the Warden retired, a new chapel or at least a smaller room in which to hold services was constructed.

There are not many dull moments working with young adults. In each of the five years I was assigned there, we had a disturbance or a riot.

The first one had been brewing all summer long. Our food service was poor, and we did not have many programs relating to African-Americans. There was no air conditioning in the dormitories and during the summer, the men were swelteringly hot even at night.

One Monday morning I decided to come to work early and get some work done before my afternoon and evening programs began. As I pulled up, I noticed there were State Police stationed around the fence line. I walked into the institution and down the hall to the grill that led to the compound yard ("the Pound"). The gate was locked and I told the officer to let me through.

"The inmates are on a sit-down strike," he replied. "They might even riot soon. You sure you want to go in?"

I looked into the Pound and saw inmates milling around and shouting to one another. My knees turned to jelly. I felt sure I did not want to go in! On the other hand, I felt it was why I was there. *To be God's representative even during a riot.*

"Please let me in," I requested, turning back to the man at the gate. Somehow, I got my legs to move me into the yard. The yard was crowded with inmates who were standing, sitting on the lawn, and just walking around. I walked around talking to various groups.

"What's happening?" I asked the first group of inmates I encountered.

"We aren't going to work any more," said one.

"Why is that?"

"The food's bad, Chaplain, you know that," said another.

"Yeah, I know. But is there anything else?"

"The heat in the dorms. No one can sleep. We need air conditioning."

At this point the PA system blurted out, "Chaplain Ames, Chaplain Ames. You have a phone call."

I turned to one of the inmates. "Hey John, go tell them I'm busy."

I went to another group.

"Our complaints! Hell, Chaplain we don't want to be here!"

"Shut your mouth, Tommy," said another. "I'll tell you our problem. We need an inmate committee to decide on the movies they get here."

"Yeah, also to help decide on what they sell in commissary," broke in another.

I stood around listening for a couple of hours. Every so often, there would be an announcement for "Chaplain Ames" to report here or there, or that I had a phone call, but I ignored them. Then, I felt a hand on my shoulder. It was Jim, the Chief of Utilities.

"What's up, Jim?"

"Yuh better come into the administration building now," Jim said in his slow Southern drawl.

"Why?" I asked.

"There are some students here for a tour."

"They're not supposed to be here for several hours yet."

"Well, I don't know. You'd better come in and talk to them."

"I guess so. They can't tour today. I'll be back out in a few minutes," I said to the inmates around me.

Jim and I walked through the grill and into the administration building.

"Where are the students?"

"Hell, Chaplain there ain't no students. I was told to get you in because you was the only staff member in the compound."

"Where are the dorm officers?"

"The union made the Warden pull them out three hours ago. They said it was too dangerous."

"I'm going back out."

"No you're not," said a lieutenant standing nearby. "Warden's orders."

I went to the Warden's office. We had changed wardens six months prior, and the current one was unfortunately very weak. I liked him, but felt he was in over his depth. The Warden was surrounded by the Associate Warden, the Captain, and some Lieutenants.

"I want back out in the compound." Anger made my voice shake.

"Can't go out," said the Captain. "It's too dangerous."

"Shit," I said, my anger leaping out. "What the hell is everyone doing just sitting around? Someone should be finding out what the problem is. I bet you all don't have any idea what complaints the inmates have. You probably don't care either!"

"What are the complaints?" asked the Warden, attempting to take control of the situation.

I told him and added, "You should be talking to them, not just sitting here waiting for things to explode."

At about this time the sit-down strike became a full-blown riot. The commissary was broken into, inmates ran around with whatever they could find for a weapon. Things were approaching a critical stage.

"You're right, Chaplain," the Warden said. "I'll go to the control room and talk to them over the PA." He marched to the control room and attempted to talk to the inmates, but the system was so bad they could not understand most of what he said.

"Maybe you should talk with them face to face," I suggested, calming down a bit.

"I don't know," he said.

"I'll go out there with you."

"All right. Let's get a bull horn and go out on the steps." We finally found a bullhorn that worked and went out on the steps of the administration building. The Warden attempted to raise the PA to speak, but his hand was shaking so badly he could hardly hold it. I stepped over and held it for him and he asked the inmates to send in a committee to discuss their grievances.

"The Chaplain will be there to guarantee I keep any agreement I make," he concluded.

Within a few minutes, we were talking to eight inmates selected by the others. They stated their complaints and the Warden promised he would get better food, showed them our plans for a new forced air circulation system for the dormitories, and promised they could have an inmate committee.

After they went back into the compound, the riot began to break up. My clerk came to the grill and said there were a lot of inmates who wanted out of the yard because they were afraid of what might happen to them. We opened up the doors into the cell-house ("segregation," where inmates were placed when in trouble. It segregated them from the general population.) and put as many into it as we could, about two hundred in an area built for fifty. There were still more who wanted out of the pound.

"Where can we put them?" asked a lieutenant.

"What about the small yard next to the segregation unit?" I suggested.

"That's a good idea," agreed the Associate Warden.

"Go out there and unlock that gate, Lieutenant. Get some officers to frisk and strip search them as they come in."

"We can't go out there!" exclaimed the lieutenant. "It's too dangerous."

"Give me the keys," I said. "I'll go and unlock the gate." I walked out and the inmates surrounded me. They wanted to know what was happening. I told them I was going to unlock the gate and let anyone off the pound who wanted to leave. I also warned they would be strip searched when they went in.

The inmates let me through and lined up to get off the yard. There was a scattering of weapons where they had been standing. Within half an hour, the compound was cleared except for about twenty inmates who refused to leave. We sent out the riot squad and brought them in.

By early evening, the inmates were being returned to their dorms and things began to cool down. I spent most of the evening walking through the dorms and talking.

The next day I went to see the Warden, who introduced me to the head of custody from the Central Office.

"Warden, I feel we need to move on the promises we made yesterday." I said to the warden after being introduced. "Things are still rather hot and if we show that we'll keep our promises, they'll cool down."

"What did you promise them?" barked the man from the Central Office.

"That we would try to provide better food, work on completing the renovation of the air handling systems in the dorms, and have an inmate committee," replied the warden.

"What the hell!" he yelled, slamming his fist into his palm. "You can't have an inmate committee. Forget it!"

"Oh," said the Warden. "If you say so, we'll forget it."

"Excuse me, Warden," I interrupted. "You remember you told the inmates you would keep your word. You said I would be there to insure that anything you agreed upon you would do. Now you have to keep your word."

"Warden," commanded the Central Office man, "there is no way in hell you can allow an inmate committee."

"You can do as you want," I said. "You're the Warden. However, if you go against your word, my ministry here is over. The inmates will never again believe anything you or I say."

"You're right, Chaplain. We'll go ahead with the inmate committee. Make up a memo instructing each dormitory to elect a representative and post it on the bulletin boards before noon today."

"Yes sir," I said and left the room.

The Central Office man became Warden at Tallahassee just six months later.

I was sitting in a chair across the office from my desk preparing the next week's program schedule when two inmates walked in with their hands behind their backs.

"Uh, Chaplain, I have to go to Education for that book. You remember the book you ordered?" asked my clerk Robert as he headed out the door. I had no idea what he was talking about, but I trusted him and told him to go.

"This is it chaplain," said one of the inmates. "You going to give us more time in chapel?"

"That is not under my authority. You know that only the warden can give you more time. I asked him and he refused."

"I don't believe you," said the other inmate taking his hands from behind his back. They had two by fours about four feet long in their hands.

I tried to get to the telephone, but one of them blocked my way. It crossed my mind that Robert had been part of the plot, but I really could not believe it. I had to get to the desk to dial the security alarm or at least knock the phone off the hook, which also caused an alarm to ring in the control room.

"We got you now chaplain. You can't get away." He hauled back with the two by four, holding it like a baseball bat. I tried to cover my head with my arms, waiting for the blow to land.

The door crashed open and five officers burst in, grabbing the weapons and controlling the inmates.

"Right on time," I said letting my breath out. As usual, the shakes began. "How did you know what was happening?"

"Your clerk came running into the Lieutenant's office calling for help," said the Lieutenant. "Looks like he saved your skin."

CHAPTER TWENTY-SIX

"There's a rock or something just off our port bow," Judy called from the foredeck.

"I don't see anything," I called back.

"Look there," she said, pointing. "See the water splash up on it?"

I did see what looked like mist shooting up. I shifted the helm to take the boat to starboard. We were sailing off the coast of St. Martin and heading for St. Barts.

"There it is again," she called.

"It's a whale," I yelled excitedly. We saw his fluke slowly rise and the huge animal sounded. Although we looked for him for an hour or so, he never reappeared.

We had left St. Martin and were heading for St. Barts, where we planned to spend a few days before going on to Antigua. The trip to St. Barts was beautiful as we wove our way through little islets, and at sunset we dropped our anchor in the beautiful Anse de Columbier Bay.

It was a beautiful anchorage with goats bleating and peacocks screaming on the shore. The latter made an eerie sound, but we soon became used to it. In the morning we walked the cliff path to a little French town, Anse de Flamandes. What a beautiful walk, with the sea breaking at our feet and a breathtaking view of the coral and rock reefs.

Stopping by a store, we bought some bread and cheese, beer and a coke for Judy. Going back across the cliff trail we stopped at a cave-like rock formation and sat in the shade to have our lunch.

That evening we were invited over to another boat for a potluck dinner. As we were leaving our boat, we noticed that the wind had picked up a bit. While we nibbled on snacks and had a drink, the wind became stronger. I was sitting right behind the boat's wind speed indicator on our host's instrument panel and I watched it hit fifty miles per hour with a steady breeze of thirty-five. I always worry when we leave the boat unattended, but in a blow like this, I was terrified that Butterfly, with all her awning up, would drag anchor and come up on some nasty looking rocks.

We said our good-bys rather quickly and dashed back home. Happily, she was downwind or our little four horsepower engine would never have made it against the wind and waves. In seconds we arrived and managed to board in the heavy chop without falling overboard. Then we struggled to get our large awning down in the gusty winds. An hour later, we were able to have a bite to eat. While I was eating, I kept watching some sharp rocks lying about one hundred feet off our stern. Our anchor seemed to be holding well, but I thought we should keep an anchor watch.

For the next three days the wind blew and we sat at anchor, keeping anchor watches at night. The waves crashed on the rocks off our stern and some of the huge swell came into the bay, but otherwise we were comfortable.

In the afternoon of the fourth day, the wind moderated. We were able to put our aft awning back up, but did not trust the weather situation enough to put the big one up. Then we got into the dinghy and went to shore. The beach was crowded with sunbathers and it was then I noticed the poverty of the St. Bart's population. They were so poor they could not afford bathing suit tops. Some were so poor they could not afford bottoms either. I walked along the beach trying to keep my eyes from straying.

"You can sure tell which ones are true blonds," said Judy.

"What?"

"Look over there," she said, "You can tell which one of those three blonds is a real blond."

I looked and sure enough she was right. I blushed. My mind was in great conflict. On the one hand I wanted to go back to the boat to get my binoculars, but, at the same time, it made me uncomfortable. Judy just laughed, as I hurried her back to the dinghy and the boat.

The next morning we left for Antigua.

After my first few months in Tallahassee, I got the lust to sail again. We were only about forty minutes from the Gulf of Mexico, where there was a marina at Shell Point. Most of the boats were Morgan 22's. I checked on the prices for a Morgan 22 and found they were six to eight thousand dollars. I had paid two thousand five hundred dollars for a thirty footer in Honduras and was not about to pay such an extravagant price for a twenty-two footer. I could not afford it anyway.

For months I looked. Every Saturday Judy would cringe when I suggested we go for a ride. She knew we would end up looking at boats, and she was very sure she did not like sailing after her experience in Honduras. However, we looked in Sopchoppy, Panacea, Carabelle, and St. Marks. In the little fishing harbor of St. Marks, I found a sloop with a FOR SALE sign.

"It looks kind of old," Judy said, trying to discourage me.

"We could fix her up."

"Maybe we should look for something smaller?" She pleaded with her eyes. Judy did not want to buy a boat.

"But this is only a thirty-two footer."

"How can we afford a boat like that?"

"I don't know." I was getting a little irritated. "We don't know how much the owner wants for it."

Judy was silent. I wrote down the phone number and called that evening.

"Hello," I said when a female voice answered. "I'm interested in the boat you have for sale."

"Wait a minute, I'll get my husband." As I waited, I thought I heard some cheering in the background.

"Hello," said the husband.

"Yes," I said, "I'm interested in the boat you have for sale."

"Well it's thirty-two feet, has a Waukesha diesel, stove and everything."

"How much do you want for it?"

There was silence for a minute or so. I almost thought the man had hung up on me.

"Well," he said, "I'll let you have it for two thousand five hundred dollars."

"Did you say for two thousand five hundred dollars?" My heart was pounding. I could maybe afford this.

"Well," he said, "tell you what. Let's make it two thousand even."

"When can I see it?"

"How about tomorrow afternoon?"

"Make it five o'clock," I replied. "I have to work until four."

"That's fine."

I could not hold still. We might be able to afford a boat!

It would cost even less than El Marinero. I shared the news with Judy, but she did not seem very ecstatic.

"It's an old boat." Judy stabbed her knitting needle into the ball of yarn she was working with. "When was it built?"

"I don't know. I didn't ask him."

"What condition are the sails in?" she asked.

"I don't know. I didn't ask him," I repeated feeling very incompetent. The lust for a boat had overcome all reason.

"Don't get your hopes up," she cautioned. "It's an old boat."

In my mind it was a beautiful boat. It had an old-fashioned wheel. I went to sleep dreaming of standing behind the wheel as we sailed through the Gulf of Mexico with the sun sparkling on the waves. Judy and the girls were sunning themselves on the deck. Then the bilge alarm started ringing.

"We're sinking!" cried Judy.

"Get your life jackets on!" I yelled in return. I could see water in the cabin. The boat started to shake.

"Wake up, Ames." Judy was shaking my shoulder. "You're having a bad dream. Anyway, the alarm went off and it's time to get up."

I heaved a great sigh of relief and got out of the bed. This evening I had a date with my dream girl. *What will I name her?* I thought as I shaved. I am not sure how I got through the day, but at four o'clock, I was out of the institution and on my way to pick Judy and the girls up to go see the boat.

Judy was curiously silent during the ride to St. Marks. When we arrived, a man was painting the toe rail. *How wonderful a toe rail.* (This rail runs along the edge of the deck. El Marinero did not have one.)

"Ahoy, there," I called somewhat timidly.

"Oh, hi. Come aboard." He helped us onto the boat and into the cockpit. *Wouldn't it be grand to spend an afternoon painting a toe rail!*

"You want to take a look around?"

I looked, but I was not sure what I was looking for. It was all painted very nice. The forepeak was a huge double bed. There was a settee in the main cabin across from the galley, which consisted of a propane stove, a five-gallon plastic tank for water, and a sink. There was a head on the port side. The engine was located under the companionway.

Judy and I could sleep up forward and the two older girls could share the other bunk. The youngest could sleep on the floor. *Yes, we could have a lot of fun with this.* The boat looked all right to me. I even looked in the bilge and asked to see the sails. The fact that I had no idea what I was looking for did not seem to bother me at all. She was pretty. Not like those Morgan 22's. This boat had character. She was traditional. This was the kind of wooden boat a real salty sea dog would have and be damned with fiberglass.

We set up an appointment for sea trials the following Saturday.

Our bank loaned us the money and I had the check in my pocket when the family went to have our sea trial. The owner dropped the dock lines and out we went down the St. Marks River, a wide river filled with oyster beds. The channel was well marked and oyster shoals or mud flats lay on either side.

It was a beautiful day, and lots of boats were out. We motored for about twenty minutes, and then the owner suggested we try it out under sail. He hoisted the sails, tacked around and headed downwind back towards the dock. He shut off the engine until we were almost at the dock and then we dropped sails, started the engine and maneuvered into the slip.

I had noticed he had a strange way of starting the engine. He took a hammer and placed it on a starter knob of some sort down in the engine compartment. I asked him about this.

"Oh this engine came out of a tractor and is a marine conversion. I have to use this hammer to reach the old foot starter plunger."

It made sense to me. He showed me what to do if the worm gear came off the rudder head.

"Put it back on and hit it a couple 'a times with this wrench." He held up a massive pipe wrench.

I was beginning to have doubts, but every time I looked at her, I could visualize the whole family having a great time out sailing.

When the owner had gone to shore to buy a couple of beers, Judy asked,

"Are you sure you want to buy this boat? It looks like an awful lot of work."

"She's beautiful!" was my reply.

When the owner came back, I gave him a check, he made out a bill of sale, and we toasted each other with a cold beer.

The following weekend we went for the first real trip on our still un-named boat. We figured an appropriate name would come to us. I started the engine; we backed out of the slip, and started down the channel.

Now the channel is seven miles long so we were still motoring some twenty minutes later when Judy yelled,

"The engine's on fire!"

I opened the engine hatch and saw smoke billowing up.

"Get the sails up!" I hollered as I shut down the engine, and then ran to the foredeck to help with the sails.

We were in a wide spot in the channel so I was able to tack her around and sail downwind. There was not much wind for sailing. About a mile from the marina, we had to tack through a very narrow part of the channel.

"We get through here," I told Judy (who was wearing an 'I told you so' expression) "and we'll have it made."

"Blaaaaast" sounded a boat horn. A fifty-foot sports-fisherman was heading toward us at top speed.

"We have the right-of-way!" I yelled, but he could not hear me over his roaring engines.

"Blaaaaast!"

We were barely moving, but I was able to tack out of his way.

"Blaaaaast!" he said, as he swept by us at what seemed like twenty knots. His wake was four foot high and it tossed us up on a mud bank.

"That %1\&***(())) +!!!!!" I screamed in frustration and anger. "That dirty *()*(&1\%\$@!!!! Let's put out the *&1\%@ anchor and see if we can get off," I added, still furious at the captain of the powerboat, at the guy who sold me the boat with a bad engine, and at myself for having been such a sucker to buy it.

However, it was no use. The tide was going out faster than we could take corrective measures. Soon we were completely high and dry.

"At least I can see how the bottom looks," I said, as if I had planned the whole thing.

The next day we had enough tide to get the boat free from the mud.

Things just got worse as the months passed. The old girl's engine would have to be replaced. It would run fine for twenty minutes and then smoke billowed out. That is why during the test run the ex-owner had decided to "sail for a while!"

There was dry rot in the foredeck-I fixed it. The hatches were rotten-I fixed them. The mast needed painting-I painted it. The bottom needed painting and when I pulled the boat, I found rot there-I fiberglassed the bottom. Then the cabin top rotted out-I fixed it.

I replaced the engine with a new one, but for a while it would only run backward in forward and forward in reverse. I needed a different propeller-I bought it. Then the rudder rotted out and I built another one.

We named the boat Questa, which was a play on words. A quest is an adventure and cuesta (pronounced questa) in Spanish means expensive. We were having an expensive adventure.

After we got the new engine, we did make a few trips up the St. Marks River. Anchoring on the upper St. Marks was interesting. One time I asked Debra to drop the anchor. When she did there was a great splash and I was afraid she had fallen overboard. She had not, she had dropped the anchor on an alligator thinking it was a log. Later she refused to go swimming.

"I'm not going," she stated. "That alligator might still be mad."

I thought she might be right and did not go swimming either.

Two years later, I put an ad in the paper:

> "32 ft sloop for sale. New
> engine, good shape. Galley,
> head, sleeps five. Call . . . ."

Judy called me to the phone about three months later. "It's a man calling about the boat," she said.

"Yeah!" shouted the kids.

"Hello," I said to the man on the phone.

"I'm interested in that boat you have for sale."

"Yes," I said hopefully. "She's a fine boat, ready to go anywhere. We've even taken her up the St. Mark's river."

"How much do you want for it?"

"Well," I said as I searched my conscience for the right price. "I'll let you have it for two thousand five hundred dollars."

"What did you say?" he asked.

"Well," I said, "let's make it two thousand even."

CHAPTER TWENTY-SEVEN

I like sailing at night better than at any other time. When the moon is out the waves become a wonderland of charging horses. I wonder if a sea monster will raise its head and sniff the wind. When there are stars, it is even more beautiful. They draw me into the heavens while I lie back in my favorite little corner of the cockpit to watch them. The mizzenmast circles around first this one and then that one, as if it cannot make up its mind which one to point out to me.

I can make out the loom of the lights of Antigua on the horizon and I slow the boat down. We will arrive before dawn if I do not. In the early morning light, I spot the entrance to English Harbor. This is a historic place with the ruins of the British Navy's seventeenth century dry dock. Lord Nelson himself spent time here and so did Captain Hornblower and many other fictional characters.

I could see the remains of two old fortresses on the cliff tops and feel the spyglass of Nelson on me, checking to see if I ran a taunt ship. I reached down and shut off the engine.

"What are you doing?" asked Judy in her concerned voice.

"We're going to sail in."

"But the harbor is crammed with boats at anchor," she said.

"Hornblower could do it. So can I!" I said with bravado.

The harbor was indeed filled with hundreds of sailboats since it was Race Week. However, all I could see were the many towering masts of the frigates and the ships of the line, which were anchored there in the days of long ago.

"Avast ye, hearties," I called. "Let's enter yonder port and show them lubbers what seamanship really is!"

"Maybe you ought to go below for a rest," suggested my mate.

I was elated as the boat, under main alone, was now making six knots on a beam reach. We were headed for a narrow opening between the cliff to port and a reef to starboard.

"Have you gone out of your mind?"

"Go up forward, me hardy," says I, "and prepare to lower the main on my hand signal."

We fairly flew through the narrows and I rounded her up between two mega racers and headed directly up wind. I made the thumb-down hand signal and the main slid to the boom with a rattle. The boat slowed and I looked for a likely anchoring spot. Steering to starboard around another anchored boat, I signaled Judy to lower the mainsail and as we drifted into a clear spot, I ran forward to drop the anchor.

I turned and looked at Judy, who did not look at all happy.

"Wipe that silly grin off your face." She scowled.

We were at anchor, and now I was no longer the ship's captain, but once again just a husband.

"I bet Lord Nelson was impressed," I mumbled as I started to help furl the mainsail.

One of the most frustrating parts of my ministry in Tallahassee was the constraint of working with only one part of the problem, the criminal. Almost all of the inmates had wives or girlfriends who, if nothing else, knew about the criminal activity of her man. Many of them had been involved in the crime actively, but the judge would let them off because they were women. They do not do that very much these days, due to the woman's liberation movement, and a lot more women are now sent to prison.

"Chaplain, you got a minute?" the resident (we called inmates residents in the 70s) was a curly headed blond of about twenty. His name was Casey and he was a member of my Family Living Group, formed in an attempt to keep families together while the men were in prison.

"Sure, Casey. Come on in."

"You asked us the other night to see if we could determine what it was that got us in prison. I've given it a lot of thought. I don't want to cop-out. I want to find the truth because I don't want to come back here."

"I hear you."

"Well, like I said, I don't want to cop-out. But I think I have the answer. My wife Alicia is a very beautiful woman. In fact, she was the prettiest girl in school. The cheerleader type, you know."

"Yes."

"Well we dated and got married. I was always afraid of losing her. I wanted her to be happy, so I bought her things. But she always wanted more. I was afraid if I didn't get them she would leave me. I had to get a second job at night in order to pay for all the things I'd bought. Then she complained that I was never home. I didn't know what to do, I was so afraid of losing her. One day I was walked past a bank and decided they had lots of money there. So I just walked in and told them to hand it over."

He laughed. "I tell you, Chaplain, I didn't even make it to the door before they had me."

Other men repeated this story enough times that I realized there must be some truth to it. Many wives or girlfriends wanted more things: a better TV, dishwasher, new car, or whatever. Some of the men had worked two jobs. When even this income could no longer keep up with the demand, they would rob a bank or steal cars and sell them. The wives and their 'wants' were the motivating force behind many of the crimes.

We were working with the man and providing him with an education, a vocational trade, psychological counseling, religious counseling, a bed and three "squares" a day. Meanwhile, the wife had to work hard to exist in the community. She might get some welfare, but not much else. If we were able to change the man to where he wanted to support himself in a socially acceptable way, we still had not changed the wife. She continued to want all those "things."

"I can hardly wait until Tom gets out," said one nineteen year-old wife. "I'm going to make up for having to scrimp the last two years."

The Bureau of Prisons frowned on chaplains working with the families, yet I was forced into it many times.

"This Chaplain Ames?" asked a voice over the phone. I glanced at my clock, which said it was about two-thirty in the morning.

"Yes," I said, trying to get my tongue loosened up so I could speak.

"This is Deputy Johnson," the voice stated. "One of the wives of your prisoners just had a fight with another wife here in a bar."

"Yes."

"Well, what are you going to do about it?" asked the officer.

I had no idea what I was going to do about it, but decided I should do something.

"Where are they now?"

"Down at the Sheriff's office."

"I'll be down in half an hour."

When I arrived at the Sheriff's office, I found the two women slumped in chairs on opposite sides of the room.

"They tried to tear each other's hair out," said Deputy Johnson.

"I should lock them up, but felt that you might help them get out of town."

I turned to the women. "What happened?"

"Well, Chaplain," said one of the women. I had seen her visiting her husband earlier that afternoon, no, yesterday afternoon. "We were bored and started to drink. Then she," she said pointing to the other woman, "started flirting with a man in the bar."

"Well, what do you expect me to do? Be a nun for three years?" asked the blond.

"That's unfaithful to your man," snapped the first woman.

"Hold on," I interrupted. "It's no use discussing the matter. You heard what the deputy said. Are you willing to get on a bus and go home?"

"Sure," said the first. "I don't want to go to jail."

"Ah . . ." said the second.

"What?" I asked her.

"I spent all my money in the bar. I was hoping the man I'd met might loan me a few dollars to get home on."

"How much is the bus fare?"

"Twenty dollars."

I pulled out my wallet and gave twenty dollars to the deputy.

"Will you see they get on the proper bus?"

"I sure will," he replied.

Driving home, I thought about the problem. The women came from great distances (Miami, Atlanta, Savannah, and New Orleans) to visit their husbands or boy friends. During the day, it was not so bad because they were involved in their visits. However, at night it was different. They were bored, so they would go out and drink. I wondered if the blond was planning to prostitute herself or roll the man she had met.

The warden called me in one afternoon. "Chaplain," he said, "we have a problem."

"Yes sir?"

"We just received information that one of our resident's wives might attempt suicide. Could you go and check it out? Here is where she is staying." He handed me a slip of paper.

"Sure I'll check it out, but first let me see if my wife can go with me." There was no way I would go visit the wife of an inmate alone.

I picked Judy up and we drove to the motel where the wife was staying. We got out and knocked on the door of her room. There was no answer. My anxiety rate zoomed. I knocked again, much louder, and called her name.

"Ruth! Ruth, are you there? It's the Chaplain!"

Soon I heard some movement and the door opened a crack.

"What do you want?" she asked. Her eyes were red from crying.

"I'm Chaplain Ames from FCI," I said, "and this is my wife, Judy. Can we come in a minute?"

She heaved a sigh. "Might as well."

"We heard you were feeling down and thought maybe we could help."

"Down," she said with a laugh, "I'm at rock bottom. In the pits."

"Would you like to talk about it?"

"Sit down," she said, motioning to two chairs.

She sat on the edge of the unmade bed.

"I don't know how to begin."

There was a minute of silence.

"After Bill got into trouble and went to jail, I had nowhere to live. My folks are mad at me. They never liked Bill anyway, and when he got into trouble . . . well, they told me not to come running to them for help.

"Bill's family let me stay with them, but they weren't very happy about it. Except for Bill's uncle." She gave a sick laugh. "No, he thought it was great that I moved in."

She started weeping. Judy got some tissues and went and sat next to her and put an arm around her. After awhile, she gained control of herself. "Bill's uncle, Fred . . . he raped me. He told me if I said anything to anyone the family would throw me out. I would have to submit to him any time he wanted me to, and that was almost every night. If I resisted he slapped me around and threatened to have me thrown out.

"I have no place to go. If I tell Bill, he would do something awful. If I tell the family or the police I'll have no where to stay. I don't know what to do."

This was to become a familiar theme. The young women whose husbands were in prison seemed to be fair game for male relatives. My concern about the plight of the families of incarcerated people increased.

One of the responsibilities I had was as sponsor of the Florida State University, Master of Social Work, field work students at the institution and one semester the university sent me a woman who was working on her

Masters in Social Work and Criminology. Her name was Maureen Fenlon and she was a Catholic nun from the Adrian Dominican Order.

Feeling she should become more involved in counseling, I arranged for her to counsel inmates one on one.

Traditionally the institution would allow female students to counsel only when there was a male staff member present. When I set Sister Maureen up for individual counseling sessions there was an uproar. The warden called me into his office.

"Chaplain," he said, "we can't have that Sister doing individual counseling. It's too dangerous and it disrupts the Institution.

"I'm sorry, Warden. She is doing the counseling in my office and there is a large window in the door. I really do not think it is dangerous for her. As far as disrupting the institution, I'll come and get you tomorrow and we can evaluate the disruption."

The following day, while Sister Maureen was counseling, I went and got the warden and we walked down to my office. Standing in front of the door and peering in were three lieutenants.

"What are you doing here?" the Warden asked the lieutenants.

"Well . . . uh . . . uh . . . we are protecting the sister, Warden."

"The only protection she needs is from you guys. Get back to work."

Sr. Maureen became the first woman to do direct counseling with inmates at FCI, Tallahassee, and perhaps anywhere in the Bureau.

I wrote up and submitted a plan to the Warden, requesting permission to ask church leaders in the community to set up a community-counseling program for wives.

"I know your concern for wives of inmates," he said. "I know that you've done some pretty good work with them also. However, the Bureau does not want to get involved with inmates' families."

After thinking this over awhile, I had an idea. Permission was granted by the warden to have a seminar for community clergy. I had done this almost every year so it was not unusual. However, the topic was to be counseling families of inmates.

Weeks before the seminar we coached the men in the family living group, who had volunteered to participate in a panel discussion and share their experiences at the seminar. Sr. Maureen got several wives to volunteer to share their problems in a separate panel.

We had thirty clergy and "other interested persons" attend the seminar. It went very smoothly and many intelligent questions were asked and answered.

A week later, the Warden again called me into his office. Sitting with him was the head of the Law Department of FSU, who had attended the seminar as a representative of the Presbyterian Church.

"Chaplain," said the Warden, "this gentleman has a good idea. He thinks there should be a community-based counseling center for wives of inmates. I would like you to help him in every way you can."

This was what I had been waiting for. Sr. Maureen and I soon set up a community committee, which evolved into a counseling center called Terrell House at Tallahassee or THAT House. Now any calls regarding wives went directly to Terrell House and I could sleep peacefully at night.

CHAPTER TWENTY-EIGHT

As I walked through the old area in English Harbor, I glimpsed out of the corner of my eye the eighteenth century sailors. When I turned my head to look they were gone, leaving only the hustle and bustle of Antigua Race Week with mega yachts, sleek racers with their crews all dressed the same, support yachts and groupies.

The crew of the Butterfly was happy to be back among friends. We, along with our cruising friends from Nona Rosa, took a taxi to the local Anglican Church at Falmouth for Easter services.

The following two weeks were hard for us as we began to deal with our feelings of grief. This was the last time we would be with Nona Rosa. They were heading across the Atlantic for Portugal and Spain; we were heading down island. The Sunday after Easter we had a service on Butterfly with a huge potluck dinner afterward with our friends.

The next day Northern Girl and Mariah left for Monserrat while we stayed to be with Nona Rosa a little longer. But we needed to be south before hurricane season began in July so eventually we brought up the anchor and headed out of the harbor.

Sailing was the only activity that kept me sane while I worked in prison. There I never saw any successes, and the failures of the system always returned. It was easy to feel that everything I did was for nothing. Sailing, however, was different. I could sail from Point A to Point B and be successful. I could race my boat against another and maybe win.

After selling Questa, I immediately started looking for another boat. While at the diocesan church camp, I discovered they had a very old and beat up daysailer for sale. I bought it for one hundred twenty-five dollars.

It was a mess. The wooden mast had delaminated, the hull was cracked and scratched, and the sails needed some stitching, but it was my boat.

I sanded and glued, fiberglassed and painted, sewed and stitched, and in two months I had a dandy fourteen-foot daysailer. Although the boat was fun, I soon needed a bigger one. I put the boat up for sale, and to my surprise I was able to sell it quickly for six hundred dollars.

With the money I put a down payment on an O'Day 16 daysailer, which we named "Tal Vez," which means "Perhaps." I could afford this fine little boat. There were a few other O'Days in the area, so we started racing.

Racing was good for Judy. She had been afraid of sailing since our experience in Honduras with El Marinero and every time she got into a boat her knees turned to jelly and her hands shook. Sailing in races, where all the boats were the same, gave her confidence since she could see that other boats were leaning over the same way we were and their crews were not abandoning ship.

After a race one day, as we were sailing back to the harbor, Judy asked to steer the boat. This was to be the turning point in our sailing lives. From this time on I had to fight to get to steer, which was fitting since she did it better than I.

Soon after we got the daysailer, I took it on a weekend cruise. Shortly after leaving the land, I was in trouble. After a very heavy squall had passed, I began a dialogue with myself:

"*Well Ames, you sure were stupid to come out here.*

"I'm so scared I wet my pants."

"*You can't tell. They're soaked in sea water anyway.*"

"I tell you, I'm scared. I cannot seem to get the boat back to shore. What am I going to do?"

"*What are you afraid of?*"

"Dying, of course."

"*Why be afraid of that? So what if you die? Aren't you doing what you enjoy?*

"Yeah."

"*Not many people get to die doing what they enjoy doing.*"

"You're right."

I whooped and yelled with a fearless joy when the next squall hit. By evening I was safely anchored, tired but joyously alive.

I have never been afraid for myself after that.

Nevertheless, even the O'Day became too small. I wanted a bigger boat, but I had no money. There was a boat dealer in town who sold Morgan sailboats, mainly Morgan 22's. Every so often, he would have a thirty-five foot boat in his warehouse and I would badger him until he let me sit in it. I would sit in the cold warehouse for hours, dreaming of owning a boat like the Morgan Out Island 35.

After he had moved into a new showroom, I stopped by one day and saw a Catalina 27 on the show room floor. I had crewed on one for the Midget Offshore Racing (MORCE) races a few times the previous summer and knew they were nice fast boats. This would be a perfect boat for weekend cruising. However, I certainly did not have the ten thousand dollars she cost.

I called Judy, who hitched a ride with one of our boating friends, and she came over to see it and fell in love with it.

"It's perfect for us!" She surprised me, for this was the first time Judy seemed excited about a boat.

"We can never afford it," I moaned.

"You're right," she sighed.

The owner of the business came over. He could see the pain on our faces.

"You like her?"

"Yeah," I replied, depressed.

"It's a good boat. We just got her in last weekend."

"Too much money for us," I said. "Tell you what. I'll give you ten dollars down on her," I joked.

"Fine," he said. "Come into the office and we'll draw up the papers."

"You're kidding," Judy said. I just stood there unable to say a word,

"No. I am not kidding. You can make extra payments until you have paid the down payment. I'll help you get the loan for the rest from my bank."

"I can sell the Daysailer and that will help payoff the down payment." I turned to Judy.

"What do you think?"

"I don't know." Judy had as many conflicting emotions as I did. She looked at me with a very serious expression. "I could see about a part time job."

"Do you think we should?" This was not a question, but a plea.

"It sure looks nice," she said. "Let's do it."

"We'll take her." I said to the dealer. "Judy, do you have any money? I have . . . mm . . . four dollars and seventy-five cents."

"Let me see." Judy opened her purse and took out a coin purse. There was a five-dollar bill and change: a quarter, a dime, three nickels and a lot of pennies. We counted the pennies and it all added up to ten dollars and one cent. A penny over!

"Here's your down payment," I said handing him the money.

We were now the proud owners of a Catalina 27. We named her ¡Viva! (Hurrah!).

A year later, I was called into the Warden's office and told that I was to be transferred to the Federal Correctional Institution at Ft. Worth, Texas. The chaplains were transferred every three to five years in those days, and my time had come.

I was ready to leave Tallahassee. I had been in one hostage situation, five riots or disturbances and had worked under seven wardens and six associate wardens in five years. Each one had his own ideas about chaplaincy, so it had been difficult to operate a consistent program.

When I told Judy we were going to be transferred, she seemed happy. I was a little disappointed that we would be located more than three hundred miles from the ocean, but I had discovered there were several lakes nearby where we could possibly sail a small boat. Nevertheless, I knew I would miss the ocean.

"Ames," said Judy. "why don't we have one last big sail before the move to Ft. Worth?" It was evident she noticed my gloomy outlook.

"What do you mean? I suppose we could get in a week or two of vacation before we leave."

"I was thinking about maybe sailing from here to Texas."

"What?" I could not believe the words coming out of Judy's mouth.

"Well, I thought it would be an appropriate last great sail before leaving the sea."

"If you really mean it, that's great." I felt like dancing I was so happy.

We immediately started planning a seven hundred mile offshore voyage from Shell Point, Florida, to Houston, Texas. We would go directly to the Mississippi River and restock at Pilot Town, then continue on through the Galveston inlet and up the bay to Houston. At one point we would be hundred miles offshore. Previously the furthest off we had been was fifteen miles.

I was very concerned about my ability to sail offshore and quickly tried to learn navigation. I borrowed an inexpensive sextant, a radio direction finder, a storm jib, and various other necessary items that we did not have and could not afford.

It was a long trip but after several days we passed the mouth of the Mississippi and, skipping Pilot Town, headed instead to Grand Isle,

Louisiana. Our battery had gone dead leaving us without running lights and I had to steer by the stars dodging through the oilrigs that clotted the gulf. At least the wind had come up and we were able to make four knots. We anchored off the entrance to the bar at Grand Isle and took a nap until daylight. Because we had only three berths without making up the dinette, Debra rolled up in a blanket on a cockpit seat while I napped on the other seat. When I woke up, I saw a sea gull sleeping at her feet.

"Debra," I said softly as I shook her arm, "wake up."

Her eyes opened and she gave me a sleepy "Oh Dad!" look.

"There's a bird sleeping with you."

"Oh Dad! Don't say stupid things!"

"I'm serious! There is a bird cuddled up by your feet."

"Let me go back to sleep." At this point, the bird, not wanting to participate in a father-daughter argument, got up and flew away. He circled the boat twice and then landed on the bow pulpit, where he stayed until we went to get the anchor up to go in.

We stayed in Grand Isle for a day to charge the battery, fill the water tank and purchase some groceries. After a party for Alaina's twelfth birthday, we left the dock and headed over the bar for Galveston.

There were four to six foot waves as we cleared the bar and the wind was getting up. This did not bother me since we had checked with the Coast Guard and were assured that the wind would be ten to fifteen knots and the seas three to five feet. Soon I was reefing the main and attempting to make headway in eight-foot seas. The boat was so light it could not punch through the waves and we would have to falloff to get past an oil rig. We were embayed, or stuck in a bay that we could not escape by sail.

A helicopter came and hovered over us, but I had no idea what he was trying to communicate. We did not have a VHF (Very High Frequency) radio on board, as there had been no stations in the Shell Point area. The helicopter flew away and a tugboat came over to us.

"Ahoy there," called a tugman from his foredeck. "There's gonna be a storm tonight. Come over to our oil rig and tie up to it."

We started to motor over to the rig, but on the way the outboard quit so we sailed over. It began to rain, and I put on foul weather gear (a K-Mart five dollar special) over my swimming suit. As we sailed up to the oilrig, I could see right away there was no way I could tie up to it. The pilings were thirty feet in circumference. *What if the wind changed and the boat swung under the rig. It would be a catastrophe!*

I sailed the boat up near the tug, which was standing off the platform, and hove to (turned the boat into the wind so she would stop).

"I can't tie up to the platform!" I yelled.

"Send us a line and we'll tow you to our mooring. When we finish our work you can tie off behind us."

I coiled the anchor line neatly, wanting everyone to notice what a good seaman I was. I had to throw the line some thirty feet upwind so I got myself ready and, as I threw with all my might, my foul weather pants along with my swimming suit, fell down around my ankles.

The men on the rig, who had come over to watch what was happening, all clapped. Judy, back in the cockpit, laughed uproariously, and our three daughters joined her. I had no dignity left!

When the tug returned to its buoy later that evening the Captain called over to tell us that they were expecting the storm to last three days and have winds up to seventy miles an hour. I took all the sails off and prepared for the blow. Suddenly the wind picked up speed and shifted one hundred-eighty degrees. We shifted with the wind, but the tugboat did not. We crashed into his side, bending our bow pulpit.

We would have to return to Grand Isle. We could not sail nor could we anchor in this storm. There was no other place to go. I replaced the sails and, with the tiny borrowed storm sail flailing and the main reefed to the numbers, we took off on a broad reach in the dark to find the entrance buoy. Stinging rain so heavy I could not see the compass battered us.

Our old friend the tug came by and called to us that the Coast Guard thought it was too rough for them to come out and help us. He said he could escort us to the channel buoy, but I felt we could get there without too much difficulty.

When we did find it, I was unsure of the compass course across the bar. I had my hands full and could not go below to look at the chart, and Judy did not know how to read it. We tacked back and forth in the storm, hoping to follow other boats going in with crews being moved off the oilrigs. After an hour, we finally got a course from the stern light of a boat heading in.

The waves were about eighteen feet high.

Approximately half way in the channel, we were almost pooped by a monster wave that we could not see coming, but could certainly hear. I was afraid the boat would not be able to handle this one, which must have been at least twenty-five feet high. We surfed on top of the wave and then headed down the front. There was a flash of lightning, and I could see a whole boat length between our bow and the bottom of the wave. I eased the tiller and brought the boat to a slight angle to the wave and we slowed a bit as we slid down the face. The wave passed under us without even wetting the foredeck. Judy later told me the cockpit had been filled with water, but I had not noticed it. In a flash, we were in the harbor and protected from the high seas.

We waited three days for the storm to end, but the weather remained bad. I fixed the engine again and we set out on the Intra Coastal Waterway. Arriving in Houston a week later, we had taken fourteen days to complete our first "ocean" voyage.

CHAPTER TWENTY-NINE

The grey clouds hovered over the ocean, reflecting their dullness and converting the normally bright blue water to a sheet metal gray. The clouds and the water reflected our spirits. The wind was behind us and the boat was difficult to handle due to a cross sea. I reefed the main when the wind grew stronger, and the boat sailed a bit better. By late afternoon we were at anchor at Daihies, on the French island of Guadalupe, in a beautiful bay.

Guadalupe, shaped like a butterfly, was the first lush green island we had seen in the Caribbean. The others had been arid with a lot of cactus. This island had trees of a deep dark green that takes the breath away. It was a beautiful sight and we sat in the cockpit watching the sunset while sipping our rum punch.

Although Guadalupe was supposed to be easy to enter through the customs office at Daihies, we had difficulty because Butterfly was only registered and not documented in the States, and it ended up with Judy and me being cleared into the country, but Butterfly was not officially there.

We took a trip by local bus up to the rain forest in the mountains through beautiful countryside and the next day headed for Iles des Saintes, after clearing out when we had never really cleared in. It was a hard two-hour battle to sail windward to these quaint islands, and we were very happy to drop anchor off the town at sunset that evening.

The Saints are a beautiful small group of islands off the west end of Guadalupe. These little islands are different in other ways. Guadalupe's population is mostly of African descent, but the people of the Saints are more French. Well, Basque to be more exact. They tell the story that the French settled here and did not want to mix with the other French on the big island. They became so inbred that the French government sent some officials to survey the situation. The officials found hundreds of retarded children and adults. Sending the retarded to special hospitals on the big island of Guadalupe, they proceeded to solve the inbreeding problem.

They mandated the French Navy in the Caribbean to have shore leave there for two weeks a year. The Navy does this even today.

Near these islands is also the site of the great sea battle between the English and the French Navies in the fight for control of the Caribbean. The English Admirals, including Admirals Hood and Nelson, hid a hundred and fifty ships in Prince Rupert Bay in Dominica. From the top of a headland, they watched for the French to come out and meet them between Iles des Saintes and Dominica. After a fierce battle, the French fled.

When we sailed from Iles des Saintes to Dominica, I was sure I could hear the echo of the battle. The blasts of the cannon, the screams of men wounded by flying splinters, the hoarse yells of officers urging their crews on filled the air. I found myself sniffing the wind for the smell of smoke, and scanning the waves for the flotsam of broken timbers.

After we arrived in Houston, we put ¡Viva! up for sale and drove the six hours to Ft. Worth. Even though I had five years experience in prison work, I was feeling some anxiety the first day at the Federal Correctional Institution, Ft. Worth.

First, the outgoing chaplain was a superstar. He had been promoted to the position of Chief of Chaplains for the Bureau and I was not sure I could follow his example.

Second, this was a very unusual institution. It attempted to help long term inmates make the transition from prison to the community and everything was different. The inmates did not wear uniforms, so it was hard to tell who was an inmate and who was staff.

When I was on the house-hunting trip, I had attended the Friday night "Fish House." This was a chapel program with entertainment was brought in by the volunteers (generally Christian rock music or a Christian puppet show) and the inmates, staff and volunteers got together informally. I was sitting drinking coffee with a man dressed in blue jeans and a checkered shirt. I asked myself, *I wonder what crime he had committed.* We chatted for a while, but I never had the nerve to ask him that question. The following Monday when I went in to meet the Warden, I discovered he was the same man. I was glad I had not asked.

Third, this institution was co-correctional. That is, it housed men and women together. They ate together, worked together, recreated together, but were not supposed to sleep together. Although this made for a more normal environment, it made me nervous. A chaplain friend of mine told me of horror stories he had experienced when he worked in a women's prison.

I had just started this new job and was sitting in the chapel located in the basement of one of the buildings. Several women came in one evening and they looked mean!

"What can I do for you?" I asked.

"Chaplain, we came here to rape you."

"How many of you are there?" I asked. They counted off seven.

"There are seven of us and we're going to rape you."

"Well, all right, but I have to warn you that six of you are going to be disappointed," I said with a smile.

They doubled over in laughter and I never had any more problems with them.

I knew that a sense of humor is necessary to remain sane in prison work. I was never given trouble like this again. They were just testing me to see if I would call for help.

The first day in the office a lieutenant came in and introduced himself. "Chaplain, do you know I found two inmates having sex in your chapel last week?"

"No. Were they two men?" There had been some difficulties with homosexual activities taking place in the chapel in Tallahassee. People are sexual and, if you remove the opposite sex, homosexuality increases.

"No chaplain, it was a man and a woman in the closet," he said scornfully.

"Oh," I was relived. "At least that's natural."

The lieutenant became very angry and stomped out. Nevertheless, I had meant what I said. In Tallahassee, I had even fought a battle to get Playboy Magazine into the institution. I did not want the young men to forget what a woman was and that she was different from the men surrounding him day and night.

The unit management staff at Ft. Worth thought they would play a little game with me. They sent me a new inmate clerk the first week. Ann, we will call her, was about twenty-one years old and a very well endowed young woman. She appeared at work the first day with a very tight skirt and an even tighter sweater.

All day long, every time I passed through a doorway, Ann would try to squeeze through at the same time. She leaned over my shoulder to ask questions. I tried to handle the situation by ignoring it, but at the end of the day, I decided to have a little talk with her. I told her to find clothing that is more appropriate before coming to work the next day. That evening I told Judy what had happened and how I was proud of myself for having handled it so well.

"Ahhhhhhhh!"

"Wake up, Ames!" Judy shook me awake. "You're having a bad dream."

I was covered with sweat.

"You want to tell me about it?" she asked.

"It was terrible. I was running across a big field covered with pretty flowers. Looking over my shoulder, I saw two huge blimps chasing me. They kept trying to crush me. I was so scared!"

"Un-huh. Two huge blimps? I can see you handled that situation with your clerk alright!" she said as she turned over and left me to my terror.

The next day Ann was dressed appropriately and she never troubled me again.

This institution seemed to me to be the least harmful for inmates than any I had ever experienced. We attempted to treat inmates as they would be treated on the streets. Of course we had to watch and not allow them to escape, but that didn't seem to be a problem. Our worry was the inmates escaping back into the facility.

The male inmates came from penitentiaries such as Leavenworth, Atlanta, or McNeil Island; the women from Alderson, at that time the only federal prison that housed women. Both male and female inmates were used to having everything structured for them: when to go to bed, when to get up, what to wear, where to work, what to eat, and what to learn. Here we did away with this structure.

They could stay up all night if they wanted watching TV, but had to be at work on time. We did not wake them up so they had to buy alarm clocks. We did not assign jobs; they had to look at the "want ads" in the Education Department. An inmate would come to me:

"Chaplain, I hear you've got an opening for a clerk."

"Yes I do. Would you take this application and fill it out?"

"An application? Why do I have to fill out an application?"

"Because that's the way we do things here. When you finish, come on back and we'll talk." An hour would pass and the inmate would be back.

"It says here," I would say as I read the application, "that you can type 40 words a minute."

"Yes sir."

"Great. Why don't you go over to the Education Department and take a typing test?"

"Take a test? Don't you believe me?" asked the inmate.

"Sure, but we always have new employees take a typing test." Generally, the test results would be much lower than forty words a minute.

"It says here that you type thirteen words a minute," I told him after reading his test score an hour later.

"I guess I'm rusty."

"Well, our standards here are forty words a minute. Perhaps you could take the typing course in the Education Department. Then when you can type fast enough we will consider you for an opening."

Some newcomers were so frustrated they would show up in my office by the end of their first week.

"How can I get back to Leavenworth, Chaplain?"

"What's the problem?"

"They don't do nothing for you here. I can't even eat my food in peace because of all the women."

"Why is that?"

"Well, Chaplain, I can't talk. You know what I mean?"

I knew what he meant. He didn't want to use swear words in front of women.

"They don't even get you up around here!" he complained.

"How do you expect to do these things when you leave here in a year or so? There will be nobody to get you up for work then."

"I'll get an alarm clock, I guess." He said after a moment of silence.

"Well, you can get one now and at least that problem will be solved."

After a while, and with encouragement, they would become organized and prepare for the reality of leaving prison.

The chapel had a program to get inmates back into church on the outside. We had nurture groups where volunteers led Bible studies and discussions. After an inmate had been a participant in one of these groups he/she was eligible to attend the volunteers' church once a week on week days. In addition, within six months of release they were eligible to attend the Sunday service at the same church. These trips were called religious furloughs. When the inmate went home, the church groups he/she attended would send a letter of reference to the same denomination in the inmate's hometown so they were waiting for them when they got out.

One year we had almost three thousand religious furloughs, with only four minor problems. However, a program like this needed close watching and a large number of volunteers. I started with about one hundred volunteers and worked up to five hundred, but found this was too unwieldy and cut back some.

Another program we had was Family Counseling. I contracted a Catholic Nun and later a counselor with a doctorate in Social Work. There was an office situated next door to the visiting room with a large sign in front of it: "Family Counseling Center." The Bureau still did not approve of such things, so every time we had a visit from the Director we had to take the sign down.

We tried to rehabilitate inmates using a medical model. Diagnose the problem, apply the proper programs, complete the programs, and the inmate would be socially well again. No one expected this to be a perfect system, but it was better than no system at all.

CHAPTER THIRTY

"Good morning," said the short West Indian man with a huge grin on his face. "It sho' is nice to see such a fat man and fat woman walkin' along holdin' hans."

"Thank you, and good morning," I replied as the man walked past us.

"Did you hear what he said? Why did you thank him?" Judy whispered, a bit taken aback.

We were both overweight. I had lost thirty pounds since the beginning of the trip and Judy had lost fifteen, but we were still overweight.

"I think that since the people of Dominica are very poor, he was complementing us on our prosperity. We have enough money to be 'fat.'"

"Oh. I hadn't thought of it that way."

We had been walking back from a hike through Ft. Sills, which dates from the 18th century, where Admiral Hood had kept a watch on Iles Des Saints for signs of the French fleet. We always climbed through every fort we saw or could get to. Judy likes walking and I am an incurable romantic.

We were anchored off Portsmouth, Dominica, for several days with some other cruising buddies. The town was very interesting, although obviously poor. We bought their inexpensive fruit and vegetables and just wandered about.

After spending about a week in Prince Rupert Bay, we raised anchor and made off to the capital, Roseau. Here you need a "boat boy" to take your line ashore. The water is so deep that boats have to lay one or two anchors off their bow and tie a stern line to a coconut tree on shore. The man who helped us was a "log boy," instead of a boat boy, as he was sitting on a floating log when we came in to anchor. I had never anchored this way before and we had to tie four lines together in order to reach the shore. Our boat boy had to work extra hard as I dropped the line into the water twice.

Roseau is a large and dirty town. The people are very friendly, but I guess they do not have enough money to buy garbage cans (we never saw even one) or renew their sewage system so that it can handle grey water. In spite of this, we fell in love with Dominica.

The Saturday market was terrific. Hundreds of people came from allover the island to sell and buy produce. Although the market opens at five in the morning and we did not get there until ten, it was still a very busy and colorful place. The fruit and vegetables were very cheap. We bought a dozen grapefruit for a quarter.

On Sunday, we attended the church in town and then went to the Castaways Hotel, one of the few tourist resorts on the island. Because Dominica does not have fancy beaches like the other islands, it is not a tourist spot. Yet it was the most intriguing island we had visited, unspoiled with a natural beauty.

We took a bus to Trafalgar Falls, which we had heard so much about from our boating friends. The bus took us within a mile or so of the falls, then we hired a guide to lead us up the side of the mountain over huge boulders.

With help from our guide, we arrived at the lower level of the falls. There was a natural pool, about fifteen feet in diameter and three feet deep, formed by the huge boulders and two waterfalls poured down into it. The one on the left was very hot, and the one on the right was very cold. We had worn our bathing suits under our clothes so it was no trouble to doff our shirts and shorts and get into the pool, where we paddled between the two falls. All this was nestled in a canyon amidst a dense rain forest and the beauty of the place overloaded our senses.

Our guide described some of the other beauties of the island for us: the boiling lake, Valley of Desolation, Titrou Gorge, Middleham Falls, and Emerald Pool. All, except the last, demands a guide and up to eight hours of hiking. However, we did not have time to see these sights, as we had to head south before the hurricane season was upon us.

After a year in Ft. Worth without a boat, I began to go crazy. I knew I was in trouble when I dreamed of standing behind the helm of a large yacht with the wind howling around my ears, only to discover that the boat had changed into a house.

We even bought another O'Day, which did nothing to satisfy my craving for sailing. We did not even name it. There were no races for an O'Day fleet and, after sailing around a lake once or twice, I became bored. One weekend we drove three hundred and three miles to Clear Lake, which connects with Galveston Bay, to boat-hunt. There we found our next boat.

She was a twenty-nine foot Erickson sloop. We named her "La Vida" (The Life), and proceeded to sail her every other weekend. This meant a six-hour drive to Clear Lake each way. We made a short sailing trip to Sabine Pass and a longer passage from Galveston to Brownsville for vacation. We found her to be a good sea boat and set about planning a trip to Cozumel, Mexico.

The coffee smell from the mug in my hand helped clear the cobwebs. La Vida was stepping along at six knots under a small storm jib. We had been riding the tail of a "norther" and were making good time to Cozumel.

The waves were large, but the boat was taking them well on a beam reach. The fog of sleep was lifting, thanks to the scalding hot coffee. I noticed that the clouds, which had been with us for three days now, were gone. In their place was a sparkling star-filled sky, topped by a huge full moon.

My watch-mate Laura, our nine-year-old daughter, had come on deck and curled up in the lee side of the cockpit. She was all bundled up in foul weather gear and wool watch cap. I had not thought the Gulf of Mexico could get so cold in May.

I changed my position at the wheel. I was more awake now and began to "feel" the boat better. The moon captured my attention. Its reflected path lay on our course line like a highway through the ocean and I drove the boat right down that road. The beauty of this night was indescribable.

A splash of icy water smacked my face as a wave, larger than most, hit the port quarter. The clock in the cabin struck two bells, and I realized it was time for me to rouse Laura so she could take the helm.

I hesitated.

It was too beautiful a night and I was at one with the boat. *I will let her sleep a little longer,* I decide.

"Wake up Laura," I had said the night before, shaking her.
"Rrrrrrr."
"Come on," I insisted. "It's time for you to take the wheel."

"Oh Daddy," she said in a wee sleepy voice, "don't you know it's not healthy for little girls to get up in the middle of the night?"

She and Alaina had always shared watches with Judy and me. They were very helpful, and once Laura kept us from being run down by a ship off the Yucatan. Parents hardly know how to raise children, and Judy and I were sure ignorant. I have asked God repeatedly why he does not provide instructions to help parents, especially in the teenage years.

The boat rushed forward on a wave and I looked down at the compass card dimly glowing in its red light. I was fifteen degrees off course since I had been steering by the moon and the moon journeys east to west through the night sky. Pulling the boat back on course I wondered how many times I had been led astray by other "bright shinning objects."

I thought how I had always struggled for success and happiness. These seemed like the moon, bright and beautiful, and I followed them. Nevertheless, I often found myself off course.

The happiness and contentment I felt sailing was almost overwhelming. *Can I keep this feeling when I return to Ft. Worth?* I asked myself. *Or will it dissipate and grow dim as the moon does at dawn?*

I could feel the motion of the waves through the hull under my feet. My legs and torso automatically adjusted for the boat's movement through the waves. Without thinking, I felt the boat direct the movements of my hands on the helm. *If all of life could only be this way,* I sighed.

I hear noises from below. Judy and Alaina are stirring. I am surprised I have been at the wheel for four hours and do not feel the least bit tired. In fact, I am a little resentful to turn the boat over to the next watch. My four-hour love affair is over. I go below to sleep.

"Ames! Ames!" said the voice. "Get up, we've got problems." It was Judy shaking me awake.

"What problems?" I mumbled, trying to wake up.

"There's a boat heading for us."

I come awake immediately. We were worried about the pirates we had heard of in the Gulf of Mexico. There had been cases where boats are boarded, crews killed, and the boat was then used to smuggle narcotics. The area had such a bad reputation that our insurance company had refused to cover this trip.

I went up on deck and looked through the glasses. It looked like a white forty-five foot red snapper boat with a red top. I went to the VHF and called him.

"This is the sailing vessel La Vida off your bow and we would like to know your intentions."

"Oh, I haven't seen a boat in a long time. Just wanted to come over for a visit," said the voice over the speaker.

"I would advise you to change course 90 degrees immediately," I said in my gruffest voice. "We are nervous about pirates and if you do not make your turn now, I will arm my crew with the AR 14's and will not be responsible for their actions."

The boat turned 90 degrees and headed away.

"Thank you," I said. I mopped my forehead. We did not even have a flare gun aboard.

Seven days after leaving Galveston, we anchored off the main town of Cozumel in twenty feet of water. After setting the anchor, I sat in the cockpit, stared at the city lights, and listened to the noises of traffic. Judy brought me a heavy shot of bourbon and the kids went to bed. I sat looking, listening and feeling the satisfaction of completing the voyage long after Judy had gone to bed. I had a great feeling of accomplishment.

The trip back was less eventful. We stopped at Isla Mujeres for a few days and then headed back to Texas. We were becalmed for a few days, which gave the girls time to catch some Dorado (also known Mai Mai) for dinner and harass three pilot fish, or Remora, that had attached themselves to the hull. The girls would tease them with a hook and bait, and then jerk it away as they darted in for the bait. One of the fish got smart, went all the way around the boat and came at the bait from the other side.

"Daddy, Daddy!" screamed Laura as she jumped up from her game with the fish and ran to the middle of the boat.

"What's the matter?" I called from the wheel.

"In the water!"

I looked over the side and saw an eight-foot shark, the biggest I had ever seen. Laura told me it had come up at the spot where she was teasing the Remora. That ended the fishing game.

I was very happy with my navigation this trip. It is hard to describe the pleasure I get from looking at the stars through the sextant and then placing little "X's" on a chart. One evening, when we were about three hundred miles offshore, I obtained a late afternoon sun sight, a moon sight, and at twilight a Polar shot. After I worked out the calculations I called up to Judy on deck.

"Judy, look off the bow. You should see a light."

"Which side?"

"The port side."

"Yes," she said with excitement, "there it is!"

It was the light from a mid-gulf weather buoy, which was an excellent check on my abilities with a sextant. Judy decided she would have to buy me another hat, one size larger.

We approached Galveston at nightfall. The entrance was surrounded with ships at anchor and tugboats and pilot boats on the move against the backdrop of the city lights. It was beautiful, but hard to enjoy when we had to concentrate on identifying all the lights.

The wind had died again and we were motoring. Suddenly the boat gave a shudder and the engine stopped.

"What's the matter?" Judy asked, with some panic in her voice. She panics a lot when the engine doesn't work.

"I don't know," I replied. "But I think something is caught in our prop." I put the boat in neutral and re-started the engine. It ran fine. I put the boat in gear, and the engine shuddered and stopped. "I was right. We have something tangled in our prop."

I restarted the engine and tried to shift to reverse to shake off whatever was there, but was unsuccessful. We put up our sails and headed for the mouth of the entrance. I was thankful when a breeze came up half an hour later and, since we were at slack tide, we had little trouble going up the main channel. We were finally able to tie up in a safe haven and get a good night's sleep.

The next morning I dove in the murky waters at the dock to check the prop, but could find nothing wrong. Whatever had been wrapped around it must have fallen off during the night.

The Ft. Worth FCI, although internationally famous as the first co-correctional facility in the world, was not appreciated within the old-line structure of the Bureau. The other Wardens laughed and called it "Candy Hill" and other unprintable names. Pressure was always on to tighten up the institution to make it more like the other institutions in the system.

The courts didn't help either. They kept mandating inmates to the institution who had never been in prison before. This was not what the program was designed for and these inmates started causing problems. It was only a matter of time before those high up in the system, who were protecting us, retired or moved from their positions.

Then the Assistant Director of the Bureau retired and the Regional Director was changed. The new Regional Director did everything in his power to discredit our programs and destroy the goals of Ft. Worth. A few of us fought it as long as we could, but in spite of positive results, which had been thoroughly researched, the end was near. The Warden was told to retire early, one of the Associate Wardens was transferred back to Washington, and soon my phone rang.

"Chaplain," said a friend of mine who was the chaplaincy administrator for the region, "wouldn't you like to go to Los Angeles? I believe you have family living on the West Coast."

"I don't know," I said, "I've only been here about five years." They had stopped moving chaplains every five years and, since we had a nice house, I was not sure I wanted to move yet.

"I really think you would be wise to put in for Terminal Island in Los Angeles."

"What are you saying?" I asked.

"That it's better to go somewhere you want to go than to go somewhere you don't want to go."

"I have to move in any case?"

"That's right. You fought too hard and the new Regional Director wants you out."

"I'll go to Los Angeles."

CHAPTER THIRTY-ONE

Off the coast of Martinique lies a small island named Diamond Rock. Roughly pyramid in shape, it gained its place in maritime history in the early 1800's. The British, who were fighting Napoleon in France, were attempting to blockade Martinique with its excellent harbor at Fort de France. Being short of ships, one enterprising English Captain sent a crew, cannons, powder, and provisions to the top of this island and named it "H.M.S. Diamond Rock." This "ship" was extremely successful in surprising French ships as they sailed through the pass between St. Lucia and Martinique. For eighteen months they held the island until a French fleet captured it.

I had read about the rock in a fictional account some years before, but had not realized it was taken from actual history. As we passed it on our way to St. Lucia we could still see what looked like pock marks where the French shelling had blasted the island. It must have been quite a feat to get the cannons up to the top, which was five hundred-seventy feet above the water.

We stayed in Martinique only one day, just long enough to pick up our mail, since we were still worried about the stories of boats being detained and fined in Guadalupe because they were registered and not documented. The officials in Martinique were very nice, but we entered and cleared at the same time. Martinique is a beautiful island but our experience in Guadalupe had spoiled it for us.

We left on a squally morning. The current between the islands pushed us to the west and by the time we were off Rodney Bay, St. Lucia, we were several miles to the west. We tacked about and started dodging fish trap buoys (clear plastic Pepsi Cola bottles). We were hard on the wind and making good time when the boat suddenly slowed and there was a knocking on the bottom. We had caught ourselves a fish trap. I put the boat in irons, dropped the sail, and went overboard to cut the trap off. My fear of sharks helped me finish the job with great speed, looking over my shoulder all the time. I was back on board, with a few cuts from the barnacles on the rudder, in less than ten minutes.

By four o'clock we were at anchor in beautiful Rodney Bay, which is a mile long and a mile wide. At anchor there were our friends which we had not seen since Dominica: Northern Girl, Mariah, and VI Rotate. We had decided not to anchor close to shore since it was Friday and I figured there would be a lot of loud music from the hotels which lined the shore.

However, as the evening wore on French boats began to arrive. The first one anchored just off our bow with about a foot clearance between his stern and our bow. Others came and anchored on each side of us. I was upset. They had the whole blasted bay in which to anchor. *Why did they anchor next to us, and why so close?* As soon as I could the next morning, I pulled up anchor and moved closer in to where our friends were anchored. If I have to be in a crowded anchorage, I might as well be with friends.

We were welcomed to the Rodney Bay Marina, which lets cruisers use its swimming pool. It was a nice place to gather in the afternoon for a swim in fresh water and a few beers. After nine days we sailed to Marigot Bay, a beautiful land locked bay overcrowded with charter boats.

Getting settled in the Los Angeles area was a nightmare. We had sold our house in Ft. Worth, put money down on a house in Long Beach, and prepared to close in thirty days as agreed.

"Mrs. Smith," I said to our realtor over the phone four weeks later, "what time do we meet to close tomorrow?"

"Oh, we'll have to delay the closing for a week."

"Why is that?" I asked. "Our financing went through all right, didn't it?"

"Oh yes, everything's in order, just a little hang-up on down the line. Don't worry, I'll call you."

I waited a week with no word, so I called back. "Is Mrs. Smith there?"

"Who is calling, please?" asked the secretary.

I told her.

"Oh, Mr. Swartsfager, she's not in just now. I'll leave a message."

There was no return call and each time I called, I got the same message. We had been living in a motel and the government only covered the bill for thirty days. Now we are on our own and I did not have that kind of money.

Two weeks after we were supposed to close, the realtor called.

"I got your messages. I had to go out of town and I just got back."

"We're two weeks past the closing date," I said with irritation. "When are we going to close?"

"Very soon, I think. Maybe next week. I'll call you."

I should have done something then, but my inexperience in these matters made me hesitate. I paid the motel bill for another week. There was no use moving somewhere else, if we could move into the house next week.

The following week I had no word from the now infamous Mrs. Smith. I called several times, but got the same run around. Two more weeks passed and I still could not get through to the realtor. We moved out of the motel and into the home of a couple we had met at church. We paid them four hundred dollars a month for the girls to live in a camper and for us to share an extra bedroom. It was a tight situation, made worse when we discovered the husband was an alcoholic. I was expected to counsel with him when I got home at night after counseling all day at the prison.

Judy and the girls found it hard to live there also. We bought and cooked our own food, but the girls were made to feel incapable of doing anything right. It was also difficult for them as they had to commute long distances by bus to school.

Still not hearing from the real estate woman, I took a day off, went, and sat on the doorstep of the office. At ten she arrived, flustered to find me waiting for her.

"I've been trying to reach you," she said.

"I've left my phone numbers and I have not had any messages that you called." My irritation was turning to anger. I attempted to control myself.

"I must have the wrong number," she said.

"Just tell me when are we closing on the house? I've waited two months past the closing date. I need to know now."

"I'm not sure. There are five houses involved in this and one down the line can't get their financing. Until they do, we can't close."

"You mean to say it could still be months?"

"That's right."

"And I can't close even though our contract says we should have closed two months ago?"

"Those closing dates don't mean anything."

"What?" I could not believe what she was saying.

"That's right. They are just an estimated date."

"That's it. I am canceling out. You've lied to me and you've hidden information from me, so I expect to get all my money back."

"You can't cancel out."

"I can and I will!"

"You can drop out of the deal, but you'll lose your down payment."

"I'm not going to discuss this with you any more. I'll have my lawyer contact your firm. I'll either get my money back or you'll go to court," I said, standing up and seething with anger, I slammed the door behind me.

I was depressed. I went out to the ocean and watched the waves for several hours. Then I called a lawyer friend of mine, who told me to relax because he thought probably a phone call would take care of the situation.

When I got home, I told Judy about what had happened. She was crushed. Our hopes for having a home were shot and we were a long way from being settled anywhere. Later that evening the phone rang.

"It's for you, Ames." Judy handed me the phone.

"Hello?"

"This is Chuck from the Yacht Brokerage in San Pedro. Do you remember me?" said the voice on the phone. When we were house-hunting, I had spoken at length with him concerning live-aboard boats. He was a wiry man in his sixties who I liked from the start because he did not try, as others had, to push a boat we could not use and did not want.

"It was hard trying to get you, but the institution finally gave me your number."

"How can I help you, Chuck?"

"Well, are you still looking for a live-aboard boat?"

"You have something interesting?"

"I have two boats that are in live-aboard slips. One is an old Cal 40, and the other is a CT 41. Both are in the price range you talked about and both can be good live-aboards."

"We'll be over tomorrow morning to see them," I said, beginning to think that perhaps God wanted us to live on a boat.

Filled with excitement, I took the kids out of school and drove the family down to the California Yacht Anchorage. We had seen a CT 41 in Clear Lake, Texas, and liked it, but knew it was not a fast boat.

When I saw the exterior of the CT 41, I fell in love with its traditional design. Her name was Butterfly and she was scruffy looking and needed varnish and paintwork, but seemed to be very solid. The interior was divided into three separate compartments so each of our two girls could have her own quarters (our oldest daughter, Debra, had gotten married in Ft. Worth). Laura's quarters was a very small compartment in the forepeak and she claimed she only had a "nickel."

"There is a lot of teak to varnish," Judy commented.

"Yes, but there are four of us. It should be fun," I replied. I could already visualize the family, sanding and varnishing to our hearts' content. It would be wonderful working together.

"Let's do it." Judy had the same gleam in her eyes as she had when we bought the Catalina 27.

"Are you sure?"

"Yes."

"How do you feel about it, girls?" I asked the kids.

After a moment of silence, they glanced at one another and Alaina said, "Sure, Dad. It has to be better than where we are now."

We put a binder on the boat "subject to sea trials, survey and live-aboard slip." This last was important, as one could not live on a boat without permission and only ten percent of the boats in this marina were given it. If we did not receive permission to live aboard, buying a boat would be useless.

The following day we took the sea trial. The wind was light so all we did was drift around, but even so, she did better than I thought she would. A survey was set up for the following week.

The next Sunday, after I had finished the morning service at the prison, I got another phone call from Chuck.

"Ames," he said, hesitating, "I have bad news."

"What's the problem?" I did not like his tone of voice. "The boat started to sink this morning."

"She what? Sank?"

"Well, her bow almost went under. Water got to the engine and the forepeak of the boat is ruined."

"I'll be right over."

The boat was in dry-dock and I looked her over. I could see nothing wrong.

"We're not sure," Chuck said, trying to brush down his unruly white hair, "but we think it was a loose fitting on one of the electrolysis control through hulls. The engine has been treated, but it will have to have a complete overhaul. The wiring and cushions will also have to be replaced."

"Will the owner's insurance pay for this?"

"Yes, he's covered. Do you still want the boat?"

"I think so, on the condition that he makes the repairs indicated on this survey, the engine, wiring, and cushions, and he pays for any structural problems found on my survey. Does that seem fair? I don't want to buy a boat that will sink on me."

"Seems fair to me, but I'll check it out with the owner."

The next day Chuck called and told me the owner had agreed to the new conditions. I was ecstatic! It would be like having a new engine and new cushions. *Not a bad deal. I wonder if God had arragned this. "Thank you Lord,"* I prayed.

The drawback was it would take several weeks to get the engine overhauled, wiring redone, cushions made and then resurveyed. At least we were on our way to a housing solution.

The marina required an interview before they would grant us permission to move in and live aboard.

"Please be seated," said the marina manager. "I understand you want to live aboard."

"That's correct," I replied. The girls and Judy were sitting patiently on folding chairs dressed in their Sunday best. They had been required to come along.

"You are a chaplain?"

"Yes."

"Your wife works where?" the manager asked.

"I work for Rockwell International," Judy answered, letting the manager know she was in the room and he could ask her questions directly.

He turned to the girls.

"What do you do on weekends?" he asked them.

They were stunned. They had not expected this question. I was anxious about their answer, especially seeing the way their faces were screwed up. I could tell they were trying to control themselves.

"Oh," said Alaina, "we read a lot."

"And we listen to music tapes . . . with earphones," said Laura.

"Sometimes we go to town," said Alaina.

"On Sundays," said Laura, "we go to church."

I heaved a sigh of relief when the manager said we could live aboard.

"What a creep!" Alaina exclaimed when we got into the car. "What did he expect us to say? That we have wild parties every weekend?"

"I was going to tell him that on Saturdays we generally run up and down the docks throwing rotten eggs at boats," said Laura with a giggle. "And on Sundays we . . ."

I was glad they did not.

It was not until February fifteenth, a month after we had moved into the "Cultural Center," an old run down apartment house in San Pedro, and six months after moving to Los Angeles, that Butterfly became ours and we were able to move aboard. We carried boxes and boxes onto the boat, positive they would not all fit. Somehow they did.

"The boat seems so spacious," said Judy, looking around her.

"Yes it does, doesn't it?"

"That was sneaky."

"What?" I asked

"Making us live in motels, other people's houses, campers, trailers, and finally packing us into that tiny apartment," she teased. "After that anything looks great." She sighed, "Anyway it is wonderful to be settled at last." Then she gave me a kiss.

CHAPTER THIRTY-TWO

We set sail from Marigot Bay, St. Lucia, just before dawn, feeling our way out the narrow passage. By the time we were clear of the bay, the sun was just cutting the horizon. It was a beautiful morning and we had only sixty miles to sail before sunset.

We were heading for the small island of Bequia in the Grenadines. Hearing the many horror stories regarding crime and aggressive boat boys on St. Vincent, we had decided to by-pass it.

We sailed down the coast of St. Lucia until we were off Soufriere where we could see the famous pinnacles, The Pitons. From here we headed toward St. Vincent. It was a beautiful broad reach and the boat romped along making seven knots.

We drifted along as we waited for the wind to come forward again. This often happened as we passed an island. This time, however, the wind slammed into us at more than thirty knots. I scrambled to take down the mizzen and ease the pressure on the boat. As I was doing this, I bumped the binnacle.

"Awak!" yelled Judy. "Help!"

The sail had dropped on her, but that had happened before and I did not understand why she was yelling for help. I lifted up the sail and looked. She was sitting with the wheel in her lap, looking up at me with questioning eyes.

"It broke," she said.

"Can you steer?" I asked.

"A little."

I opened the port lazarette (a locker) where we keep spare pieces of rope and grabbed one. Straightening the binnacle, I tied it to the guardrail rails on either side of the binnacle. With this rig, we made it to port by sunset.

The time at Bequia was spent repairing the binnacle base. I had a large piece of teak stored down in the forward bilge for just such a purpose so I loaded it into the dinghy and went to town in search of a carpenter.

Behind the Anglican Church there were a couple of work shops, one of them a carpenter shop. Inside was a newly completed coffin, some partially built cabinets, and two men. The elder one seemed to be in charge.

"Excuse me, sir," I said.

"Yes mon, can I help you?"

I explained that I needed the teak cut into four pieces and a four-inch hole cut out of each.

"I can cut them mon, but I have to saw the holes."

"Don't worry, I have a hole cutter for a half inch drill bit." I had bought the hole cutter before we left the States, but found it would not work on my three-eighth inch drill. It was a wicked looking thing with a regular drill bit in the center and an arm with a razor sharp cutter that swung around the diameter.

"That a real cutter, mon." The carpenter turned the cutting bit around in his hand, looking at it closely. "Yes mon, a real cutter."

"It goes in a drill press," I said, realizing he wasn't sure how it worked. A smile lit up his face.

"Sho' do," he said walking over to his drill press. "We make good holes with this cutter, mon."

With the aid of his assistant, he sawed the wood, then took one piece and held it on the drill press while his assistant plugged in the power cord.

"She don' turn so good," he explained.

"Perhaps you should clamp the wood down."

"No trouble, mon," he said while the cutter whirled around. "She be jus' fine."

The bit hit the wood and almost spun the man across the room.

"Pull de plug man! Pull de plug!" he shouted. The assistant leaped to comply and the drill wound to a stop.

"I think it would work better if you clamp it down," I said again.

"Not to worry, mon," he said. "Dis time I use bot' han's."

Again the helper plugged it in. I couldn't watch and waited outside, praying no one would get hurt. When it was finished, I offered the cutting tool to the master carpenter.

"No, mon! That ting is dangerous mon," he said, backing away from the tool in my outstretched hand.

With the help of Jim from Northern Girl, who was anchored nearby, I spent the next five days making a new base for the binnacle. Most of that time I was hanging upside down in the port lazarette attempting to take the steering gear apart and put it back together again.

Getting to know a new boat is like trying to make out on a first date. You know what you want to do but you are not sure how to get there. Our new boat had innumerable little things that needed correcting. To begin with, the one hundred-twenty volt wiring was in backwards and the boat was not properly grounded, so I rewired the system.

The poor gal needed intensive care for her teak and paint, so I gathered the family together for our first "Teak Weekend." It was going to be great fun.

After eight hours we stopped.

"We've sanded, scraped and bleached," said Judy, mopping her brow. "Will we ever get done?"

"Sure honey," I said as I lit up the bar-b-que. I knew that after we all had a wonderful dinner everyone would be ready to continue on the morrow.

"We'll have the sanding done by tomorrow night," I said, turning over the ribs. "Next weekend we can start varnishing."

"Who's we?" asked Alaina, looking up from her book. "And who said anything about tomorrow, as far as that goes?"

"Well, I thought we should finish what we start," I said confidently.

"I have to go to a birthday party tomorrow, Daddy," said Laura, who was trying to comb her long chestnut hair after having showered.

"I have a date," announced Alaina, who was always quick thinking.

"Don't look at me," said Judy, busying herself making a salad.

I really could not expect the family to work on the teak every weekend, so I decided to have only one "Teak Weekend" a month.

Over the next three weeks, I was able to finish the preparation of the teak by myself, in time for our second teak weekend.

"I have a band rehearsal," claimed Laura. "It's in the afternoon, but I have to practice in the morning."

"Gee, Dad," said Alaina, "I've been invited to go racing on the Cal 20's."

I looked at Judy, and she looked away. I could tell she was trying to think of a good excuse.

"No you don't Judy. We have to get this finished."

It was not always this bad, but there were many times when my daughters had "things to do" on Teak Weekend. Somehow the boat was patched and painted and began to look great. Even though we got it in February, we did not make our first sail until the end of March. The official reason was that I had many repairs to do. The unofficial reason was she was a huge boat and I was afraid to sail her.

"Look at the sea lions, Dad!" cried Laura as Butterfly made her maiden voyage with us as owners through the Los Angeles entrance. The sea lions were sitting on the buoys, bobbing in our wake. There was a nice wind this afternoon and the sun shown through the hazy moisture laden air while pelicans floated on the air over us. We sailed a few miles out and Alaina yelled and pointed ahead of us.

"There are porpoises! Lots of them!"

The school of porpoises joined us for a few minutes and then disappeared.

"What was that?" cried Judy, looking over the side. "That's the biggest porpoise I've ever seen!"

"Shhhhhhhhhhh!"

I jumped. To my starboard was a waterspout. It was a whale.

"Shhhhhhhhhhhh!"

There was another whale to port. This one dived, went right under us and came up on the other side.

I was mesmerized by the massiveness of these creatures. They were longer than the boat. Their backs were grey and had barnacles scattered over them. One of them, I swear, looked me right in the eye. Suddenly they were gone. There was silence from the crew.

"Did you see what I saw?" asked Alaina in a hushed voice.

"Yes," said Laura thoughtfully, "but I'm not so sure I liked those whales being so near."

"They were bigger than the boat," Judy added in wonderment. I was too shocked to speak.

When we got back in, we were unusually quiet. All of us were thinking about the wonderful marine life we had seen.

"They all came out to welcome Butterfly!" explained Laura.

For the next few years, we enjoyed sailing the islands off Los Angeles: Catalina, Santa Barbara, Santa Cruz, Anacapa, San Clemente and Santa

Rosa. They were interesting and fun places to go for weekend (for us this was Fridays and Saturdays) cruises.

As I gained confidence, I began to dream of longer cruises. Consequently, the day after Christmas in 1982, we dropped our dock lines and headed for Cabo San Lucas at the southern most end of Baja California.

My daughters were unhappy because we had to take down the Christmas decorations on Christmas afternoon.

"I don't feel like Christmas," complained Laura.

"I don't really want to make this trip." Alaina was pouting, knowing she would not see her boyfriend for a month.

I was ready and could hardly wait, but leaving would have been better if the girls had been happy. It was difficult for Judy to get a month off from work and Christmas was the only chance she would have for an extended vacation.

The first night I was on watch with Laura.

"Dad look!" she shouted. "It really is Christmas!"

I looked to where she was pointing. Gamboling along in our bow wave were porpoise. As they swam alongside, they would leave the water luminescent with a phosphorescent glow. Moreover, when they leaped through the waves, the running lights reflected red on the starboard ones and green on the port ones.

"It's like having red and green reindeer porpoise pulling our boat," she laughed. "It's really Christmas now."

We froze to death the first four days, three of which we had to motor since there was little wind. After passing Isla Cedros the weather changed drastically. One day we were wearing long johns, jeans, long sleeved shirts, wool sweaters and foul weather gear topped with wool hats, and the next we were running around the deck in bathing suits.

The wind came up and we sailed the next three days, dropping anchor in Cabo San Lucas exactly seven days from the time we dropped our dock lines. It was a strange new world of warmth and clear waters.

Lest we become too complacent, the engine refused to run the following day and I found a cracked fuel line fitting. While the family shopped and had fun, I shopped for a new fuel fitting. After several days, I was able to jury rig another fuel line.

Then I spent the next two days doing the paper work for obtaining fuel, buying the fuel, and clearing port. We had been at anchor eight days, but I saw very little of the country.

We had planned to sail back in three stages. The first leg would be to Bahia Marguerita, the second to Tortuga, and the third to San Diego. We had to hold up in Bahia Marguerita to wait for a storm to subside and my "Montezuma's revenge" to go away. Huge schools of porpoise that stretched from horizon to horizon and the sighting of many California Gray whales punctuated the trip to Tortuga.

When we left Tortuga and headed up past Isla Cedros the weather became wild and cold. Back in the long johns and coats, we slogged to windward with the main set and the engine doing the best it could, which was about three knots. For two days we were battered, and then the engine developed fuel problems. It would run for about twenty minutes and then quit. I changed fuel filters twice, but that was not the problem. I would bleed the engine, start it again, and twenty minutes later end up repeating the whole process.

"Now for the Baja Net weather report," said my short wave receiver. We did not have a Ham radio at the time, but I had borrowed this little receiver.

"All you folks in the harbors should stay there. There is a big storm coming your way. If you are not in a harbor, we suggest you find one as soon as possible. We are expecting very high winds with this one. It should hit the upper coast of Baja sometime late this morning . . ."

I looked over the chart and found the nearest safe port was St. Martin, an island ten miles directly to windward and close to the mainland. It was already nine in the morning. I could not trust the engine to get us to a safe harbor so we fell off and boadreached with reefed main, mizzen and working jib directly away from the land.

As the day passed, the wind and waves increased. They were coming straight from Japan with nothing to slow them down. My goal was to get as far offshore as I could. We were making three or four knots and the wind began to get even stronger, so I went up and furled the main.

Just after dark, a huge wave crashed over the bow as it buried itself in its crest. Water came sluicing down the deck two feet deep. There was a crashing on the hull at the bow.

I made my way to the bow and found that the lashings on the anchor had been torn loose. I called to Judy to come forward to help. As we worked, we would be up to our waists in cold sea water and then, as the bow rose, be tossed into the air. It took an hour and a half of pure determination to get the anchor back on deck and secured to the bollards.

No sooner had we gotten back to the safety of the cockpit than we heard a loud ripping and flapping sound from forward. The jib had split about a third of the way up the luff. *This is as far as we are going* to *get,* I thought, as my stomach knotted with anxiety.

Judy and I were so beat after the anchor foray that I sent Laura and Alaina to the foredeck to take down the jib before it ripped more. Laying the boat to the wind with the reefed mizzen, I thought they would never get it down. It was very hard to wait while they struggled but I knew I could not do it right then. I was just too worn out after getting the anchor aboard.

I heard shouting from the foredeck, but little by little the sail came down, and was taken off the stay and pushed down the forepeak hatch. When the girls got back to the cockpit Alaina raced below to lock the fore hatch while Laura slumped onto the stern cushion. I asked her what she had been yelling.

"I'm not sure whether I was praying or cursing," she said as exhaustion played across her face. "I kept yelling 'Jesus! Jesus!'"

I went down and figured our DR (dead reckoning) position. We were forty-five miles from the mainland, and, if we drifted with the wind, would probably stay clear of land.

"Ames," called Judy, leaning into the companionway hatch, "the mizzen is going."

I came up on deck to see the reefed mizzen shred itself and disappear into the howling wind.

"Let's take it down," I yelled above the wind to Judy. The girls were below, exhausted after their wrestling match with the jib. Feeling safe in the protected cockpit, I did not snap my lifeline on. As we were lowering the remnants of the sail, I grabbed the halyard shackle to take it off, and at the same time the boat healed over as it climbed the side of a steep wave. I lost my footing and found myself hanging over the water, one hand on the halyard wire to keep me on board. The wire cut through my hand as I waited for what seemed like hours for the boat to get back on its feet again. We finally leveled off and I opened the shackle and secured the line as fast as possible. Before I had finished the boat heeled over again, but this time I was ready.

Grabbing the wheel, I turned it to windward and locked it down. Now the boat lay with its starboard bow toward the waves and she rode a lot easier. After assigning crew to keep watch from the companionway, I went below and fell into an exhausted sleep.

I awoke to sun streaming into the cabin. It was quiet and peaceful.

The storm is over! I rejoiced as I made my way to the companionway. Opening up the hatch, I stuck my head out. The wind, which had been muted down below, screamed at me. I looked up and saw a wave higher than our spreaders coming toward us. The boat lifted to it like a duck on a pond and then, at the top of the wave, heeled a little more with the blast of wind and slid down the backside. I closed the hatch. Butterfly was doing just fine.

I rechecked the engine, trying to find out what was wrong with it, while Judy and the girls lined up in the forward compartment to sew the jib. After several hours, I decided that the problem was in the fuel tank air intakes. There was water in them, and I figured a vacuum was being created in the fuel tanks so the fuel could not get to the engine. I was wrong, but it seemed logical at the time. Actually, the problem was rusty scale the size of a quarter, which plugged the fuel outlets.

The next morning, when I had the engine running again, I went topside. It had calmed down so I decided to raise the main and head for San Diego. I took off the gaskets and hauled the sail up. Going back to the cockpit, I let the boat falloff a little to fill the sail. No sooner had I done this than I realized the wind was still strong . . . much too strong for that old sail.

As I ran forward to untie the halyard there was a loud ripping sound. The main had ripped across the first set of reef points. Getting the sail down as fast as possible, I decided to wait until the next day before getting underway again.

With the wind down to less than ten knots we motor-sailed with the main reefed to the second set of reef points. A day and a half later, we motored past Ensenada, Mexico. As night fell, the weather deteriorated and numerous thunderstorms with squall lines crossed our path.

At times, the light off Point Lobo was completely obscured. I was fearful the engine would quit as we went through the entrance channel to San Diego. I knew I could clear the engine in less than ten minutes, but in ten minutes, we could get ourselves in real trouble. The wind had backed to the north-west and was blowing fifteen knots between the squalls. I decided to sail in under reefed main alone. After an anxious hour sailing down the long San Diego Channel, we docked at the customs dock, where I fell into an exhausted sleep. We had made it back to the States, but our sails were ruined.

We borrowed sails from our friend Edie, who also had a CT 41 (Pacific Wind) and was tied up across from us at our marina. Judy and I had an uneventful sail up the coast to Los Angeles. Our girls had left with Edie saying they wanted to get back to school. Except for being very cold the whole time, the trip was not bad. We arrived back at our slip at three in the morning on the second day, and after catching a few hours sleep, I left for work at seven-thirty.

CHAPTER THIRTY-THREE

We left Bequia and sailed past West Cay and Pigeon Island to Canouan Island, a tropical island about three miles long, and a mile and a half at its widest point. The sail, which took only a few hours, was uneventful. The steering worked fine, but we were aware that the compass needed adjustment. Sailing from island to island, one does not really need a compass, as the islands are easy to see and fairly close together. But we knew we'd have to deal with it sooner or later.

We sailed past the north end of the island with its low hills and eased our way into Charleston Bay anchorage. Northern Girl and Mariah were at anchor and had already gone ashore to clear from the Grenadines for Grenada. After lunch, Judy and I decided to do the same. We tied up our dinghy at the pier, climbed the rickety ladder to the dock, and walked into "town." There was no real town, just a collection of houses along a muddy rutted path that served for a road. Tethered along the road were goats which eyed us mournfully and occasionally bleated at our passing.

We had been told to go to the police station to get our clearance out. At the station, we waited for some time before being told to return in the morning as the customs man was at the airport and would not return today.

"Come back at eight in the morning," said the uniformed police officer. "He will be here for sure."

As we walked down the road, a man riding a burro came up on us.

"Good day," he said with huge smile. "How are you doin' dis fine day." He was seated on the rump of the small animal, with his feet hanging just off the road. He wore a beat up straw hat, a shirt full of holes and denim pants that were much too small.

"Good afternoon," I replied.

"That's a cute burro," Judy added.

The man's smile increased. "It's not a burro. It's my taxi."

"Your taxi?"

"Yes man, I have two taxis. I am rich." The burro became a little skittish and he swatted it with the switch in his hand. "Stand still now girl," he said. "Yes, I rich man to have two such fine taxis."

"This is a nice looking burro," Judy said as she reached out to pet it. The animal shifted her weight and looked back at Judy, who quickly removed her hand. It started to turn towards her but was stopped by the owner's switch.

"She not very polite," he explained. "How you like our island?"

"It's beautiful," I said.

"Very pretty," Judy added.

"Yes Very pretty. Soon they's goin' to build a hotel over there," he said, pointing to the hills with his switch. "A big one and lots of people come. I make more rich with my taxies."

"I'm sure you'll do well," I lied.

"Be very rich. Got to go now. Have to pick up someone. Good day." With a few swats from his stick, the animal began to move down the road.

Judy and I continued walking, slower so we would not pass the taxi.

That night it rained. That morning it rained. At seven-thirty it was still raining. Maybe raining is not the correct word. If you have ever stood under a lukewarm shower at full force, then you have some idea of the way it was raining.

I jumped into the dinghy and bailed it out. As I headed towards shore, I could see Judy waving to me from the cockpit. *What a miserable day,* I thought, as I tried to ignore the water running down my neck.

I arrived at the police station at eight, happy to get inside out of the downpour. The office was very dark but a police officer sat behind the desk.

"Good morning," I said.

"Good mornin," the officer replied.

"I've come to make my clearance to Grenada."

"The custom man not here yet, but he com' anytime."

"It's kind of dark in here."

"We have no power all night. Dis telephone do not even work."

"That must make things difficult for you."

"Oh yes, sometimes. But nothing happn' here. If someone steal where he gonna go?"

"I guess you're right about that." I looked at my watch and saw it was almost nine o'clock. "Do you think the customs man will come soon?"

"I t'ink so. He's sure to be here now."

"Can we call him?"

"The phone do not work," he said with a shrug of his shoulders.

The wind was blowing hard from the south-east and the rain was coming down even harder than before. I went out on the open porch and stood surveying a couple of goats pegged across the street. They did not look too happy.

An hour later, I was bored out of my skull.

"Is there any way we can find out what happened to the customs officer?"

"I don't know," said the officer. "Maybe he went to clear the plane. There was supposed to be a airplane from Union Island dis mornin'" He looked up at the sky and frowned. "It might not come though. He not here yet, mon I sure he get here soon though."

At eleven a new officer came on duty.

"I'll stop by his house," he said, "cause I got to go to the airport to look for the plane."

A half hour later the lights came on and the phone rang.

"The customs man say fo' you to go to his house. It too wet from him to come here."

I got the directions and found myself scrambling up a trail through the mud to a road that ran on the ridge behind the station. I fell in the mud a couple of times, but did not really mind because I was soon to see the elusive customs man.

I turned right on the trail past the "rusty truck that's broken, you know," went to the front door and knocked. The customs man took one look at me and told me to come around to the back. I could understand why when I glimpsed myself in a mirror inside the house.

"It being too wet to go out today," he said with a smile, as he brought his rubber stamp down with a thump. "Best to stay inside."

The institution at Terminal Island did not have any special programs, nor did it provide much action for volunteers. The chapel consisted of a Chapel, a small group room and two offices. We could manage four groups at night, or ten groups a week. This was very different from the fifty to sixty groups I had in Ft. Worth. I was bored.

To find excitement, I looked outside the institution to sailing and to singing sea shanties. I had been collecting sea songs for ten years or more and even before we left on our missionary adventures in Honduras, I had bought a banjo and Judy a guitar. I knew a banjo must be easier to play because it only has five strings while a guitar has six.

I was wrong!

Over the years, we had learned a few sea songs. One night we had a dock party to entertain our friends and, to our surprise, they really enjoyed the music we made. One of them asked us to play for a dinner, and soon we found ourselves playing for yacht clubs, Maritime Museums, colleges, and even a tour of Wyoming libraries. Our favorite place to play was Canetti's Seafood Restaurant in San Pedro. We played there the first Friday night of each month and had a great time. We did not make a lot of money playing, but we were able to buy better instruments and an amplifier.

Meanwhile, things were popping at the institution. The objectives there changed so quickly that each day we had to ask what our mission was for the day. We were given two months notice that we were going to have to stuff three hundred jail prisoners in our already overcrowded institution. The staff worked day and night to prepare, but the work took its toll. Several mid-management and executive staff became so stressed out that their marriages began to crack. They were seldom at home, and when they were, they did not communicate.

We started taking staff out for an evening cruise of the harbor. At least one Monday evening a month we set forth with ten to twelve staff members and their wives or significant others (children were not allowed). The rules were to hold hands, enjoy the sunset, and watch the city lights trying to compete with the heavenly stars. Anyone caught talking about work would be made to walk the plank.

In 1986, Los Angeles was preparing for the Olympics. The institution was also in the throes of preparing emergency action plans. These plans became huge documents that weighed about twenty pounds each and covered every imaginable situation (and some that could not be imagined). The plans were never used, but many hours of staff time were spent on them.

Part of this plan included the possibility that the island could be completely cut off from the mainland by terrorists. I suppose this might have been possible, as Terminal Island is separated from Long Beach and Los Angeles by just three bridges and the institution was to be the Federal jail for the event. We were expecting some eight hundred detainees (mostly people trying to assassinate the president), or Russians, or maybe even spies trying to steal our state secrets.

The plan included me as the "Commodore" in charge of three Coast Guard boats because I was the only licensed captain on the staff. These boats could bring staff to and from work, as well as prisoners to the institution. They were going to charter my Butterfly to help bring food to staff housing. I met and had a quick run through with the Coast Guard. The Olympics came and went and we processed a total of three jail prisoners due to the Olympics. I did not even get to be a "Commodore."

After eight years in Terminal Island, I was asked to transfer to another institution. Actually, I was told I had been in one place too long and they needed my expertise in opening a new institution in Marianna, Florida. Looking at a map, I discovered Marianna was located fifty miles from the Gulf of Mexico.

"You'll have to sell your boat," said the Controller. "We'll pay for the broker's fee."

"I would rather have the time off to sail it through the Panama Canal and around to Panama City, Florida. It'll only take six weeks or less."

"You heard what the Warden said," the comptroller cut in. "They need you now."

"I know, but I have ten weeks of vacation on the books and it wouldn't cost the system anything."

"Nope. They want you there in 30 days. Sorry."

"You will have to move the boat then," I stated.

"We don't move boats."

"You move mobile homes," I said.

"Yes we do."

"Then you can move my boat. There's no difference. I have lived on it for eight years, so it's certainly not only for recreational purposes."

"I don't think we can do that."

I spent the next two days looking through past GSA decisions regarding moving and then I found it. A staff sergeant in the Air Force had his boat moved because it was his residence. I took the information to the business manager.

"Well," he said, "this does look like a precedent. "Let's try it."

Watching poor Butterfly hang in the air as the flat bed truck maneuvered under her was a sad moment. We had taken off her railings, bow sprite, and taped up all the teak trying to prepare her for the long journey. The crane operator lowered her gently onto a cradle and the driver tied her down. Several friends who had come to share in the experience produced beer and we all said a sad "Bon Voyage" to Butterfly as the trailer pulled away.

CHAPTER THIRTY-FOUR

We sailed from Canouan the next morning, rounding Glossy Hill Point at eight. I was disappointed we did not have time to stop at Tobago Cays, one of the most beautiful snorkeling areas in the Caribbean. We passed Mayeau and headed through the beautiful clear water in the channel between Palm Island and Union Island.

"Look out for a reef ahead," I told Judy. Grand de Coi reef was shown on the chart with a buoy marking it.

"I see it," yelled Judy from the bow. I looked and saw water breaking with the brown color of reef and rocks. The reef was much bigger than it looked on the chart, and the buoy seemed to be right in the middle of it instead of on the west side as indicated.

I swung the boat to starboard and watched the depth sounder go from thirty feet, to twenty-five, then to twenty; the shoaling continued to fifteen feet. This always makes me nervous. I knew the water should go back up to at least twenty feet soon. However, time stopped as the depth said thirteen feet. I was about ready to turn one hundred-eighty degrees, when the sounder flickered back to fourteen feet, then sixteen, and when we reached twenty I was greatly relieved.

The wind picked up as we sailed on a broad reach south to Carriacou, the first island of the Grenada group, and we were really flying when we passed Rapid Point. Coming into the wind off Jack-a-Dan Rock, we motored into the anchorage off the town of Hillsborough. It was still early in the afternoon so we went to shore to clear customs and immigration. The town was very interesting and clearing customs was easy-too easy. We had read in a cruising guide that we had to obtain a cruising permit at this point. After customs, the man at immigration stamped our papers.

"Don't we need a cruising permit?" I asked.

"What is a cruising permit?" the officer asked.

"Some kind of official paper that says it's all right to sail in Grenada," I explained.

"Oh no," he said. "The stamp in your passport is all you need."

"Oh, all right." I thanked him, happy not to have any more paperwork to fill out. It was strange, as always before we were given an official document to show the boat was cleared into the country. It made me nervous.

We drove across the country to our new home in Panama City, Florida, with me driving one car and Judy following in the other.

At lunch the first day she said, "What's wrong with you?"

"What do you mean?"

"You're normally a good driver, but you're driving me crazy."

"How is that?" I asked

"You slow down at every underpass. I almost ran into you a few times."

"Oh," I said, "I'm just looking."

"For what?"

"I'm looking for scrape marks. The boat was sitting high on the trailer. What if they hit an overpass?"

"Oh Ames!" she said disgustedly. "Just drive normal from now on, or they may have to scrape you from an underpass!"

After eighteen years in the Bureau of Prisons one would think I would not be nervous starting at a new facility. I was. There is a minute of panic when I enter a new institution for the first time. I feel as if I know absolutely nothing.

I felt anxious as I walked up to the door of the warehouse that housed the temporary offices of the Federal Correctional Institution at Marianna, Florida. The Warden welcomed me and had the staff find me a desk. The warehouse was filling up with the furniture and supplies needed to furnish a complete prison. This institution was to be different from any other in the Bureau. It would have the first Federal Women's Camp for minimum custody women (two hundred-fifty); the first Federal Women's High Security Unit, which housed one hundred-fifteen of the toughest women in the United States, in addition to a five hundred man (turned out to be a thousand man) Federal Correctional Institution.

It was a very windy day when Butterfly was lowered into the water in Panama City. After checking the through hulls and bilges, I started the engine. As I backed her out of the loading slip, I knew immediately I was in trouble, as the wind caught the boat and shoved her downwind toward the dock we were supposed to tie up to. I threw the engine full throttle into reverse and we still passed the dock, doing three knots. After several attempts I got the boat stopped. During a lull in the wind, I was able to back up to the dock and get her secured.

"It looks like she wants to head on out," said Judy.

"She's been away from the water too long," I agreed. "We need to take a trip soon."

Our first trip was to move the boat to our marina, which was about five miles away through very shallow water. We ran aground within one hundred yards of the dock. I was used to the bouyage system on the West Coast where there was plenty of deep water around markers. In Florida, one has to scrape the markers in order to stay in the channel. Since I did not scrape, I thumped aground. After two hours of tugging with various small boats that came by, we were able to get out of the mud and motor to St. Andrew Marina.

St. Andrew Marina was not much. There were no bathrooms or showers, and we had to side tie. It was not bad until a thunderstorm came along to throw us up against the dock. We had problems even after we put out a breast anchor to windward. The price was right, however, and the people great.

After a few trips to Shell Island, five miles away by a narrow channel, we were bored with it and did not spend many weekends sailing. We did decide to take a sail the following September to the Dry Tortugas, a small group of islands located about fifty miles to the west of Key West and twenty-five miles north of Cuba.

With our middle daughter Alaina, we set sail for these interesting little islands. Butterfly danced and curtsied through the choppy waves of the Gulf of Mexico, always happiest when off on a long voyage. As I stood at the helm, I could hear her talking to me.

"*Well, we're finally off!*" she cried exuberantly, the wind singing in her sails. "*I was tired of that crummy bay. I can stretch my sails in the wind and breathe deeply of the salt sea air. My spars creak from lack of use when I plunge my bow into each cresting wave. I am alive again! At last, finally, I am alive!*"

We romped through the thunder squalls we could not avoid, and in three days arrived at the Dry Tortugas. Navigating the narrow channel around Ft. Jefferson, we dropped our hook in twenty feet of water.

"*Is that all?*" Butterfly sighed. "*I was just getting started. How long are we going to be here?*" She wiggled down and settled in at the end of her anchor line.

Pirates used to hang out here and attack ships plying the channel between Cuba and Florida. Fort Jefferson, almost one hundred years in the building, sits on one of the little islands. It is a true fortress with a moat, ramparts and the works. It has a small temporary chapel, but the permanent chapel was never built.

"Dad! Hey, Dad!" called Alaina as she waded toward me. We had been snorkeling on a small reef, about a half mile from the beach at Ft. Jefferson.

"What is it?" I called back.

"What kind of fish is that following me?"

I looked and saw a silver fish about three feet long. Then he turned his head and looked at me and I saw a mouth full of very sharp needle like teeth. It looked as if he were grinning at some joke he had heard.

"It looks like a barracuda," I said, trying to keep the panic I felt out of my voice. "You and mother go on back to the shore."

"What's the problem?" yelled Judy, who was a few yards away from us.

"Go to shore! You and Alaina go to shore!"

"Now," I said to the mouth full of teeth. "It's just you and me." I started swimming slowly toward shore.

"They turn sideways toward you when they are about to attack," someone had told me. This fish was turning sideways. *Is he attacking? Do not panic.*

I was swimming on my back, as I did not want to make a lot of splashing with my hands. "A barracuda will sometimes attack a bright flashing object like a ring," someone else had said. *A ring!* I covered my wedding ring with one hand so Mr. Teeth would not see it.

Is he still there? I wondered. Lifting up my head, I looked. Yes, there he is, about three inches from my flippers.

Maybe he'll bite my flippers and not me, I hoped.

"Sometimes before they attack," I remember someone saying, "they open their mouths."

Is his mouth open or *closed?* I did not remember. Again, I raised my head and as I did, I lost buoyancy and started splashing.

My hand! The ring! It's flashing! I could almost feel the teeth of the monster raking the bones of my hand as he gulped my ring.

"No," I said aloud, "don't panic. Nothing's happened yet." *But was his mouth open or closed?* I could not remember. I rose up again to see, being more careful this time. It was open.

"0 God," I prayed, *"Help me get out of this."*

Clunk!

My head hit a stone on the bottom. I was ashore. I looked at my flippers. No barracuda there. Mr. Teeth had given up.

Judy ran to me as I came out of the water.

"Are you all right?" she asked as she hugged me tightly.

"Sure, honey."

"I was so afraid!" she said. "I'm so scared of sharks and . . ."

"No, no. It was just a barracuda," I said.

"Weren't you afraid though?" asked Alaina.

"Who me? Afraid of a little barracuda? You have to be kidding."

"Well, if it wasn't a shark, let's go back in over here," said Judy. "It looks like good snorkeling."

"**I** think we should all just lie on the beach for awhile," I replied. To myself I said, *I'll be damned if I give that toothy monster a second chance.*

We stayed in the Dry Tortugas a few days, but we ran out of gas for the dingy. One of the gas cans, which we had left in the dingy on the stern davits while we were sailing, had spilled. Without gas for the dinghy engine, we were unable to explore.

We set out one evening for Tampa/St. Petersburg. As we looked back at the sunset, we saw a huge cloud cover the island. For the next several hours we could see lightning lashing the island and were very happy we had decided to leave when we did.

The sun was rising as Butterfly slipped through the channel into Tampa Bay and passed under the new suspension bridge. We were able to sail the rest of the way to the Yacht Harbor in St. Petersburg.

Spray was flying and the boat pounding into the head seas as we left the channel headed for home after only a few days exploring St. Petersburg. The first northerly of the year had hit and the wind was blowing twenty knots from the northwest. The weather report predicted it would slowly shift to the north, then to the north-west, and finally die down some.

It took forty-nine hours to sail from St. Petersburg Marina to Panama City, a distance of two hundred twenty-eight miles. For us, under a reefed mizzen and working jib, this was a record run.

The institution at Marianna was an extremely difficult one for me. We could not find a Catholic Chaplain, and it took us a while to find a second Protestant Chaplain. Meanwhile, I was either conducting or supervising six services every Sunday. When we finally were assigned a second Chaplain, he joined the Army Reserve and took three months off for training. Because we lived in Panama City (this was my decision, so we could live on the boat), the commute took an hour and a half. Many times I had to stay in a motel because there was not time to get home to sleep and return the next morning. I was worn out, exhausted, and pretty much burnt out. I was considering retirement.

For all of this, I enjoyed the institution. I had always believed that the way a chapel program started out would affect the future programs. If the first programs had no support from the staff or inmates, the chaplain that followed would have the same problems. For this reason, I worked doubly hard to create a good program with a lot of depth.

Both the inmates and the staff gave the program support. It did not take long to fill the chapel to overflowing. Our services were in three languages: English, Spanish and French (for the Haitians). It was a place of peace, a place where religious groups (Islamic, Jewish, Seventh Day Adventists, Jehovah's witnesses, Catholics, and Christians) met without tension.

One holy week we had a service in the men's unit. We had no Catholic priest at the time. I set up a Christian service for Catholics and Protestant inmates in the large assembly room by the Chapel. We had three choirs and three bands (rock, Latin, and Haitian) who had written special music for the service. There were so many inmates there that the lieutenant became worried. He and six officers came to the service to see what was happening.

At the Peace, where everyone greeted those around them with a handshake or hug, I noted that inmates greeted all the officers. Later at the Lord's Prayer it was our custom to hold hands and I noticed the officers holding hands with the inmates. It was unheard of to have officers hugging and holding hands with inmates.

One year at the women's high security unit I held a Maundy Thursday (Thursday in Holy Week which celebrates the first Lord's Supper) service for the women, because there was no Catholic chaplain at the time. I decided to do the traditional foot washing ceremony. I washed and dried the feet of all the women, about thirty. When I finished, one of the women said through tears,

"Thank you chaplain, now we must wash yours."

All the women came up and washed my feet. Tears were streaming from their eyes-and mine. One of them dried my feet with her hair. I will never forget this experience.

I had mixed feelings of compassion and sadness working with these high-security women, some of whom were awaiting the death sentence in the states from which they came. They needed someone to talk to-to cry with. It was not unusual for me to go through a case of Kleenex a week. Men, when they were upset, generally went to the iron pile (weight lifting area) and worked off their problem. The women went to their room and ate. Gaining weight lowered their already low self-esteem. Moreover, these women had lost almost all contact with their families and received very few visits.

"Hello, Ames," said my boss, the Associate Warden, on the phone one Friday morning two years later.

"Yes," I replied, "how are you this morning?"

"Fine. I have some good news for you."

"What's that?"

"You've been selected as Regional Chaplaincy Administrator in the new Mid-Atlantic Region."

"Oh shit!" I said without thinking.

"What was that?"

"That's great," I replied. "Just great. When do I report?"

"In July sometime. Congratulations."

I told Judy when I got home.

"Stay right here," she said. "I have to go out for a minute."

I puttered around the boat pondering this new development in my life. I had been thinking about retiring soon. I had my twenty years in, but due to misinformation given me some years before I would not be eligible for retirement health benefits for another six months. I had been thinking about retiring from Panama City in six months.

Being promoted to a regional job was a great opportunity to work within the system in a new way. I would be in charge of eleven states and more than twenty chaplains. Maybe I could do something to help them.

Judy came back about an hour later with a gift-wrapped package in her hands.

"Here," she said, as she handed the package to me. "This is for you."

I opened it. Inside was a pair of purple boxer undershorts. "What's this?"

"I figured this is as close to being a bishop as you'll ever get. Now you can wear purple, at least purple under shorts!"

The next few months were a whirlwind of activity as I tried to tie things up at the institution, start training for my new, and do my part in setting up my part of the program for the National Chaplain's Conference to be held in Phoenix in June.

If this was not enough, I was selected "Chaplain of the Year" by the Bureau. I felt totally inadequate and overwhelmed by all the attention and recognition. I was happy, but knew that if it had not been for Judy and my fellow workers I could not have accomplished anything.

The last week of June we set sail from Panama City for Annapolis, Maryland, where we would live while I worked in the nearby town of Laurel. We had invited our youngest grandson, Luke, to join us for this trip, which was to take three weeks. Since his mother, Debra, was going to spend several weeks in Russia as part of an archeological team, we decided to keep him all summer.

Early one morning we left our dock at St. Andrew and headed out, taking two crew members to help us. It was dead calm when we left and the calm lasted three out of the five days it took us to reach Key West. Even so, we crashed and banged through the steep chop caused by a tropical depression off the Yucatan Peninsula.

We stopped at Key West to make a repair and on Monday evening, we set sail again, this time to the great Gulf Stream, which runs between Florida and the Bahamas. Butterfly never flew so fast, at times nine and ten knots with the current.

The following morning we discovered the gooseneck on the main had broken. Since it was the day before the Fourth of July, we kept on sailing under jib and mizzen until we reached Cape Canaveral.

The Fourth was Judy's birthday and Luke made her special cinnamon toast for breakfast. I pushed the boat under power because of the light winds and because I wanted to get to Cape Canaveral by nightfall so Judy could enjoy a dinner ashore.

It was our custom on the boat for everyone to take turns at cooking. The two men who were crewing for us, being Southerners, did not believe they should have to cook and complained they did not know how. Nevertheless, Judy and I convinced them that they could at least open a couple of cans and heat their contents.

That evening as we steered toward the entrance to the Canaveral Channel, one of the men got out two cans of chili, since it was obvious we would not make it in by dinnertime. I was sad because I really did not want Judy to have chili for her birthday dinner. Just as the crew was getting ready to open the can, I heard,

"Grandpa! Hey Grandpa."

"What's up?" It was Luke, sounding very excited.

"The fishing line is acting funny."

Sure enough, we had caught a fish. It was a King Mackerel, just big enough to feed us all.

"Hold the chili!" I called down. "We're going to have a real feast tonight."

Twenty minutes later we were all eating pan broiled fish.

"Grandpa, do you think God sent that fish for Grandma?"

"I'm sure of it," I replied with confidence.

As we entered the channel later that evening, we could see the sky light up with fireworks from a dozen displays. What a welcome!

After settling down at a dock, I brought out the lopsided chocolate cake Luke and I had made and Judy opened her presents. My sister, Dianne, had sent a card for me to give to Judy on her birthday. She had written:

> "I am praying you will be able to have your birthday on shore
> so you can really enjoy it."

"Her prayers were certainly answered," said Judy, happy wonder in her voice.

After spending two days at Cape Canaveral getting the gooseneck repaired, we headed for Beaufort, North Carolina. The trip continued to be windless, but we sped up the coast riding the Gulf Stream.

We entered the Intercoastal Waterway at Beaufort, North Carolina and traveled up to Norfolk, Virginia. The trip was mostly uneventful as we watched the charts and waited for the bridges to open.

At Norfolk, I pulled out the charts for the Chesapeake Bay. I had sent away for them and they had arrived shortly before we had to leave, so I had not really looked at them closely. I opened the first one for the entrance, noted it looked fine, and folded up the others.

As we reached the end of our first chart, I dug out the lower Chesapeake to find a place to spend the night. Then I saw these next two charts were for ocean-going vessels: there were no soundings of less than twenty feet. Because I knew the Chesapeake was shallow in some places, I had no idea where or how to get to a secure anchorage. The wind had been building all day and we were really flying with sail reduced to the working jib and mizzen. At this rate, we would arrive off Annapolis at dawn.

As night fell we attempted to keep track of the ships in our area, but this was difficult since the ship channel wound back and forth across the bay. Overall, the ships were wary and respectful of our little boat, as I tried to keep to the edge of the channel.

"Ames, come on deck," Judy was shaking me. I struggled with my weariness.

"What's the matter?"

"I think a bad squall is coming."

I went on deck and looked around. The night sky to the east of us was black. Out of this blackness were distant flashes of lightning.

"Get the crew up," I said. "It looks like it's time to drop the jib and mizzen. We'll motor until the squall passes."

Just as Judy went below I saw something flash past our bow lights and there was a scraping along the sides of the boat. I saw what looked like tree branches going by. *"My God, we have hit a tree,"* I thought as I heard and felt a solid thump on the keel. The boat hesitated a moment and then continued. I turned the helm to port and we were out of it. By this time, everyone was on deck.

"Drop the jib and mizzen! Start the engine!" I yelled, panicked. "Judy, take the helm."

I ran below to check the bilges. No water was coming in. I went back topside. *Could we have hit a tree? Maybe it was a fishing weir.*

I had heard there were many of these fish traps in the Chesapeake Bay. I took a Loran reading, which showed us well within the edge of the channel. There was a red buoy to our starboard where it was supposed to be. The more I thought about it the more convinced I was that we had run through a fishing weir that had been placed inside the edge of the main channel.

I decided to stay on deck the rest of the night. The wind was blowing over thirty knots so we used just enough engine power to make steering easy. I did not want to arrive off Annapolis before dawn. My head kept drooping and in order to stay awake I took bearings and plotted them against the Loran.

As we closed with the Thomas Point light, dawn started to fill the sky. The chart did not show the entrance to Annapolis and the channel and area around it was less than twenty feet. I did not know how I was going to find our way in.

"Here's some coffee, honey," said Judy.

"Maybe we can follow a boat in," I said, sipping the hot coffee and hoping the caffeine would help me come up with a better idea. How many boats would be entering Annapolis at six on Sunday morning?

"I've got an idea," said Judy as she darted below. In a few minutes she was back up with the brochure for the marina, which was to be our home, in her hand and a small magnifying glass.

Look," she said, "there is a chart on this."

Sure enough, there was a very tiny reproduction, the size of a postage stamp, of a chart with the entrance to Annapolis and Back Creek, where we were headed. I used this "chart," magnifying glass, and course-protractor and charted a course to the first buoy. From there on it was easy.

When we got into Annapolis Landing Marina, I tied up at the fuel dock. In five minutes I was fast asleep. The dockmaster, Alex, let us stay there for two hours so I could get a nap, and then kindly helped us into our new slip.

CHAPTER THIRTY-FIVE

"What a wonderful place" Judy said as we worked our way into a little bay of the Island of Grenada.

"I don't see any other boats here," I noted, as I wound Butterfly through a narrow opening while keeping my eye on the depth sounder.

"Look at all the birds. There must be a dozen pelicans at least."

"It's beginning to shallow, now." I told Judy as I put the engine in neutral and let the boat coast. The depth sounder read twenty feet.

I gave the wheel to Judy and walked forward to drop the anchor. There is nothing I like seeing more than a boat come in and drop an anchor with no other sound than the splash of the anchor. This cove was so beautiful I wanted to do it without even that splash. I gave Judy the hand signal to back down slowly. In a few minutes, we had the anchor set, and were looking around at the most beautiful little harbor we had ever been in. There were palm trees lining and giving shade to a little beach, a cliff on one side of us, and a hill on the other. There were some children splashing around in the shallows.

I stood with my arm around Judy on the bow of the boat, thinking how wonderful this was. We were the only boat in the anchorage for the first time on our cruise. I had lecherous thoughts about chasing her around the deck.

"You want a drink, honey?" she asked, unexpectedly. *Was she thinking the same as I?* "The sun's past the yard arm."

"Sure. That would be nice."

"Ames," she yelled a minute later from below.

"What?" I ran back to the companionway.

"Look!"

Looking below, I saw that the whole cabin was alive with flies. They were buzzing so loudly it sounded as if the engine was on. The floor, the curtains, the cushions were all black with flies.

"Now we know why we are the only ones here!" Judy cried. "The cruising guide said there were some flies here, but this is ridiculous."

Judy flopped down in the cockpit and sighed wearily. "What are we going to do?"

"It's too late to go further. I guess I will have to kill flies."

We put up the screens (too late of course) and I started killing flies and shooing them out the portholes. I killed them left handed. I killed them right handed. As I walked around, I was killing them with my feet. In an hour, we had things more or less under control. I figured I had killed more than ten thousand flies.

"El matador," muttered Judy.

"What?"

"That's what you are. 'El matador.' The killer. A mad killer of flies," she explained with a laugh.

We left at dawn the next morning and by the time we were away from the shore we had gathered more flies. It took us three days to rid the boat of the pests. We discovered later that the island's garbage dump was located near the anchorage. It was such a beautiful place, too.

Dropping anchor in Prickly Bay, we went ashore to check in, as we had been told to do in Carriacou.

"Where are your papers from Carriacou, Captain?"

"They didn't give me any," I said.

"They didn't give you any papers?"

"No sir," I repeated, "They didn't. They stamped our passports, and when we asked them for other papers, they told us we didn't need them."

"Oh my, Captain. They was supposed to give you papers. I guess they's a new man there."

"What shall I do?"

"Not to worry. Everyt'ing's OK."

"I don't need to do anything?"

"No Captain. Goodbye for now."

We sailed around to St. George and anchored in the lagoon, a nice protected anchorage. It was protected from the elements, but not from the thieves. Our friend Dave from Ty Dewi rowed over and told of thieves coming aboard at night and stealing things. We decided to lock up at night.

The anchorage was right in the middle of things. There were two grocery stores (which even had fresh meat) and the center of town was within dingy distance. We made a beeline for our mail, which we had not received since St. Lucia.

I began thinking about that dirty word that ends in "K": W-O-R-K. There was a balloon payment due on the boat in December, just a few months away. Then I was going to have to find the money to pay the taxes and penalties on the IRAs and Thrifts we would have to cash in to pay the balloon payment. I had to come to grips with reality. I would have to go to work again.

My work in the regional office was interesting, but I was away from home two or three weeks each month. I am a homebody, and I like to be with my wife. My big raise had turned into a wage reduction after paying state taxes. I was taking home one hundred dollars less a month and the cost of things was much higher than in Florida. Each month I watched as we dug into our savings just to survive.

Judy signed up at all the temporary agencies and tried to help out, but we still had to get a loan to pay our annual slip fee. We thought about selling the boat and even listed it with a yacht broker, but I was only half-hearted about selling her.

My first assignment in the regional office was to check out a situation where a chaplain was about to be fired. I talked to both the Warden and the Chaplain and set up a trial period in which the Chaplain, who had alienated most of the staff and many of the inmates, could try to straighten out the situation.

The trial period did not work out and I had to go back and help pack the Chaplain out. This was not what I had expected to be doing, but there was no resolving the situation.

Most of the work was enjoyable, however, and I was able to help the chaplaincy by pushing for and eventually getting a higher pay grade for them. I had spent twenty years as a chaplain in institutions and for more than seventeen years was at the same pay grade, because there were only two grades for chaplains. In several cases, I was able to help chaplains get the money and space they needed to operate a solid chaplaincy program.

I was ready to retire after a year of this.

CHAPTER THIRTY-SIX

We set sail for Puerto La Cruz, Venezuela. After settling Butterfly into a marina there, we flew to the States for my daughter Alaina's wedding. She had announced her engagement in Annapolis just before we started on this journey and I was very happy for her. I enjoyed all the excitement of the wedding preparations and the ceremony itself, but I was worried about money: all we owed and all we did not have. *Would we be able to get enough money together to payoff the boat or would we lose her?* I called the Chief of Chaplains, a long time friend, in the Bureau of Prisons.

I dialed the number with a trembling finger.

"Hello, Chaplaincy Services."

"Charlie," I said, "You don't happen to need an old broken down, retired, seafaring, chaplain anywhere, do you?"

"Ames, you're just the man I was looking for. I've been trying to track you down. You speak Spanish, don't you?"

"I speak some Spanish, but I'm not bi-lingual."

"That doesn't matter," Charley said. "We could use you to open up the new Metropolitan Detention Center in Guaynabo, Puerto Rico. They need someone very badly. The person we had lined up for the job quit and no one else wants to go. We need someone for about six months. What do you think?"

"Sounds good to me," I lied. I did not want to go to work, but at least this would be better than tossing hamburgers at the Golden Arches. The pay was better, too. "I can be there about the first of November," I said, hoping he did not want me earlier.

"That's good enough. I'll call and confirm this, but I don't think there will be a problem."

I was afraid I had forgotten what chaplains do, and I knew I was out of touch with policy. After my experience in opening FCI, Marianna, I swore I would never open another institution. Was I really up to fighting the battles for space and money?

However, it could be an adventure. I would meet new people and maybe see some old friends. I would certainly have a chance to improve my Spanish and perhaps even add to our cruising kitty. After all, six months is not forever.

When we returned to Venezuela, we found the boat in good order. We took some time to refinish the cabin floor, and then sailed for the Gulf of Santa Fe, the island of Caraca del Oeste, and Mochema, a group of islands and bays to the east of Puerto La Cruz.

While in these lovely islands of Mochema I decided to make a table for the cockpit. This had been a project I had been thinking of doing for many years and while at anchor here I finally figured out how to do it. Dragging out a piece of half-inch plywood from under a bunk mattress, I went to work. I used a piece of brass piano hinge I had stowed in the forepeak. While using a hack-saw to cut the hinge to size, my hand slipped and the saw made a deep cut in my left thumb.

Blood poured from the thumb.

"Ouch!" I said a little loudly. I might have added a few other words, but I do not remember.

"What happened?" inquired Judy as she came up on deck. Seeing the blood, she turned pale. She always does.

"Get me something to keep the blood off the teak deck," I said.

Judy brought a clean rag, which I quickly wrapped around my thumb.

"Wash the blood off the deck," I commanded. Blood stains teak black, and I did not want that to happen.

"But your hand, how bad is it?" she asked.

"Wash the deck. I'll take care of the thumb."

I have to admit I was feeling a little queasy, especially since I noticed some "saw dust" from my thumb bone on the teeth of the saw. Since there was no place to get medical help, I knew I would have to take care of the situation myself. Judy feels faint at the sight of blood so not much help would come from that corner.

I went below and rinsed the cut, then fixed it up with antiseptic, sewed the cut closed and finished with butterfly bandages. It did not hurt because the nerves were severed. I felt very fortunate.

We spent a week or so in the bays before sailing for Laguna Grande in the Bay of Caracas. The bay was beautiful and so huge one could anchor several hundred boats there, though we were the only one at anchor. It was like sitting in the middle of the Painted Desert and I spent long hours looking at the brilliant oranges, yellows and reds change colors as the sun moved across the sky.

In order to check the rigging before starting the hard slog eastward toward Trinidad, I climbed the main mast. I found that a mast tang—which holds one of the heavy wires supporting the mast—was broken.

In order to fix it we sailed to Cumana, a large Venezuelan city just seven miles from the lagoon. It took several days to get the tang off and repaired and Judy was elated to dock at a real marina. She could step right off the boat onto the dock and did so about forty times, just to show me.

When I got the tang re-installed, we sailed north and then headed east for Punto Pargo and Trinidad.

It had been a serious mistake to tell the Regional Director I was going to retire in August. Although I asked him not to spread the word, it spread anyway. I was a lame duck administrator.

Even so I pressed on, trying to do my best for the inmates and chaplains of our region. There were eleven states and some twenty-five chaplains (Roman Catholic, Protestant, and Islam) under my authority. Some of the institutions were under-manned with chaplains and others needing a financial boost.

When I was not doing audits in our region I helped audit other regions, so there was always a lot of travel and paperwork. Nevertheless, I missed the inmates, the counseling, the church services and even the hectic pace of institutional chaplaincy.

CHAPTER THIRTY-SEVEN

One either loved Trinidad or hated it. We formed part of the latter group. It was not the people we disliked, it was the boat facilities. The anchorage was so rolly we had to come ashore every afternoon and the heat was terribly oppressive.

There were some good things though, like the steel bands. Some of the cruisers became very involved and even played in one of the bands. Judy, being a percussionist, was very interested, but we were not going to be able to stay long enough for her to do anything. We did attend a couple of steel drum contests. One was a solo contest and the winner, who had written his own piece, played so fast we could not see his hands or sticks.

We went to a band contest also and enjoyed a night of unbelievable music. It did not sound like a steel band, but more like a symphony orchestra. When a band played rhythmical popular music, the people in the audience became involved by standing and dancing.

There were vendors selling drinks and cow-hoof soup, which many seemed to enjoy. Judy and I looked at this greasy clear soup with a cow hoof floating on the top and we decided it was not something we wanted to try, especially when we did not know where the cow had been walking.

After two weeks in Trinidad, we set sail for Grenada, an overnight trip. Entering Grenada at Prickly Bay, we moved to Hog Island for a week and then stopped a few days in the lagoon at St. George to fill up on water and get our clearance papers.

On November second the hurricane season was officially over and we motored out of the channel at St. George and headed for the U.S. Virgin Islands. As the day wore on, I became very ill with nausea and diarrhea. It was probably caused by a Chinese dinner we had eaten the night before. Judy went into her "save the Captain" mode, letting me sleep past my watch several times.

On the third day, I felt better and could take on my normal responsibilities, and by one-fifteen that afternoon we were anchored at

Charlotte Amalee at St. Thomas. Before we could clear into the islands, we needed to get money from the bank at the passenger ship dock. Then a short bus ride got me to the customs and immigration office just before they closed the door. After clearing into the U.S., we moved to Honeymoon Bay, a favorite anchorage.

The following morning was an easy downwind sail to the Puerto Rican Island of Culebra and the next day we continued on, dodging the many reefs as we went, to Isla Palaminos. From there it is a short downwind sail to San Juan.

Entering the harbor of San Juan was spectacular. As we approached, we saw the fortress of San Cristobal sitting on a tall cliff. Below the cliff was a picturesque settlement we thought must be a fishing village, but were later told it is where thieves and cutthroats live. Even the police refuse to go into its precincts. We turned toward the harbor entrance, trying to keep the large waves on our port quarter as we rolled down the channel. On our port were reefs and high above on another cliff was the great fortress of El Moro. Running along the city wall of Old San Juan, we turned east up San Juan Bay to the anchorage.

We picked up a mooring at a marina on the eastern end of San Juan Harbor. Normally we would have anchored, but we would be leaving the boat alone a lot and felt more secure on a mooring. The dock slip rental was close to four hundred dollars a month which we couldn't afford. The mooring was expensive enough.

During the months before I retired, Judy and I found ourselves almost swamped with preparations for cruising. We had lists for everything: things to be repaired or painted on Butterfly, and equipment needed to be purchased, charts found, food lists made, and an etcetera list had to be compiled.

The biggest job on the boat was not discovered until the Spring when the snow melted from the deck and we found the aft deck separating from the fiberglass hull, leaving a half inch space between the deck and the stern. With the help of a friend, I ripped out the deck and rebuilt the complete stern section.

Judy signed up for a navigation course so she could take star sights with a sextant. The teacher was not very good so she supplemented her studies with my knowledge. The more we crossed off our lists the longer they became. We knew if we waited to do everything we would never leave, but we tried to do as much as possible. Every bit of free time was given to repairs, shopping and planning. At times, we wondered if we would ever get off.

The day came for retirement and the Regional Office gave me a great retirement party. Judy and I had attended innumerable of these boring affairs and were determined that my retirement celebration would be different. It started as usual with the presentation of certificates and gifts, and the usual speeches were given. A serious thank you by the Regional Director, a funny speech by his Deputy, and then it was my turn to reply.

I said a few words of thanks and then started taking my clothes off. So did Judy. Eyes widened. There were a few gasps. The Chaplain and his wife were taking off their clothes!

Under the party clothes, we had our Bitter End sea chantey costumes. We had come to the restaurant earlier and installed our amplification equipment and, taking up our guitar and banjo, we serenaded the crowd with a few songs we had written for the occasion, including "Kosher Kitchen Blues" and "Chaplain's Lament."

I am not sure if anyone else had fun, but we did. The party was definitely not boring.

CHAPTER THIRTY-EIGHT

The staff greeted me enthusiastically upon arrival at the Federal Detention Center in Guanabo, Puerto Rico.

Sadly, we had not been there long before Judy went to Michigan to be with Laura, who was having a difficult time with Multiple Sclerosis. After work one day, just as the sun was setting, I got into the dingy to row home. The mooring was around the end of a pier and I always enjoyed rowing around the corner and seeing Butterfly after a long day at work. It reminded me why I was working. She would be sitting at the mooring, her image rippling in the small waves of the harbor, the setting sun's rosy glow reflecting on her masts. It was beauty and serenity combined. My heart always skipped a beat as I rounded the pier.

This time my heart stopped beating completely.

Butterfly was not on the mooring. There was no reflection on the water, no sunlight on the masts. There was no Butterfly at all.

Trying not to panic, I rowed faster to the spot where she should have been.

"I know I left her here." Looking around stunned, I did not know what could have happened. *"Maybe she dragged the mooring in the afternoon wind."*

I looked down the bay, but did not spot her. I rowed through the anchored boats. There were people on some of them, but I could not bring myself to ask them, "Have you seen my boat? I've lost it." *How could anyone lose a fifty foot boat?*

Could someone have stolen her? Maybe, but then where was the mooring buoy? No one would steal the buoy. *So she wasn't stolen and she hadn't drifted down the bay.*

I rowed back to where I had left her that morning.

Maybe she sank and took the buoy down with her? I looked into the water to see if I could see her on the bottom.

"Impossible, stupid," I scolded myself. *"The water here is only twenty-five feet deep. The masts would be sticking out of the water."*

I sat, wondering what to do next, while the dingy drifted where Butterfly's reflection usually was.

There was only one more place to look. Rowing along the marina's docks, I spotted her tied up in a slip. I climbed aboard and could find nothing wrong. *Why had they moved her here? Where was the mooring buoy?* I asked around the dock, but no one could tell me anything and the marina office was locked up tight for the night.

The next morning I delayed going to work until the dock manager arrived.

"Why did you move my boat into a slip?" I asked the dock manager when he finally arrived.

"We decided to pull the mooring and service it," came the calm reply.

"But why didn't you tell me? I about had a heart attack last night."

"Well, we didn't think about it and we weren't sure where you were."

"When are you going to put the buoy back?"

"In a few weeks, maybe a month. Meanwhile, I'll tell you what. You can have the slip at the mooring price. Will that be OK with you?"

"Well, I guess that will be all right," I replied, calming down. In fact, it would be great.

"How long will you be here?" he asked.

"Until June," I replied.

"Oh. That's almost five months from now."

"Yeah, that's about right."

Each month the manager would ask, "When are you planning to leave?" They still had not replaced the mooring when we pulled out, five months later.

After having worked for seven months, we were ready to leave the dock. We had been working morning and night for the last ten days to reach this point. I am convinced that when a boat stays in one place it slowly begins to disintegrate.

We generally do not tell our friends when we are going to leave since it puts more pressure on us than we like. This time, however, they were so insistent we gave in and told them June 4.

Planning to get away at six in the morning, I double-checked everything from rigging to engine. All was in readiness for the upwind sail to Los Palominos Islas, which lie to the east of the main island.

When it was time to leave, one of our friends was at the dock and others were going to take pictures as we passed the fortress of El Morro at the entrance to the harbor. I started the engine and helped Judy take off the bowlines, then went back and took off the stern lines and said goodbye. I put the engine in gear and gave it fuel. Butterfly just sat there.

Drat, I thought. *Not in gear!* I jiggled the lever and tried again.

Nothing happened.

By this time the boat was beginning to turn sideways in the slip so I ran forward and secured the bowlines. My friend on the dock helped secure the aft lines.

Going below I found that the shifting cable had just about disintegrated. There would be no sailing today. I would have to replace the cable with the spare we had onboard.

The gear cable was repaired and we were ready to go before dawn the next day. Just as I was about to start the engine, Judy called.

"Ames," she called in her "something's wrong" voice.

"What is it now!" I replied, exasperated. I had checked everything twice.

"Honey, we have a problem with the head. It won't flush."

I went down and looked and sure enough, it refused to flush. I would have to take it apart to fix it. That meant another day in San Juan. I felt like screaming.

"Forget it! We'll use a bucket!" I yelled in frustration at Judy.

After leaving Puerto Rico, we stopped by the Virgin Islands and then went on our way to Grenada. Two days out of the Virgin Islands, we had a visitor come aboard Butterfly. Judy and I were sitting on the cabin top letting LAD, our self-steering machine, take the helm. It was our tradition to sit there, drink in hand, and watch the waves. We watched them carefully, looking for one we might have seen before.

Suddenly something hit me on the head, knocking my hat off. At first I thought a fitting had fallen from the masthead, but then I heard a noise behind me. I saw a large bird tangled in the starboard lifelines.

He was a large brown booby, who we named Charley. He (we assumed Charley was a "he") had big yellow webbed feet and a six inch long beak. He was brown except for a white stomach.

Judy and I got him untangled and he stood on the deck looking at us balefully over his long beak. I wondered if he had hurt himself. After a while, he stretched out his wings and messed up the deck in a big way.

Deciding that he was not hurt or ill, I helped him overboard with a stick. I was afraid of that beak. Charley hit the water and took off flying, circling the boat and coming to rest on our life ring. Again, I helped him off and again he circled it and this time came to rest on our brand new cockpit cushions.

Remembering the mess he had made on the deck, neither Judy nor I wanted him to stay there. I tried to move him but he would not budge. After a short time, he moved of his own accord, to the helmsman seat. My chair. The Captain's chair.

I began to wonder if he was trying to take over the boat. Judy was doubled over with laughter. I did not know if she was laughing at Charley or me. Again, I tried to move him, but he would not budge.

"Charley," I said, "You are not the Captain. I am. If you want to stay on the boat, you'll have to move to the foredeck." I was hoping he would not mess the helm seat as I took my "bird stick" and gently tried to move the stubborn bird.

The fight began. Charley grabbed the stick with his beak. I, by pulling hard, got the stick back and tried again. This time he snapped at my hand. It did not hurt, but it sure scared me. I moved to the other side of the chair and pushed him off.

"Now," I commanded in my firmest voice, "you go forward. You can stay there if you want."

Charley looked at me with beady eyes then, slowly, stomped up the weather deck to the foredeck. He did not much like it there, as every so often a wave came aboard wetting him down.

Later that night I went up to take the mainsail down. Charley did not appreciate my being in his territory. He snapped at my bare legs and feet.

On my way back to the cockpit, I found a few flying fish flopping on the deck where they had landed. I picked them up and gave them to Charley, who quickly ate them, but he did not thank me.

When I went back in the morning to raise the mainsail Charley was still there. I looked around and found some more flying fish for him, then returned to the cockpit for my own breakfast.

Judy was sad when we saw Charley take off a few hours later. I was not sad. The foredeck was white with his unsanitary habits, and I was convinced he was a potential mutineer hoping for the job of Captain.

It was a drizzly day when we arrived in Grenada, but we were happy to be here as this island was one of our favorites.

CHAPTER THIRTY-NINE

We left Grenada and headed back to Venezuela, anchoring along the coves on the north shore. In Cumana we overhauled our masts and made a couple of trips inland. From Puerto La Cruz we sailed to Tortuga, and then to Los Rocques, an archipelago of islands off the coast of Venezuela and on our way to Bonaire and Curaçao.

There I was on night watch, lying on deck with my eyes closed, reliving a great Dorado dinner I had just feasted on and planning on grilled fish for breakfast. Hearing a noise over my head like a rag in the wind or a loose line flapping around, I opened my eyes and saw a bird hovering over my face, trying to land.

"Well, hello there," I said quietly. The bird heard me and terminated his landing approach. For the next twenty minutes he attempted to land on the mast peaks, but in five foot seas they were moving too much. Then he tried the spreaders and jumper struts.

As he swooped over the cockpit during one of his landing runs, I called out, "Little bird, it looks to me as if you're going to have to trust me or drown."

At last he made his decision with great care, glided down, and landed on the stern light near where I lay.

"Grook . . . grook," he said, which I interpreted to say, "Hi, I'm Billy Bird. I'm so tired I don't care what you do. I'm staying here."

"That's all right, Billy," I replied. You're welcome to stay as long as you want. Try not to mess up the boat too much."

I looked Billy over but could not tell much about him in the dark. He looked like a dove with a needle-like beak. His feet were not webbed, so I knew he was a land bird lost at sea.

Billy preened and then tucked his head under a wing and slept. I disturbed him several times while keeping watch and he became a little upset when Judy came out to take over, but soon he settled down.

Four hours later, Billy was still sleeping on the light.

At five-thirty, just as the horizon was beginning to lighten, Billy woke up and stretched.

"Grook ... grook. Grook ... grook," he squawked, and then, jumping into the air, he flew away. I felt warm allover.

He'd said, "Thanks for the ride. I'm glad I trusted you. Good-bye."

I raised my hand and waved good-bye, though by this time the early semi-darkness of the dawn had swallowed him.

We anchored several places in Los Roques and then headed west through Islas Los Aves, where we spent the night, and on to Bonaire to dock.

After a few days of rest we let go the dock lines and left for Curaçau, where we navigated the narrow and shallow channel into Spanish Waters, a large bay almost completely surrounded by land. We settled in for fifteen days and painted the cabin top between rain showers, checked navigation lights, GPS, corrected the barometer, scrubbed the hull, and had a heck of a time ashore with our friends at a local clubhouse for cruisers.

But I was worried. Judy and some of our friends had talked me into visiting Cartagena, Colombia. I was not worried about going there; I was worried about leaving. I had heard of cases where the U.S. Coast Guard harassed cruisers who had stopped there.

Another worry was directed toward the weather. All our books and pilot charts indicated that November and December were the worst months for high winds in the area. It was already the end of October and I felt the need to go, but it was hard for Judy, and me, to leave this great protected anchorage.

At last, on November third, we headed out the channel with a boat from Texas. Two days out the weather kicked up to twenty to thirty knots out of the east, northeast and the waves built to a fifteen to twenty-foot chop. The Atlantic and Caribbean waters are certainly different from the Pacific. This is probably why Pacific Ocean cruisers are sometimes intimidated when they leave Panama on the Caribbean side.

I listened to the NOAA weather report and it forecast ten to fifteen knots today and fifteen knots tomorrow. Carefully, I climbed up the companionway ladder, but before I got to the top a huge wave came crashing aboard bringing a foot of water into the cabin. It had ripped out the starboard weather cloth. I closed the companionway doors.

"Wow!" exclaimed Judy. We had been hand-steering since morning, mainly because we enjoyed it but also because the autopilot was reacting a bit slowly. We had just the working jib up and were doing a steady six knots, surfing to eight.

I made my way over to the port pin rail to watch the seas, which were massive. We had not seen anything like them since our trip to Bermuda and years ago on a trip to Baja California.

"I think the wind is getting stronger," Judy says. "Must be blowing more than thirty knots."

"No," I reassure her. "It's only blowing ten to fifteen. The forecast says so."

"Sure," she replies, giving the wheel a twist as the stern rises to another large swell. Butterfly lifts and slides down into the moving valley below.

I cannot stop watching the seas. They are a deep indigo blue, except where they start to curl prior to breaking, when they become a translucent green. The boat lifts to the top of a larger than usual wave and I can see for miles. I am on a mountaintop, looking at the valley twenty feet below where there is foam and spume. After hesitating a minute at the crest, she slips down into the valley.

Butterfly seems to be dancing through the waves like a ballerina, twisting here, leaping there, and pirouetting through the huge energy force of the waves. What joy! I cannot help but smile at the interchange between boat and wave, nature and man. The smile turns into laughter.

We were three days out from Curaçao, and it was right at dusk, when I call up to Judy from the navigation area.

"The GPS doesn't work." I had gone down to take a fix and there was nothing but a blank screen. We were one hundred miles from Cartagena, with currents going every which way at variable speeds, and the GPS goes out!

"What are we going to do?" The anxiety was evident in her voice.

"We'll just have to use the old method of navigation and piloting. We've done it before," I reassured her. We had not had a GPS until just before we left Annapolis, and I figured I could get us in all right. It was just going to be a lot harder.

"You're right. We've done it before, and we can do it again," she half-sang, relaxing a little.

We had planned to arrive off Cartagena at dawn, but now I was concerned we might get too close to land during the night. I figured that if we could get to a point off Punta Canoas, where there was supposed to be a reliable light with a range of twenty miles, we would heave—to until dawn.

It was a good plan, but of course it did not work. I plotted dead reckonings every hour, trying to figure in the various sets and drifts of currents. We reached the point where we should have seen the light at eleven. We could see nothing, not even a glimmer, in the dark moonless night. We went six miles further, and still no light.

"We'll have to heave-to until daylight." I called to Judy. We had done this before in large seas so we anticipated a little relief from the constant battering.

We brought her through the wind and backed the jib with a huge "bang," and Butterfly was now heaved-to. We were wrong about the relief. The boat's motion had been bad before but now, in the short steep chop, it was miserable. The wind, by hand anemometer, read a constant thirty knots with gusts to fifty.

At dawn, we got underway again. I climbed on the cabin top to look for land that I thought sure should be there, but all I could see were mountainous waves. At one point, I thought I saw a hill, but it disappeared. It must have been just another wave.

We continued on our heading until the DR (dead reckoning) position indicated we were five miles inland. Since I had not felt a bump or crossed a beach, I figured my DR was off and we had drifted further out to sea.

"I'll have to dust off the sextant," I told Judy. "Maybe I can get a line of position at ten. I can get a noon position and we'll be home free. Meanwhile, we'll head due east, toward where land should be."

I climbed onto the cabin top one more time for a last look, but it was so hazy I could not spot anything.

I took over the wheel and headed on a compass course of one hundred-sixty degrees, which seemed comfortable. I would change to due east after the sun shot at ten. Then I saw a shadow in the haze ahead.

"Judy! There's a huge rock ahead!"

"Hmmm . . . kind of a strange looking rock. Kind of square shape," she called back.

"It's a ship," I said with relief.

Now navigators and pilots have all kinds of tricks up their sleeves. I decided that here was a good chance to dust off an old one.

"Judy, get on the VHF and ask the ship their position."

"Why don't you do it yourself?" she replied, frowning. She hates to use the VHF. She also hates to be a go between. We have probably had more arguments over her using the VHF than over any other thing.

"The ship will answer a woman, but she won't always answer a man." I was relying on my knowledge of piloting and seamanship now and I was speaking from a great wealth of experience.

"Oh, all right!" she exclaimed disgustedly while going for a pencil and paper. You see how smart she is. I would have called and then fumbled for the pencil and paper.

"To the ship on a northbound course, off Punta Canoas: This is the sailing vessel Butterfly off your port bow. Please come in," said Judy. I did not know how any captain could resist her sweet and sexy voice.

"Butterfly, this is the northbound vessel. How can I help you?" came the slightly accented voice.

"Our GPS went out and we would like to have your present position, please."

"We are at 10^0 32.7'N and 075^0 05.2'W. Is there anything else we can do?"

"No, but thank you for your help. Butterfly clear."

I took the information and ran down to plot it. Something was wrong. His position was 40 miles inland. He could not have been at 075^0 05.2'W.

I went to the VHF and called.

"To the northbound ship, Butterfly calling."

No answer.

I repeated the call several times with the same result. I took the wheel and told Judy to call.

Seconds after her first try, the ship answered. She asked him to repeat his position. After a few minutes, he came back.

"The ship is exactly 10^0 34.3'N and 075^0 5.2'W."

Judy shook her head and thanked him.

"You're right about ships answering women faster," she conceded.

I went back to the chart. He was wrong. He could have been at 076^0 05.2'W or at 075^0 52.0'W. I took the former for a fix, as it seemed more reasonable.

The GPS instruction books make it clear that one should not rely solely on GPS for navigation. They are correct. One needs to have those secret navigational tools: a woman, a VHF radio and a ship. I hoped the next time we would get a ship that knew where it was.

By twelve-thirty, we saw the buildings of Cartagena and knew we would be in a sheltered harbor by nightfall.

Coming into Cartagena is not as easy as it may seem from the sea. You see the city and a big opening into the bay, called Boca Grande (Big Mouth). However, you cannot enter here. In order to stop pirates from attacking the city, an underwater wall was built in 1778 to within four feet of the surface. There is one small opening but it takes "local knowledge," a hard commodity to find when at sea.

Instead of entering the enticing bay, you sail about eight miles south and enter through Boca Chica (Small Mouth), which lies between two islands. The Spanish had built two forts here, one on the port side entering and another on the starboard side about a half a mile farther in from the entrance. This second one was built to strike at the water-line of attacking ships. One dare not anchor here, as the locals will steal anything, including the boat itself. They must be descendants of the aforementioned pirates.

After passing these fortifications you sail up the inside of the island back to Boca Grande, another eight miles. On the north side of this larger bay there is a smaller bay, which is very shallow. The anchorage for small boats is in front of another small fortress, which has been made into a marina, and in the distance looms the towering fortress of San Felipe.

We dropped our anchor off Club Nautico, a broken down but famous marina and were surprised to find about fifty other cruising boats anchored here. We planned to stay there for two weeks, but Butterfly was not to leave Cartagena for almost three years.

CHAPTER FORTY

Making contact with the Episcopal Church in Cartagena, I assisted the local priest, Fr. Ricardo, who had his hands full with two churches and a mission.

One day the bishop showed up at our boat after talking someone into bringing him out to the anchorage in a dingy. He convinced me to go to Cali, where an English-speaking congregation and two Spanish-speaking congregations needed help. I was ready for a change and thought this might be an interesting experience as long as I could break even financially. I agreed to go for one year.

In Cali, Lois and Bill Murray, members of the congregation, greeted us warmly. They showed me Trinity Church, which held interdenominational services even though it was under the auspices of the Episcopal Church. There were Presbyterians, Methodists, Lutherans, and even Roman Catholics (the wives or husbands of Colombians) who wanted to worship in their own language. I was impressed with their desire to have a full time priest in residence.

"I hear you won the Chaplain of the Year Award for the Bureau of Prisons. But what do you feel you can do for a non-prison congregation?" one woman asked.

Thinking about this question, I was not sure what to say. I did not really feel there was a difference. People are people, although some are in more difficult situations than others are. What had I given my inmates? Love . . . God's love.

"I can only let God's love flow through me. Everything else is not very important," I replied. After the words left my mouth, I felt they were pompous-sounding. Nevertheless, evidently I had said the correct thing, since they asked me to come and minister to them.

After much rushing around to get our residency papers, finding a place to keep the boat, and packing everything in the boat that we were going to take to Cali with us, we finally boarded a plane for Cali.

I held my first services there Easter Sunday, one in Spanish at my home located in a barrio called Los Guaduales and the other at Trinity Church. It was a wonderful experience, as it had been a long time since I had conducted a service in my own church.

Soon after my arrival in Cali, I was contacted by the Columbian Cartel trying to get money from me to "save a man who was going to jail if he could not come up with . . . ." I was also contacted by the Columbia Secret Police, which was attempting to discover who I really was, and by our own Drug Enforcement Agency (under cover, of course). I was a real puzzle to everyone, as I was almost the only American who did not live with guards at my door.

Almost a year later I started the service on Maundy Thursday.

"The Lord be with you," I said in Spanish, lifting my arms in invitation to the great Prayer of Thanksgiving.

"And also with you," came the enthusiastic response from the little congregation of La Sagrada Familia in Cali, Columbia.

"Lif up hur arts" came out of my mouth instead of the expected "Lift up your hearts."

"Ift uh yuh arts," I tried again. Sweat broke out on my forehead as I looked at my wife sitting at the organ at the back of our living room/chapel. She announced a hymn in Spanish and the congregation sang heartily.

Holy Week is not a good time to lose your voice, particularly since it was only Thursday. I needed to have services at two churches, this one and Trinity, the English-speaking congregation. *How can I if I have no voice?* I thought. *I hope I have just strained it.*

The hymn ended and I cautiously intoned, "Lift up your hearts." Better, but I could feel my voice on the edge of going nasal again. By taking long rests between sentences and speaking softly, I finished the prayer and relaxed a bit as the congregation recited the Lord's Prayer.

After everyone left following the service, I slumped into a chair, exhausted. Judy brought cokes and sat down across from me.

"What happened?" she asked anxiously.

"I don't know! My voice just quit on me." I took a long drink from the glass. "It's not sore or anything. I just don't understand."

"How are you going to get through Good Friday's three hour service?"

"I asked the seminarian to preach part of the sermon. I don't know . . . ." I did not want to admit to Judy or myself the fear I felt. "If it gets bad, I'll just add in some silence for meditation."

"Do you think this has anything to do with the other things that have been happening? You know, with your eyes?" Judy asked.

"I can't see how they would be connected."

Just before Christmas of 1994, I had begun having difficulty with my eyes. They jumped around, making it hard to see. I went to an ophthalmologist who told me it was an allergy and gave me some drops. On Christmas, my right eyelid drooped so much it looked as if I was continually winking at the congregation.

Then I went to an American-trained ophthalmologist. He took me more seriously and did a brain scan, but found nothing suspicious.

"Must be stress," he said.

"But I don't feel stressed," I replied.

"Everyone in Cali is stressed," he assured me.

A few weeks later the eye was normal again, so I forgot about it. However, I found myself becoming very tired in the afternoon and it was difficult to make my pastoral rounds. I thought it must be the heat, or perhaps, I was just becoming lazy. Surely none of these things had anything to do with the loss of my voice.

"I'll rest my voice as much as I can," I told Judy. "I hope I can make it through the Easter Services." This was not only the most holy of Christian days, but it would be my last service with the two congregations in Cali and the people I had come to love.

Somehow, I got through Good Friday and Easter without completely losing my voice as I had on Holy Thursday. Without warning I would feel it begin to go and with great concentration and several unscheduled hymns, was able to make it through the services.

During the past year, I had been able to build up the little Spanish mission at our home church, La Sagrada Familia, and Trinity increased its membership and attendance. It had been a great time and I began to regret contracting for only one year.

However, we were anxious to get back to sailing, and the following week we packed up the house and moved back aboard our beloved Butterfly in Cartagena. After loading our boxes on the boat, I discovered I could not hold my head up. For a week, all I could do was work for twenty minutes and rest for ten. Then my neck was strong again.

"I must have pulled a muscle," I told Judy.

"Maybe," she said, giving me her suspicious look. She does that when she thinks there might be something else wrong but does not want to admit it even to herself.

My voice was still going out on me so Judy pushed me until I went to an Ear, Nose, and Throat specialist. He looked me over and announced that I needed to practice elocution. He gave me some pills and directed me to come back in a week. I did not think elocution was the problem, but I had no idea my world was about to collapse around me.

The following week we returned to the specialist.

"I can't find anything wrong with you."

"But doctor," I said in Spanish, "why do I keep losing my voice?"

"Have you ever had any psychological problems?" the doctor asked.

"No," I replied.

"I think you might now. You might be trying to get out of preaching."

"I think you are wrong," I said with some force and anger.

"Let me look at your throat again. Mmmmmm."

"Mmmmmm," he repeated.

"Well?" I asked.

"Strange. It looks as if one side of your throat is lower than the other. It sags."

"What does that mean?" I asked, wondering if this was some other strange theory of his.

"I think you ought to go and see a neurologist. Immediately!" stated the doctor.

"Why?"

"I think you may have a neurological problem. There is a very good neurologist at the Epilepsy Clinic here in Cartagena. You need to see him."

The next day Judy and I went to the Epilepsy Clinic on the edge of town. It was modern in architecture and ancient in methods. We had called for an appointment but when we arrived were told to wait in line "over there." It was a long line and some people said they had been waiting over three hours. We asked what the line was for. To make sure we were in the right place.

"To get an appointment," said an older woman who had a young boy with her. "You have to wait here until you are called to get your appointment," she explained in Spanish.

It was hot outside and there was no place to sit. One hour, two hours went by. Soon it was past noon and we still waited with the others. At one, our turn came.

"What is wrong with you?" asked a nurse.

"I don't know," I replied. By now, I was hot, tired and irritable. "That's why I'm here."

"Do you fall down?" she asked.

"No. I have been told I have a droopy mouth."

"A droopy mouth?" She looked at me with a strange expression.

"Yes. That's what I said."

"I'll set you up with a doctor's appointment. Come back at four this afternoon."

At four-thirty, we were in the doctor's office. He looked at my throat, had me do some exercises, and used a tuning fork on my head.

"I see what the ENT doctor was talking about. The right side of the throat is sagging. Has anything else been happening over the past few months?"

I told him of the eye problem, the voice and the neck problems. He gave me orders to get a blood test and to come back at eight a.m. in two days for more tests.

During the next two days, I tried to put the problem out of my mind, but could not. I covered up my fear by running around trying to get the boat ready to sail to the San Blas Islands, our next destination.

We arrived at our scheduled time, the doctor took me into a room with a computer and some patched-up equipment. Then he tortured me for about forty-five minutes. This test, I later learned, is called an Electromyography or EMG. The computer sends shocks through an electrode attached to a muscle, which makes it jump. For normal people it jumps the same every time, but for me each jump was consecutively smaller. He tested my eyes, face, neck, arm, and hand. It was extremely painful.

The test completed, Judy and I were taken to the doctor's office where we sat in metal chairs and nervously awaited the results. Sweat ran down my back from the Cartagena heat as I waited for the doctor to look up from the graphs and papers on his desk. I looked around the shabby examining room/office, noticing it definitely was not up to U.S. standards. The walls were dingy grey and I wondered if they had once been white.

After what seemed a long time the doctor glanced up and took off his glasses, saying nothing for a minute. After clearing his throat he said in Spanish,

"Well, it looks as if you have Myasthenia Gravis, a neuro-muscular disease. I'm sorry to say, it's incurable." He sat back, more relaxed now that he had given his diagnosis.

Judy looked at me and I at her. We had never heard of this disease.

"What is Myasthenia Gravis? Will I die? What will happen to me?" There was more than a little hysteria in my voice.

"Oh, don't worry," he said. "Myasthenia means muscle weakness and Gravis is the name of the doctor who discovered it."

Now I had not been the greatest Latin student, but I knew that Gravis means very serious.

"Can I go on sailing? We're planning to leave next week."

"No. I don't think so. We may have to put you into the hospital . . . . I'm not sure. But I don't think you should go sailing."

"Where can we find out more information in English?" Judy asked.

"Go to the university library. They may have something. Meanwhile, here are two prescriptions, one for steroids and the other for a drug called Mestinon. And come back next week on Friday."

The next day Judy went to the university and came back with a copy of a very recent article in the *New England Journal of Medicine* by Dr. David Drackman, the most well known authority on Myasthenia Gravis. Among other things, we discovered that the medications the doctor had given us were correct.

"Did you see this?" she asked me, pointing to the article.

"What?"

"It says you could stop breathing. I don't like that!"

"Me neither. It would be difficult to live that way," I said, trying to make a joke.

"Maybe you should go back to the States."

"I don't think so. At least not yet. I don't want to leave the boat. Maybe with this medicine I'll get better."

Judy did not reply.

The only thing I wanted was to forget the whole thing and set sail for Panama and the San Blas Islands. The boat was ready and all we had left to do was provision her with food for the trip.

"I don't think we should go," Judy stated with finality.

"Let's get away from here. I'll be all right once we get back to sea," I countered, trying to deny there was anything wrong.

"Please, Ames, we can wait here a little while to see what happens, can't we? I mean we have the time; there's no rush." She was becoming adamant.

"Oh, all right" I gave in. "If it makes you feel better we'll wait one week. But no more." I used my authoritarian voice, which failed me in the end by becoming nasal.

The following week I started to have trouble swallowing and chewing. Judy did not want to wait any longer.

"You are going back to the States now!" she blurted out as tears ran down her cheeks. "I don't want you to stop breathing here. I wouldn't know what to do."

"But Judy," I pleaded. I knew I had lost the argument by the tone of her voice, but I thought I might give it a try. "Where would I go? To one of our daughter's homes? I think it's better to go to Panama. We might find another doctor there. Besides, I'm feeling better."

"You are not better! Anyway, I called Laura this morning and she asked her neurologist who we should contact in the States. He referred us to Dr. Drackman at Johns Hopkins."

"Where is that? We don't have the money for me to stay at a hotel while I look for a doctor."

"It's in Baltimore. We can call Jim and Judy Stevenson to see if they will pick you up and take care of you there."

As usual, Judy was ahead of me. The Stevenson's had cruised with us for almost a year and were good friends. When we called, they readily agreed to help.

That afternoon we bought a plane ticket to Baltimore and put Butterfly up for sale with the marina owner. I flew to the States while Judy stayed and tried to decide what she had to bring back with her on the plane, what to sell, and what to leave aboard in case Butterfly needed to be sailed up to Florida.

On the flight back to the States I kept my face turned toward the window, trying to hide the tears rolling down my face. I had lost everything: my ministry, singing sea shanties, and my whole life style of sailing. I was not sure what else would happen to me. It was unclear if or when I might get better . . . or worse. Where was I going to get the money for doctors and medicines? I only had a small pension and I was sure we could not live on that in the U.S. I hoped that in a few months I could go back and continue on the trip to Panama. I also hoped the boat would sell soon. My mind was very confused. To sum it up, I was devastated.

At Johns Hopkins in Baltimore, they confirmed the diagnosis after another torturous EMG and blood tests. The doctors were very kind and patient. A woman met me as I was leaving the office. She told me I had a Muscular Dystrophy disease and was eligible for help and the Muscular Dystrophy Association would pay for some of my expenses, which included some doctors visits, referral to eye specialists, EMG tests, and a long list of other things. This relieved my mind somewhat of financial problems, as we had a good insurance policy to take up the slack.

Judy arrived three weeks after me. She was exhausted from making many very difficult decisions regarding the boat and its care. I was happy to have her with me again, but I was worried about how she would hold up under the pressure and stress.

As the days went by, I began to discover the effects of Mestinon and the problems it causes. One of them is diarrhea. One afternoon, returning from the doctor's office on the light rail system of Baltimore, I was hit with Mestinone's call to nature. The commuter train had no bathroom and the stations we passed had none either. I squirmed and wiggled. I finally got off the train, hoping to find a nearby service station or store with a bathroom. All I found in either direction was a street lined with trees. The situation was becoming critical, so I crawled under the ramp to the station and relieved myself. I was extremely embarrassed.

Other problems developed. I could not walk as well or as far as I used to. Washing my hair, brushing my teeth and shaving all were problematical. I could not hold up my arms or hands long enough to do these things. Some days I washed my hair and brushed my teeth and other days I shaved and brushed my teeth.

One very nice event took place while we were in Baltimore. Two of our three daughters flew out to be with me. The third daughter, occupied with four of our grandchildren, could not come. We had a great time, especially on the Fourth of July, having a picnic in the rain. Laura, my youngest and a victim of Multiple Sclerosis, helped me deal with some of my problems, as there are some similarities of symptoms between the two diseases. Alaina was empathetic and for a while I forgot my fear and self-pity.

After they left, time dragged by and I became more depressed each day. I was living a bad dream.

"It's not so bad," a friend told me. "You could have a worse disease. And you still have your life."

"What life?" I exploded. "I've nothing left. I can't preach or even perform a service, let alone sail. And my singing sea songs is a thing of the past. Don't you understand? My whole lifestyle has been wiped out in a few weeks!"

My friend took a step back, afraid to say anything more. However, I had not finished.

"I had planned as a last ditch fall-back to earn money by using my Captain's License to run charters. I cannot do that now . . . and how am I going to get Butterfly back from Colombia? The doctors say I can't go back there." I broke down in tears. I did not realize at that time that one of the effects of prednisone was emotional explosions.

My friend, uncomfortable and not knowing what else to do said, "Would you like a beer?"

It was like falling off that cliff I had climbed to get out of the Mission District. I had been hanging onto this cliff for the last forty years. I was afraid I could not support my wife and myself. I panicked, as I did not know how far this disease would take me. Would I suddenly stop breathing?

The symbol, and ministers believe in symbols, of the whole experience was epitomized by my twelve string guitar, which American Airlines crushed to matchwood. I too was crushed. By whom? God? I did not want to believe so.

I was angry. I was undergoing grief. I suppose I was mostly in shock. It seemed that one day I was climbing masts and the next I could not even turn a screwdriver. The worst part was losing control: control of my body . . . control of my life!

There were many times in the night I broke down and cried, feeling very sorry for myself. "Why me!" I cried. "What have I done to deserve this?" Rationally I knew my autoimmune system had malfunctioned and getting this disease had nothing to do with what I deserved.

Even at my lowest, I tried not to communicate my depression to Judy, who was having trouble enough adjusting to our new life. Once she could lean on me, now I was leaning heavily on her.

She would watch me all the time at first.

"Why are you looking at me that way?" I asked.

"Just looking at you," she replied.

"No you're not. You have a funny look on your face."

"I do?" she asked, trying to brush off the conversation.

"You are looking at me as if I'll stop breathing any minute. That's not going to happen."

"I'm scared it will and I won't know what to do." Tears now, streaming down her face.

I took her in my arms, and we searched for strength in each other.

"Honey, if something like that does happen . . . the worst happens and I die, we've had a wonderful life together, haven't we?"

"Yes." More tears.

"You heard the doctor say it would not happen quickly anyway."

"Yes, but I'm scared."

After a hesitation, I said, "So am I."

Almost a year later, Judy went to Cartagena with a crew to sail Butterfly back to Florida, where we hoped to live on it. After a rigging problem, she took the boat to Panama where repairs were made, but the crew had to leave. She hired another Captain to sail Butterfly back, then flew home. During this time, I felt useless.

When I saw Butterfly lying to the dock, tears welled up in my eyes. She was scruffy and needed a lot of tender loving care. We took her to a yard to clean her bottom and do a survey. I found I could do very little. I would work ten minutes and have to rest fifty.

After the haul-out, we moved her to a nice slip, but I had trouble getting on and off the boat and doing such simple work as fiberglassing. We made the decision, very painful for the both of us, to sell her.

Doing what we could, and with the help of a few paid hands, we put the boat in a little better shape and then left her . . . this time never to see her again. She looked like an old woman covered with makeup in an attempt to look young, and I could swear she wiggled her stern, trying to get me to return. I walked away not looking back, tears running down my face.

Putting Butterfly up for sale marked the end of a life style. I had come a long way from the Mission District in San Francisco where I ran through back alleys, trying to outmaneuver the gangs chasing me. I had graduated from college, received a Master of Divinity Degree, been ordained and become a successful prison chaplain highly regarded by my peers.

I had also fulfilled by childhood fantasy of sailing the seven seas, although I had only sailed three seas. I was a licensed Captain and successful navigator and had been able to take my own boat apart and put it back together again. I had found paradise in cruising among the islands.

Yet I continuously felt I had to keep pressing on or I might find myself again in the Mission District where I had started. This time it was a disease pursuing me. Holding onto the cliff top was becoming harder. My fingertips were slipping and in addition, someone was stomping on them. I was going to fall at any moment.

What the hell does God want from me anyway! I cried. What does God have in store for me? Maybe he is calling to me as I called to Billy Bird, who was also lost.

"Ames, it looks to me as if you're going to have to trust me or drown."

"All right," I pray. "I'll trust you to give me a safe harbor, but it won't be easy."

"It never is, Ames," I heard him reply. "Just stay with me and I'll give you rest."

EPILOGUE

It is now fourteen years since the point where I felt I had lost everything. The first four of those years were the worst. I was in the hospital many times for plasmapheresis, and went from one doctor to another, mainly dealing with the side effects of the drug prednisone, a steroid.

My disease was worse than normal. Even my neurologists used me as a case study. On top of all this, I was confined to a wheelchair, because I could not walk more than a half a block. There were times when I was in the hospital for infections, pneumonia, calcium toxicity, and other physical problems.

Over the next few years, I was placed on Intravenous Immune Globulin (IVIG), and my health became better and I could walk more. I was able to exchange the wheelchair for an electric cart, and started to work as an honorary assistant at a church in Lewisville, Texas. Soon I was working part-time.

In order to keep my mind alive, I tried writing every day in the morning. In the afternoon I worked building small ship models, some in bottles. I learned to cook since Judy was working, and I wanted to help her. As the years went by my life slowly improved and I stopped blaming God for this sickness.

By the year Two Thousand, I had purchased a seventeen-foot Catboat, which I could sail while sitting in one position. We sailed this little boat in the Florida Keys, and in Texas lakes. It was fun, but at the same time a little sad. I could no longer hope to sail in the Caribbean. Five years later, we sold our little house and moved to Olympia, Washington. Here we bought a forty-two foot Glasply powerboat, "Sea Song", and sailed in the Puget Sound from Olympia up into Canada.

In Two thousand seven, we had to leave our boat because I could no longer keep up her maintenance. In addition, the grayness and rain of Olympia depressed us, so we put "Sea Song" up for sale. As we were in the process of this change, our daughter Alaina called.

"Where are you going to move now you're leaving the boat?" she asked.

"I don't know. We'll probably just RV around the country."

"We are moving to Singapore because Enrique has a job there as plant manager. We need someone to do some house-sitting. Since you have no place to go, could you come to Connecticut and live in our house?"

"Sure," I said. "We will be happy to."

No one can tell me that God does not watch over us all. I remember preaching my first sermon in a prison, the New York Correctional Institution in Napanock. "You too can escape" was my theme, which made the correctional officers a little worried. I was trying to put across that ever since living in the Mission District of San Francisco I had attempted to escape from the oppression of gangs, from sin, and from failure. It was only with the grace of God that I was able to escape personal danger from people who wanted to kill me, sailing through mighty storms, and now, through Myasthenia Gravis.

However, the truth is you too can escape. When we are imprisoned with the cares and problems of our lives, when we think we are at the end of our ability to cope, there is a place of safety. Just like the birds that sought safety on Butterfly, we can climb aboard God's ship and leave the navigation to him.

####

1 ↑   3 ↓   2 ↑   4 ↓

1. Padre Ames at his mission, La Sagrada Familia, in Cali, Columbia.
2. Trinity Church in Cali, Columbia.
3. Padre Ames at Trinity with Lois Murray, parishioner.
4. A group of members of Trinity Church with Padre Ames.

5 ↑ 6 ↓

7 ↑   8 ↓

5. A Mass at La Segrada Familia.
6. Judy helps play the organ for the Spanish services.
7. A mass is held at a coffee "finca" (farm) in Armenia, Columbia.
8. Rowing the dingy from boat to shore in Puerto Rico.

On left: SV BUTTERFLY, the sailing ketch Ames and his wife, Judy, lived on for 18 years.

Below: Cruisers gather on Sunday mornings for a service. Here they are listening to an informal sermon by Ames. Sometimes these gatherings were followed by a potluck lunch and "yarning" or the singing of sea shanties.

Left to right: Jim, John, Kathy, Jim and Judy

Above left: Ames and Jeep in Puerto Cortes,
Honduras. (1965)
Above right: Judy, Laura, Alaina and Debra in Middletown,
New York (1968)
Below: Docks at Puerto Cortes, Honduras

Above left: The Swartsfager family (L-R: Joy, Dianne, Ames, Jackie; Front: Grace and Vernon)

Above right. Ames (second from left) and church friends.

THE BLUE NOTES: Ames' band at Lowell High School. L-R: Ken Polson, Nancy Wood, Dick Burke, Manny Goldman, Irene Lanterman, and Ames. Ca. 1955.

Get Published, Inc!
Thorofare, NJ 08086
11 September 2009
BA2009254